A POT TO P*SS IN

A MEMOIR

SAGASHUS T. LEVINGSTON, PhD

LITTLE CREEK PRESS
MINERAL POINT, WISCONSIN

Copyright © 2025 Sagashus Levingston, PhD

All rights reserved. No part of this publication may be reproduced, distributed, or transmitted in any form or by any means, including photocopying, recording, digital scanning, or other electronic or mechanical methods, without the prior written permission of the publisher, except in the case of brief quotations embodied in critical reviews and certain other noncommercial uses permitted by copyright law. For permission requests or other information, please send correspondence to the following address:

Little Creek Press
5341 Sunny Ridge Road
Mineral Point, WI 53565

ORDERING INFORMATION
Quantity sales. Special discounts are available on quantity purchases by corporations, associations, and others. For details, contact info@littlecreekpress.com

Orders by US trade bookstores and wholesalers.
Please contact Little Creek Press or Ingram for details.

Printed in the United States of America

Cataloging-in-Publication Data
Names: Sagashus Levingston, PhD, author
Title: A Pot To P*ss In. A Memoir
Description: Mineral Point, WI Little Creek Press, 2025
Identifiers: LCCN: 2025909000 | ISBN: 978-1-955656-89-4
Classification: BIOGRAPHY & AUTOBIOGRAPHY / Personal Memoirs
SOCIAL SCIENCE / Women's Studies
FAMILY & RELATIONSHIPS / Parenting / Motherhood

Book design by Little Creek Press

Disclaimer

This is a work of nonfiction based on the author's personal experiences, memories, and perspectives. While every effort has been made to present events accurately, certain names and identifying details have been changed to protect the privacy of individuals. Some dialogue has been reconstructed and events have been condensed or re-ordered for clarity and narrative flow.

The intent of this memoir is not to harm, defame, or misrepresent any person, community, or organization. The views and reflections expressed are solely those of the author and do not represent those of any institutions with which she is affiliated.

I dedicate this book to my father, Isaac Levingston.
I miss you, old man, and I love you.

I dedicate this book to Winnie Ledbetter, my grandmother,
and Janet McFarland, my aunt. Thank you both for your wisdom,
for showing me the power of prayer, for always answering
my calls, and for always showing up. I miss you more
than words can express.

I also dedicate this book to the little girl in me who
refused to take no for an answer, the young woman
in me who refused to give up on love, and all the
versions of me who refused to die.
Thank you for carrying us here.

A LETTER FROM THE AUTHOR

Dear Reader,

To my Versies—my fellow truth-tellers, story-weavers, and warriors of the IMverse—this one's for you.

Writing *A Pot to Piss In* wasn't just about filling pages with words. It was about healing, growing, and telling the truth—even when it hurt. I didn't just write this book; I lived it. I cried through drafts, laughed at old memories, and sat with truths that were hard to swallow. I wrote it because I needed it. And because I knew someone out there might need it too.

If there's one thing I hope you take away from these pages, it's this: You are enough, even when you feel like a hot mess. You don't have to have it all together to start. You don't have to be perfect to be powerful. And you sure as hell don't need anyone's permission to be the fullest, boldest version of yourself.

Every story I shared, every truth I uncovered, was with you in mind. I wanted you to see yourself in these pages, to feel less alone, to find the courage to chase your wildest dreams—even if you're still battling yesterday's demons.

And listen. In this book, you're going to see how I went through some things over the course of nine months to accomplish what others thought was impossible. But let me tell you—those nine months paled in comparison to what I went through in the three years it took to finally complete this book—especially this last year.

But that tells me that this message was so important that hell was sending its big dogs to make sure you never read this story. It tells me that whatever you have brewing in that brilliant brain and big heart of yours is so bold, so fantastic, and so revolutionary that a force did all it could to keep you from getting this inspiration, love, confirmation, and affirmation.

But "tuh," by God's grace, here we are.

May this book unlock something extraordinary in you and give you the permission you never needed to do the thing you were always meant to do.

Thank you for trusting me with your time, your heart, and your story. I'm rooting for you. Always.

Now go make some noise. The world is waiting.

With love and grit,
Dr. Sagashus Levingston

PREFACE

When I set out to write *A Pot to Piss In*, I did it because, quite frankly, I needed this book. I needed it for myself, and I needed it for the women I coach—the ones who, like me, often feel like the world doesn't speak to them or see them in their fullness.

When I started Infamous Mothers, the question that kept me up at night was: Who is inspiring moms like we inspire CEOs and athletes? Who is speaking life into them, letting them know they can do it—even when it feels impossible? The same question pushed me to write this book, but on a bigger scale.

I think about the women who come to me with bold, audacious dreams. The ones who want to make money, start businesses, build successful families, and thrive in their marriages. The ones who have all this fire but are a little skeptical of the experts who tell them how to live. Why? Because those experts don't look like them. They don't share their stories. They give just enough of their story to show they aren't perfect but not enough to help my women feel like they, too, can overcome the weight they carry.

There's this myth that before you can go out and be extraordinary—before you can make an impact and accomplish your wildest dreams—you have to clean up every single part of your life. And listen, if I had waited until I had it all together, I'd still be stuck somewhere I had no business being.

I wrote this book to help you unlock the *both/and* within yourself. To show you that you can chase your dreams and heal at the same time. You can build an empire and still be a work in progress. In fact, pursuing those dreams often forces you to address the things you once thought you couldn't handle.

So let me be clear: This book isn't about perfection. It's about courage, resilience, grit, and bold moves. It's about showing up even when you feel vulnerable and imperfect. It's about finding power in the messy, in the not-yet-there, and in the "I'm doing it scared."

To be fair, I'm not the first to explore this idea. Dr. Venus Opal Reese, for example, built an incredible brand around being the "Hot Mess Millionaire." But I felt called to speak specifically to mothers because, let's face it, we're often not given the space to be messy and magnificent at the same time.

I also wanted to bring my faith to the table. Not in the way you might expect. I'm not a pastor or a preacher. I'm not here to convert or condemn. I'm just a woman who talks to God every day—who laughs with Him, cries to Him, seeks His advice, and shares my deepest fears and wildest dreams. My journals are full of our conversations, the strategy sessions where He offers wisdom, comfort, and direction. When I say I have strategy sessions with God, I mean it. My journals are filled with prayers, plans, and promises. And while I know I'm brilliant—no imposter syndrome here—so much of what I've accomplished is because I've had the ultimate consultant guiding me.

I'm a hot mess who cusses, has sex, isn't married, and lives with my share of flaws. And yet, God has been my bestie through it all. He's loved me in my brokenness and used me to serve others in ways I never saw coming.

This book is my coming-out story—not as someone who has it all figured out but as someone who knows what it feels like to lean on God not just when there's nothing else, but in every ordinary and extraordinary moment. It's for those who believe but feel too imperfect to pray. For those who want to draw closer to God but feel they have to clean themselves up first.

And this book is about value. We live in a world that often measures worth by numbers—bank accounts, followers, milestones. But I believe there's an asset we all possess: *our story*. Your story is your power. It's the key to leveling the playing field, to showing up in spaces that weren't built for you and making them work in your favor.

When you read this book, you might raise an eyebrow or two. You might wonder how my kids feel about my transparency. Trust me—they know it all. We've had the hard conversations, and they support me fully. My kids taught me about body positivity and the importance of speaking openly about taboo topics. We've built a family culture where honesty isn't just encouraged; it's the norm.

This book isn't about shock value. It's not about being provocative for the sake of it. It's about calling out to those who have felt powerless—those who have been disempowered in the most foundational parts of their lives: their bodies, their money, and their stories.

At its core, *A Pot to P*ss In* is about relationships. The relationship you have with yourself, with others, and with the institutions that shape our lives. It's about discovering the power of your story and daring to tell it, no matter who tries to silence you.

ACKNOWLEDGMENTS

First and foremost, to **the family I birthed and built** with—my children and my partner—thank you for your unwavering support. I am so grateful for the way we move as one, standing together through every season.

To my **mom** and to my **dad**, whom I miss so much, thank you for raising me to be resilient, down-to-earth, and real. Your candor and support have been a constant source of strength.

To my **brothers and sisters**—including my in-laws—and to my **nieces and nephews**, thank you for shaping my identity and giving me a profound sense of belonging. Your love, care, admiration, and respect fuel me every day, no matter how near or far we are. Please know that the love and pride I feel for you are every bit as strong and mutual.

To my **extended family**—my aunts, cousins, and uncles—thank you for always showing up. You have been my extended parents and siblings, and I cherish the love and community you provide.

To my **Holy Angels family**, thank you for being my day ones and my foundation. You all gave me roots that I continue to draw strength from, no matter where I go.

To my **Lake Forest family**, thank you for being the blueprint for the intellectual life and community that makes me feel safe, challenged, and inspired. You set the standard for what a vibrant and supportive community should be.

To the **team that helped me buy this house**—thank you for believing in the vision and for making what seemed impossible a reality.

To my professors and colleagues at the **University of Wisconsin–Madison**, there is no place I would have rather completed my graduate studies. You all are my family away from family, and I am forever grateful.

To my professors and colleagues at the **University of Illinois at Chicago**, my momma told me that my grandfather used to always say, "If you can make it in Chicago, you can make it anywhere." You all taught me exactly that. I was my biggest mess with you, and yet you helped me find my way through.

To my **Paul G. Stewart family**, I still have not been able to make memories anywhere that top the ones I made with y'all.

To my **Eagle Heights community**, thank you for being family to my children when I was away from my own. You were my respite, my support, and my biggest advocates, and you provided us with a place to heal.

To the folks at **641 W Main Street**, thank you for helping me cross bridges, for understanding my vision, and for keeping a roof over my head when I struggled to do so.

To the **Madison, Wisconsin community**, thank you for making it possible for me to build a company with a worldwide reach. You have been my village, my testing ground, and my launching pad.

To all my **baby daddies** and their families, thank you for doing the best you know how with what this world has given you.

To my **publishing team**, thank you for allowing me to tell my story unfiltered and whole. Thank you for trusting me and for giving me the freedom to show up fully on the page.

To my **coaches**, thank you for letting me fall apart, faint, and fall out so I could come back together again. You helped me to offer the world my gifts and talents uninhibited.

To my **"textie bestie,"** you're the only friend on the planet I only talk to by text, and somehow, your support lands with the weight and warmth of the best in-person conversations. Your presence, even from a distance, has meant the world. I'm deeply grateful for you.

To **myself**, thank you for being relentless in your pursuit of the impossible. Your courage, grit, and vision have carried you through.

To my **ancestors**, I am determined to believe that you are walking with me and petitioning on my behalf. Thank you for continuing your work on the other side.

To my **pastor** and my **church**, Christ the Solid Rock, thank you for creating a space where everybody is somebody. I definitely feel like somebody when I am there with you all.

And finally, to **God**, my Father who protects and keeps me, thank you for never failing me.

INTRODUCTION

This Is Bigger Than Me

A Pot to Piss In is not just my story. It is the story of what it means to take up space in a world that often wants you to play small. It is a book about leadership and business, yes, but also about power, trauma, and permission—the kind of permission we need to give ourselves when the world withholds it. It's about what happens when you stop asking for a seat at the table and start building your own damn table, with mismatched chairs if necessary.

My journey started with raw emotion. My mother's sharp words—"Y'all over here destroying my stuff, and you know your momma ain't got a pot to piss in or a window to throw it out"—cut through me, exposing my vulnerabilities. But those words also ignited something fierce. I needed to respond in a way that was more than just a rebuttal. I needed to build something that would not only push back but propel me forward. I needed to show what it looks like to take a wound and turn it into a weapon.

The Power of Taboo: Leadership, Vulnerability, and Permission

Some might question why "The Orgasm Project" and "Naked" are part of a book that is, among other things, about leadership and entrepreneurship. They might ask what power, trauma, fulfillment, body, and story have to do with building businesses, leading teams, or creating legacies. The truth is, these chapters are not here for shock value. They are not the book's version of "clickbait." Instead, they are strategic explorations of how unresolved trauma and shame can keep us from fully embodying our success and greatness, even when we have reached the height of it.

This isn't just about personal healing; it's about leadership. When we do not own our power privately, we often abuse or misplace it publicly. When we fail to address our trauma, our unfulfilled needs, and our unspoken stories, those shadows show up in our leadership. They influence how we negotiate, how we advocate for our worth, and how we navigate opportunities.

This book is not suggesting that we talk openly about our most personal stories in professional spaces. It is not advocating for bringing our trauma into the workplace without discernment. But it is about acknowledging that our private experiences have public implications, whether we speak of them or not. They shape how we show up as leaders, partners, parents, and visionaries.

We've seen what happens when power and trauma collide without healing. Harvey Weinstein, Sean "Puffy" Combs, Bill Cosby, Russell Simmons, Les Moonves, Matt Lauer, Charlie Rose, Kevin Spacey, Jeffrey Epstein, Roger Ailes, Bernie Madoff, and countless others. Their stories are not just about personal failings. They are about the cost of leadership without introspection, of influence without healing. They show us what happens when private shadows cast public consequences.

But this isn't just about avoiding scandal. It is also about the quieter stories—the leaders who achieve monumental goals but cannot rest in their own accomplishments. Those who give generously to others but struggle to receive anything for themselves. Those who advocate fiercely for their teams but can't ask for a raise, a promotion, or simply the respect they deserve. These are the impacts of trauma and shame on leadership. They create ceilings in our careers and in our capacity to experience joy, satisfaction, and peace.

A Pot to Piss In offers a different path. It creates a space where readers can begin to dismantle the narratives that keep them small. It is an invitation to explore the places where shame has silenced us, where trauma has stalled us, and where unspoken stories have limited us. It is a call to step into the fullness of our power—not just for our own benefit but for the impact we are meant to make in the world.

The Hero's Journey: Redefining the Protagonist

As I started shaping *A Pot to Piss In*, I knew I wanted it to follow the structure of a hero's journey, but not in the way we typically see it. In popular culture, the hero is often white and male and faces an external battle. I wanted to challenge that narrative. My protagonist wasn't going to look or act like the typical hero we're used to seeing, yet her journey would be just as profound—if not more so.

The hero in my story is a full-figured, forty-something Black mother of six. She is complicated and contradictory. On one hand, she holds a PhD from a top university; on the other, her relationship choices are often questionable. She is a woman of faith with a deep relationship with God, yet she is openly sexual. She has a credit score under 500 but is talking about becoming a millionaire. She is a hero that many people might not recognize as such, but still, she is doing what so many women like her are doing daily: surviving, striving, and, eventually, thriving.

But her journey isn't just about achieving a personal win. This story isn't simply about buying a home. Although, for her, that was nothing short of extraordinary. It's about showing how a woman can turn a private victory into a public triumph. It's about demonstrating how the act of reclaiming your story, finding your footing, and stepping into your power can shift the ground beneath you and those who walk behind you.

In a world where stories about Black mothers with many children often end in quiet redemption or quiet struggle, I wanted this story to make noise. I wanted it to show what happens when a woman like me doesn't just find peace but finds power and uses that power to build something that changes lives, creates opportunities, and disrupts the status quo.

Embracing Legacy: From Brothels to Boardrooms

By starting this book with my great-grandmother's story, I'm drawing a line through history—from brothels to boardrooms, from survival to strategy. She may have been a madam, but she was also a businesswoman, a leader, a visionary in her own right. She did what she believed she had to do in a world that offered her few choices. I honor that legacy not by repeating it, but by evolving it.

Today, I am using what I have—my story, my experiences, my voice—to build something new. I am leading with the same grit and ingenuity, but I am also showing what it looks like when that legacy is paired with opportunity, education, and unapologetic ambition. This is what generational progress looks like.

The Power of Hip-Hop Feminism

I drew heavily from hip-hop feminism as I wrote *A Pot to Piss In*. With its grit, glamour, struggle, and success, hip-hop offers a cultural framework that embraces complexity. It is a space where contradictions live openly—where vulnerability and bravado, healing and hustle, coexist without apology. Hip-hop gave me a language and a structure to tell my story, not through a fictional character but as the protagonist of my own life.

This book is not a novel. It's not an imagined narrative with a crafted heroine. The woman you read about—the full-figured, forty-something Black mother of six who holds a PhD in one hand and her messy, beautiful, complicated life in the other—is me. Hip-hop feminism allowed me to show up fully, to write not just about surviving but about overachieving, not just about healing but about helping. Like the artists who rise from impossible circumstances, I am grinding. I am making it happen, balancing motherhood with my dreams, refusing to wait for the perfect moment to pursue what's mine.

From a rhetorical standpoint, hip-hop influenced every aspect of this book. It shaped my **invention** process—the brainstorming and the boldness to tell my story authentically. It guided my **style**, infusing the narrative with raw, unapologetic language. I wanted the book to feel like a cypher, where truth-telling isn't just encouraged but expected. The title, *A Pot to Piss In*, is a nod to this rawness—a refusal to sanitize the struggle or make my story palatable for mass consumption.

Hip-hop also shaped the **delivery** of this book. It influenced the cover design, the politics and economics of the issues I explored, and the overall vibe of the project. Like a powerful hip-hop track, I wanted this book to offer a rhythm that gets under your skin. I wanted it to be both poetry and prophecy—something that moves you and makes you move.

At its core, this book is about showing that the quiet wins matter, but so do the loud ones. It is about amplifying the moments of private prayer and transforming them into public programs that change lives. It is about taking the intimate healing from trauma and building a platform where others can reclaim their bodies, money, and stories. Hip-hop taught me that you don't need permission to take the mic. You just need the courage to speak your truth—and this book is my verse, my remix, my contribution to a larger movement that demands we show up fully, lead boldly, and live without apology.

Rest and Resilience: Softness in Hard Places

At its core, *A Pot to Piss In* is as much about rest as it is about resilience. It holds space for the quiet rituals that keep us whole—the small, sacred practices that offer refuge when the world demands more than we feel capable of giving. It explores the interplay between pleasure and work, meditation and production, and the balance of emotional labor with the need for restoration. It embraces softness not as a retreat from hard conversations but as the very strategy for engaging them.

This story doesn't present rest as an extravagant escape or a grand, curated experience. There are no weekend getaways to remote islands or luxurious spa retreats. Instead, rest shows up in staycations at local hotels, where the goal isn't to impress but to decompress. It is found in showers where prayers are whispered, in walks where thoughts unravel, in journaling sessions where chaos is sorted. It is found in sex that isn't performative but grounding—an act of reclaiming the body, of finding pleasure even when the world feels heavy.

And it doesn't get it right all the time—if ever. There are moments when rest is an afterthought, when resilience looks more like survival. But what matters is the constant questioning, the pursuit of balance in some seasons and integration in others. It is the willingness to sit with the tension of wanting a soft life while knowing that hard actions are required. It is the practice of finding moments of ease amid the hustle, not as a reward but as a right.

In this book, rest is not a pause from the work—it is part of the work. It is a reminder that pushing forward doesn't mean pushing through to the point of breaking. It is about learning to let softness be the strategy, not just the sanctuary.

The Call to Action

This book is more than a personal journey. It's a challenge to the limited ways society defines success and struggle. It is a call to action for every woman who has been told her life is a failure because she doesn't fit the mold of a "successful" woman. It is for those who are doing the work, showing up, and pushing forward— sometimes with nothing more than faith and grit.

In these pages, you won't find a hero who has it all figured out. Instead, you'll find someone figuring it out as she goes. Someone who understands that sometimes the bravest thing you can do is wake up, show up, and try again. This isn't just my story—it's our story. And my hope is that as you read it, you see yourself in it. That you find your own power, your own voice, and your own unapologetic heroism.

PROLOGUE

CORA

It's late, around ten o'clock, and the night has settled into that quiet stillness that only comes when the world outside is finally at rest. I'm on a three-way call with Mistee and Renee, laughing as we often do during these late-night catch-ups. Mistee, my sister-cousin and the family griot, always has a good story to tell, and tonight is no different.

The conversation flows easily, the kind of banter that only family who know each other inside out can share. Renee, always getting the party started, suddenly sends pictures to our group chat—old photos of family members long gone. There's one of a woman in a heavy, old-fashioned dress, her eyes staring back at me from another time. The kind of photo that makes you pause and think about where you come from.

Mistee's voice streams softly through the line, full of that familiar energy. "We're from Cairo, Illinois," she starts, setting the stage as always. "And Cora—she had a brothel."

"Who is Cora?" I ask, already knowing but wanting to hear the story unfold again, as if for the first time.

Renee jumps in, her voice warm and patient. "That would be your great-grandmother, Say. She was my great-grandmother, too, and Mistee's great-great-grandmother."

Mistee continues without missing a beat. "That's Cora. And she had thirteen kids."

Renee's tone shifts slightly, a hint of sadness creeping in. "But the majority of them were deceased by their thirties."

"One of her children was Geraldine, who worked the brothel," Mistee says, her voice steady, as if she's laying out pieces on a board for us to see.

Renee steps in to clarify, "Now, Say, I know you know this, but to keep it all straight—Geraldine, your grandmother, okay? She was my grandmother, too. And she was Mistee's great-grandmother."

Mistee picks up the thread again. "And she worked in the brothel as an employee. She had a really nice body that men were extremely attracted to, so she was one of the women in the market. And she got pregnant and had my grandmother, Florine."

"Who is my mother and your dad's sister," Renee adds.

Mistee continues. "And she's the oldest of three. She got pregnant by a guy from New Orleans who was in his sixties. I don't remember his name, though."

I can't help but ask, "And how old was she?"

"Well, rumor had it she was fourteen," Mistee says, with a hint of mystery in her voice. "But I found the documents, okay? And they say she was seventeen. So, she was seventeen when she had Grandma."

Renee chimes in again, her voice a mix of admiration and reflection. "And Geraldine was a hustler who—"

"Was in and out of jail for a variety of things," Mistee interrupts, the excitement of the story building. "But her main thing was gambling and writing checks. She'd wear different costumes and go in and out of different currency exchanges to cash checks to get money. Sometimes, she'd hit one currency exchange four times in a row, go to the car, change her wig, change her clothes, and go right back in and do it again."

I laugh, shaking my head at the audacity of it all. "How would you describe the women in our family?"

Renee answers first, her voice filled with pride. "We are definitely strong."

"We're go-getters," Mistee adds, the conviction in her voice unmistakable.

"We're thinkers, and we don't take no for an answer," I say, feeling the truth of it deep in my bones.

Renee wraps it up perfectly. "Very sensual women, very sexy women, very sensual."

The conversation lingers on those words, the silence on the line thick with shared memories and unspoken understanding. These women, the ones who came before us, were flawed, fierce, and unforgettable. They made choices that shaped their lives and ours, for better or worse. And here we are, carrying their stories, their strengths, their mistakes, and their triumphs woven into the fabric of who we are.

As I sit there, the images from the photos and the stories from Mistee and Renee swirling in my mind, I'm struck by how much we've inherited, not just in how we look or the things we do but in how we navigate the world—with a blend of hustle, heart, and an unapologetic sense of self. The legacy they left us is complicated, but it's ours, and it's powerful.

This is the backdrop of my story—the history that pulses through my veins as I stand at the crossroads of my life, trying to carve out a path that honors where I came from while still being true to who I want to become. The choices I make, and the dreams I chase are all part of this ongoing story. And like the women before me, I'm determined to make my mark in my way, on my terms.

As the call winds down and we say our goodnights, I can't help but feel a deep sense of connection to Mistee and Renee, yes, but also to all the women who came before us. I carry their stories with me, not as a burden, but as a reminder of the strength in my blood that will guide me as I continue this journey.

TABLE OF CONTENTS

Chapter 1 • **Dear Sylvia and Robert** 1

Chapter 2 • **Doctor** 11

Chapter 3 • **Felons Can't Rent** 27

Chapter 4 • **Poverty Does Shit to You** 39

Chapter 5 • **Cindy Trimm** 48

Chapter 6 • **Inconceivable** 63

Chapter 7 • **Nothing's Wasted** 78

Chapter 8 • **Tight in a Bud** 86

Chapter 9 • **Dear God** 94

Chapter 10 • **Love + Business** 102

Chapter 11 • **The Orgasm Project** 114

Chapter 12 • **Perspective** 126

Chapter 13 • **Books, Bullets, and Babies** 130

Chapter 14 • **More Books, Bullets, and Babies** 145

Chapter 15 • **Mary and Elizabeth** 159

Chapter 16 • **Naked** 173

Chapter 17 • **Net Worth** 182

Chapter 18 • **Close** 195

Chapter 19 • **Breathe** 207

Epilogue 218

About the Author 220

CHAPTER 1

DEAR SYLVIA AND ROBERT

JULY 2021

Dear Sylvia and Robert,

The moment I stepped into your home, I felt something I hadn't felt in a long time—a sense of belonging. The tall windows and the way the sunlight danced on the oak wood floors all spoke to me. It wasn't just a house but a place where I could see my family's future unfolding. A place that held the promise of peace, stability, and growth

...

That's what I wrote. But what I also wanted to say, and couldn't, was this: *I don't know how in the hell I'm going to buy this damn house. Listen. It's big and beautiful, and I can't afford it. I'm broke. My credit is trash, and my life is a mess. At the same time, I keep wondering: Can I really make this happen? I guess I'm going to have to. While the financial situation leaves much to be desired (and that's putting it nicely), I can't shake the feeling that this house was meant for us. The walls seemed to whisper stories of a future that could be ours if only I could find a way to grasp it.* Yeah. I kept that part to myself.

The letter wasn't just a step in the home-buying process; it was part of a narrative I was determined to see through to the end. The pen in my hand felt heavy with meaning as I started brainstorming the first draft, every word deliberately selected, each sentence casting a spell for our future.

In a world driven by numbers—credit scores, down payments, loan approvals—it's easy to feel boxed in, suffocated by the weight of what you don't have. The anxiety curled in my stomach, a tight knot of worry that refused to loosen. *How can I ever get past this?* The thought gnawed at me, a persistent doubt that threatened to overshadow my hope. But then, a different thought flickered to life, quiet but insistent. *What if the key isn't in the numbers at all? What if the power lies in my story, in the experiences and resilience that have brought me this far?*

My story has always been more than words—it's been my way in. My ability to paint a picture and build connections through words has created possibilities for me where none existed before. I could feel the pulse of thoughts, steady and robust, reminding me of every battle I've won and every challenge I've overcome. Maybe, just maybe, it could put me in rooms where traditional financial metrics fall short.

I've always believed that stories are more than just words; they're a force that can move mountains, open doors, and mobilize nations. The memory of past victories fueled my resolve, a quiet fire burning in the center of my chest. My story has carried me through some of life's toughest challenges, and I'm betting it can take me through this one, too.

In the early 2000s, I remember sitting at my desk late one night—textbooks piled high, baby bottles lined up like they were fresh off a factory assembly line, and crumpled sheets of paper everywhere. My fingers hovered over the keyboard, the cursor blinking at me as if asking, *Are we doing this or not?* The room was silent except for the occasional rustle of pages and the distant vibrations of the refrigerator, a stark contrast to the turmoil in my mind. *How do I make them see?* I wondered. My inconsistent grades and semester withdrawals were heavy on my mind. My transcript wasn't a "good look." And I knew it.

Meanwhile, there I was, with all my audacity, applying to two top-ranked English programs in the Midwest. The pressure was suffocating, each breath a struggle as I grappled with the fear of failure. Then it hit me—my academic record only tells one piece of the story. *Give them the other parts.*

I started typing: *Books—bullets—and babies. I juggle all three.* The words flowed from me, each keystroke a release, a way of channeling the tension into something tangible. As each word showed up on the screen, I could almost hear the committee reading my statement, understanding that despite the odds, I had a history of finishing what I had started. What they do with that understanding, well, that's out of my control. But they will know.

The determination in my heart seeped into every word. *They need to see the fighter in me*, I thought, as my willpower carried me through exhaustion. The adrenaline kept me going, the late hour forgotten as the story took shape, my story—one of grit, resilience, and unwavering persistence. That story, I'm sure, played a huge role in getting me accepted into both graduate programs I applied for, with funding to boot.

But this time, it's not about getting into a program; it's about securing a home for my family—a home that, like my education, can bring another layer of peace and stability to our lives. The stakes felt higher now, the weight of my family's future pressing down on me, but so did my resolve. And once again, I'm betting on the power of my story to help drive this journey. The words I wrote felt like stepping stones, each one bringing me closer to that front door, closer to the life I envisioned.

History shows us that stories, more than numbers, have the power to start movements and inspire change. I think of Martin Luther King Jr.'s "I Have a Dream" speech. Though long before my time, the memory of that day felt vivid and real, as if I could reach out and touch the energy of that moment. I can almost hear the murmur of the crowd gathered on that sweltering August day, the sun beating down on them, sweat trickling down their backs, but no one moving, no one leaving, all eyes fixed on the podium. I can feel the electric anticipation in the air as King stepped up. The silence before he spoke was thick with expectation, making your skin tingle and your heart race. The words that followed weren't just a speech; they were a vision—a story of a future where equality and justice would prevail. As he spoke, his voice rising and falling with the rhythm of a preacher, the crowd was spellbound, the dream he wove taking hold of their hearts. The resonance of that moment, the way his words echoed through the crowd, is a testament to the power of storytelling. It was more than just the content of his speech; it was the passion, the belief, the unwavering conviction that made it unforgettable. It wasn't the facts or the figures that moved people. It was the story of his dream. A story so powerful it transcended time, igniting a fire in the hearts of millions, a fire that still burns today.

Similarly, Simon Sinek's *Start with Why: How Great Leaders Inspire Everyone to Take Action* reminds us that the "why" behind what we do can be more potent than the "what" or the "how." In his book, Sinek tells us story after story about how people transformed the world not because they had bigger budgets and the best credit but because they were able to inspire those around them with their *why*. The Wright brothers, Steve Wozniak, and Steve Jobs are all right there with Martin Luther King Jr., moving people to action with the stories they tell behind the products they sell or the aircraft they're inventing. And I'm putting myself right there with them. These examples aren't just inspiring—they're proof that a well-told story can transcend the barriers of traditional systems. My story might not start a movement or change the world, but it can change my family's life trajectory. If King's dream could inspire a nation and Sinek's *why* could drive innovation, my story can get us this house. It's not just about what I want; it's about why this home matters to us.

"You're going to need to write a letter of intent," Ruby's voice flowed through the speaker. I imagined her in her car, probably wearing a pair of those quirky, cute glasses she's known for. Maybe bright red frames or yellow—who knows with Ruby. She's magical like that.

"A letter of intent? For a house?" I repeated, skepticism creeping into my voice. The concept felt foreign, like a plot twist I hadn't expected in this complicated story.

"Yes," Ruby replied, her tone calm and reassuring. "It's a way to connect with the sellers, to show them that this house isn't just another property to you. It's a home where you see your future and your family. They need to see that."

Until that point, everything had been about numbers—scores and dollars, cold calculations that felt impersonal. But Ruby was right. That letter could add humanity to a process that often felt cold and sterile, even if it wasn't as objective as we like to think.

Numbers, like everything else, paint a picture. They tell a story about whether you check the boxes and whether your square pegs fit into their square holes. Can you meet the standard—their criteria, which seems objective? And based on the rise or fall of those numbers, a story is told, a case is made, a decision is determined. But the problem with numbers is that they're only evidence without testimony and context—a piece of a much bigger story.

Maybe that's why gatekeepers rely so heavily on them. They believe numbers can't seduce or influence them. But how crazy is that? In general, bankers, investors, and humans can all be influenced by numbers. No, seduction isn't what people are trying to avoid. And they don't prefer numbers because they lessen the risk. Listen, I'm from Chicago's Low End. I've seen people play with numbers—manipulating check stubs, stretching timelines, doctoring taxes. Numbers can lie just as quickly as words.

Nah, banks and investors prefer numbers over words because they're trying to protect their hearts. After all, they aren't robots. And a good story can convince you to give a con person your money, a slick man your body, and a dishonest woman everything you own. But we're not talking about cons, slicksters, and liars here. We are talking about the value of a really good story with a beautiful mission. That story can change everything, even when you have bad credit and have lived through poverty. After all, numbers don't start movements; stories do.

I glanced around my bedroom, and the mess surrounding me reflected the chaos in my life. But maybe, just maybe, my story could cut through the noise of credit scores and loan applications. Maybe it could reach the hearts of those who built the home I so desperately wanted.

"Okay," I said, the word coming out quickly, surprising even me. "I'll do it. If there's one thing I can do, it's write a letter."

"And make it beautiful, Sagashus," Ruby added, her voice softening. "This is your chance to show them who you are."

The letter to Sylvia and Robert wasn't just a formal expression of interest but an open and honest window into my life. I kept it as real as possible, and I was vulnerable in ways that made me feel exposed, maybe even at their mercy, but I still maintained my dignity. It wasn't just about writing a letter but asking for something more—something my family and I desperately needed. I couldn't hold anything back.

This letter was my chance to show them how much this home would mean to us. I needed to show them the surface details and the heart of my family's need for a sanctuary. So I told them my truth:

I have a big family. I am the single mother of six children. Six months out of the year, I care for a dad who has dementia. He's about to be eighty, and he lives in Chicago. I educate my children from home (we're homeschoolers) and run my growing business from it. As you can see, home is the center of EVERYTHING for me.

Where we live has to be many things to many people—a schoolhouse, a nursing home, an office, a retreat center, a place of refuge. Space is very important to us. When I walked into your home, I saw enough rooms to accommodate the demands of my life as well as offer my family and me a haven. For example, I—and a couple of my children—struggle with anxiety and sometimes depression. Your high ceilings and big windows are exactly what we need on those days. As you can imagine, laundry is a monster in our family. I'd always joked about buying a home with three washers and dryers. I joked about it because I'd never seen it before, so I didn't think it was even possible. But then I walked into your home and saw two sets of laundry units. I reimagined possibilities. I am anemic, and so is one of my daughters. We are always cold. To live in a house with heated floors, something I never even knew was "a thing," makes me feel that you imagined people like us when you designed your home.

Writing those words felt like stepping off a ledge, trusting that they would see the depth of what I was trying to say. I'd shared so much, exposing parts of our lives that I usually kept private. I was standing in front of two strangers, essentially asking them to see me, my family, and our needs—not just in terms of logistics, but in terms of who we really were. The pressure of it weighed on me as I wrote, knowing how deeply connected my sense of hope was to this house.

It was one thing to tell them the facts—how many kids I had or the challenges we faced with space. It was another thing entirely to lay out the emotional truth: This house was more than just a roof over our heads. It was the sanctuary we'd been longing for. This house could hold the pieces of our chaotic, beautiful life together in a way that no other space we've occupied could.

I had to trust that by sharing those details about our struggles with anxiety, our constant battle with laundry, or our need for warmth, they would understand that this wasn't just about convenience. It was about finding a home that could nurture us, physically and emotionally, a space that was big enough to accommodate the weight of all of us.

As I wrote, my body started to relax, slowly releasing the pressure that, just minutes before, had my shoulders tight and stiff. The fear of getting it wrong had caused my muscles to ache with dread. My ADHD had been going into overdrive, my mind running around in circles like a dog chasing its tail, even though I was physically sitting still. I had to close my eyes, take a deep breath, and try to quiet everything—my mind, my emotions, the pain in my body. *How do I make them see what this house means to us?* This letter wasn't just a step in the home-buying process; it was part of a narrative I was determined to see through.

So I continued to write:

In my wildest dreams, I wanted a space that was flexible enough for me to run my primary business but would also double as an Airbnb. I needed that space to have some level of noise control and separation from my living quarters while also being connected. I needed a kitchen island for meal prep and for serving food, and a closet big enough that could also be a prayer room. My children have lived two (and sometimes three) to a room their whole lives. But I've noticed my home is a lot calmer and more peaceful when they have their own space. Your home is big enough to make that possible. And finally, the idea that one day, one of my children can move out of the family home and live in the smaller home right in front of it is everything we've dreamed of.

This wasn't just about convincing Sylvia and Robert; it was about using my story at every stage—from negotiating with real estate agents to securing a loan from the bank to rewriting my life. Every word of that letter was a thread in the fabric of my family's future, a future I was determined to weave together piece by piece.

This wasn't just about owning a house but about creating a safe place for my family. I could see it so clearly—my children running through the hallways, their laughter filling the space as sunlight streams through the windows. The thought of my father sitting by the fireplace, a soft blanket draped over his legs, made my eyes tear up. He deserved this comfort, imagining the peace on his face as he gets comfortable in a home that would be as much his as mine. And for me, the house represented more than shelter. It would be the foundation on which I could continue building my business, empowering other women to find their own strength and resilience. The stakes were high because that house was more than just walls and a roof—it would be the future we've been dreaming of.

I wrote more ...

Finally, I have to share that the owners are also a key factor. As you can see, family is a big deal to me. Having to leave mine to move here to pursue my dreams means I had to build a support structure that felt like home. Growing up in low-income housing on Chicago's South Side, the neighbors were moms, cousins, dads, aunts, uncles, and siblings—even with no blood ties.

When I met you as a couple, two things struck me. First, I was impressed with you, Sylvia, because of your vision. You've created a space that allowed you to fulfill your vision for family and business. My hope is that I could sit at your feet one day as someone who has trailblazed a path I'm trying to make sense of. But if I can't, I love that your story is part of the legacy of that home.

Robert, you said very little. But the one thing I remember is that you built the walls thick enough for noise control. And while that was a big deal for me as a potential buyer, the bigger deal was the idea that I was in the presence of a man who was part of building a space that, from what I understood, has been connected with his wife's vision. I teach a class called Love + Business. In it, women often tell stories about how their husbands undermine their dreams, not support them.

The little you said was a big deal for both the story I'd like to share with my children as time passes and the story I'd like to share with my clients. As an English major, a collector of stories, and a storyteller, I know that narratives are important. And, for me, the "lore" of the original owners is as crucial as the ceilings, the island, and the space itself.

As I wrote those words, I felt a new wave of vulnerability, a different kind of nakedness. *But what if it doesn't work?* The thought of losing this house to another buyer was almost unbearable. My children would continue to share cramped spaces, and my father wouldn't have the comfort he deserves. Losing the house wouldn't just mean losing a piece of property—it would mean losing the future I've envisioned for us, which felt so close yet still out of reach.

I've always known that stories are powerful, but I didn't grasp their impact until I had a conversation with a childhood friend. Let's call him Omari. He graduated as the salutatorian of our eighth-grade class, his sharp mind already setting him apart from so many of us. He went on to one of the best Catholic high schools in Chicago, attended a prestigious undergraduate university, and graduated from one of the top medical programs in the country. His brilliance was evident in everything he did, from the way he spoke with confidence to the ease with which he navigated complex ideas.

One night, we were talking about the value of our respective degrees—the one he had as a psychiatrist and the one I was pursuing in English. I was sitting in the small living room of my two-bedroom campus apartment, and my three children were finally asleep, their soft breaths the only other sound in the room. The lamp's warm glow cast a soft light on the cluttered space filled with textbooks, toys, and half-folded laundry. The familiarity of my surroundings was comforting, but the conversation took on a weight that felt far beyond those four walls. We somehow got onto the subject of the value of each degree, the conversation shifting from light banter to something more profound. His voice was calm, measured, the kind of tone that made you sit up and really listen.

He said something that stuck with me: "The work you do in English keeps people from having to come visit me as a psychiatrist." His words hung in the air, their weight slowly sinking in. It was as if he had opened a door to a new understanding, one I hadn't fully considered before.

He wasn't saying that literature, stories, and writing replace the medical establishment, but he was acknowledging the healing power that can be found in those places. The way he spoke, there was a softness in his tone, a quiet respect for the work that stories do on the human soul. The kind of healing that can positively impact a person's mental health, stave off depression, improve clarity and focus, and alleviate anxiety. I could almost see the connections he was making, the invisible threads that tied the work of a psychiatrist to the work of a storyteller. Omari, a medical professional, was trying to help me understand that the healing power of storytelling is something he had come to respect and value. In that moment, I felt a deep sense of validation, as if the words I'd been writing for years had suddenly taken on a new, more profound meaning.

I think about that often. The idea is repeatedly affirmed in the emails from people who have thanked me for sharing my story at a keynote. It's reaffirmed when I break down watching a story on television that makes me feel seen. My story has opened doors I didn't even know existed and has connected me with people in ways that numbers never could. And here, once again, I was relying on my story to connect, to cut through the coldness of numbers and logic. This house wasn't just a place to live—it was the key to my family's future, and I had to make them see that.

So I ended the letter with this:

I love your home for both that lore and its ability to accommodate my family. I love it because I imagine my future there and the future of those who will come behind me. I look forward to hosting clients, guests, and family in a space that allows me to do it all. And I look forward to educating my children there as much as I look forward to hiding away from them and the world in a space that is roomy enough for me to breathe. Thank you for your thoughtful design and vision. And I hope to add to the beauty and legacy of the story that is the house on Huron, especially as it relates to the empowerment of women.

Warmly and respectfully,
Dr. Sagashus Levingston

I poured my heart into that letter, but again, there's no guarantee that my story will do what I need it to do: make a real connection. The uncertainty looms like a dark cloud, heavy and oppressive, threatening to overshadow my hope. *What if they don't see what I see?* The doubt creeps in, insidious and relentless, a cold whisper in the back of my mind that refuses to be silenced. *This is uncharted territory*, I remind myself, *navigating a world that often reduces people to numbers.*

The path ahead feels precarious, like walking a tightrope with no safety net. But I've been here before, facing impossible odds, and I know the way through. The memory of past struggles and the victories that followed give me a flicker of hope, a small flame that I nurture in the face of the darkness. It's faith, hard work, and trust in the power of my story—the story that's brought me this far. I sense the gravity of that story, its importance bearing down on me, but also its power, a lifeline I must hold onto tightly. I've got to believe it can carry us the rest of the way.

And so, with a quiet determination, I step forward, trusting the story that's carried me this far will lead me through the unknown.

After days of drafting and redrafting, I sent it to Ruby to share it with the sellers of the house. The letter was no longer just mine—it was out there, waiting to be received, waiting to speak on my behalf. The anxiety still lingered, but there was a quiet peace underneath it. I'd said everything I needed to say. Now, it was in their hands.

A day or so later, Ruby's response came through—a thirty-second video message I didn't see coming but was grateful to receive.

"Okay, Sagashus, I just pulled over to read your letter of intent. And it's beautiful," she said, her voice cracking slightly. "It's a lot more beautiful than the ugly cry I'm doing sitting out in front of the preschool. But—I just wanted to say— you nailed it."

Ruby broke out into a genuine smile and a heartfelt laugh, the kind that radiated through the screen, making me feel like maybe I could breathe for the first time in days. As the seconds ticked by, I watched her transition through a range of very human emotions—pride, joy, and something deeper.

"Knocked it out of the park. This is supposed to be your house," she said, her tone shifting to something more serious. The laughter faded from her face, replaced by a look of quiet resolve. "Where are the tissues?" she added, laughing through what I could tell was a second wave of tears. "Good job. It's awesome."

As the video ended, I sat there, phone in hand, absorbing Ruby's words. I felt the weight of her sincerity, the rawness of her reaction. If the letter had touched her that deeply, maybe it could do the same for Sylvia and Robert. Maybe it could rally a team of people behind this cause, inspiring them to look past the numbers and scores, past the barriers that had always seemed insurmountable. Maybe it could carry my story into their hearts and inspire them to take me seriously enough to help me see this thing through.

For the first time in a long while, I allowed myself to hope.

CHAPTER 2

Doctor

JANUARY 2021

It's a little after ten o'clock at night, and the kids and I are driving back to Madison from Chicago. The night sky is a deep, velvety black, punctuated by the occasional glow of streetlights and the red taillights of cars ahead. Despite the late hour, all fourteen lanes are packed, bumper to bumper with cars. The roar of engines, the distant honking, and the faint sound of bass through car windows create a symphony of city life that feels strangely comforting in its familiarity. With the worst of the city's heavy traffic behind us, I finally start to relax. The tension in my shoulders eases as the road ahead opens up, stretching out like a ribbon of quiet opportunity. It's clear for miles, and with this sense of ease, most of the kids fall asleep, just like they used to when they were small. Their soft, rhythmic breathing fills the car, a lullaby of sorts, blending with the steady roll of the tires against the asphalt.

My fourth child, my second son, remains awake, earbuds in, lightly bobbing his head as he gazes out the window. The dim light from the dashboard casts a soft glow on his face, highlighting the profile of a young man who's growing up faster than I can keep up with. I glance at my children through the rearview mirror and settle into the drive that will last at least two more hours. It's a dark, winding path that's leading us back to our lives in Madison. As I catch my breath, my thoughts drift back to the visit gone wrong, leaving me questioning how I could have made such a huge miscalculation. The weight of that misstep presses on my chest, the frustration bubbling just beneath the surface.

It's hard to believe that fifteen years have passed since I left low-income housing on Chicago's South Side with three small children, chasing a dream that felt too big and too distant—earning a master's and then a doctorate in English at the University of Wisconsin–Madison. The memories of that journey flood back, vivid and sharp: the cramped apartments, the late-night study sessions, the exhaustion that never seemed to fade. During those years, I lost friends and family—some to violence, others to illness or accidents—and gained new life in the form of three more children of my own. The bittersweet cycle of loss and renewal etched itself into my heart, each experience leaving its mark. I watched as relationships crumbled and new ones took root, as my body bore the visible marks of stress: weight gain, gray hairs, and the permanent bags under my eyes. The reflection in the mirror each morning was a testament to the battles fought and the resilience built. But somehow, through thirteen brutal winters, intense springs, too-short summers, and busy falls, I persevered. The seasons blurred together in a relentless march of time, each one a reminder of the passage of years.

Yet, nothing could have prepared me for the shock of returning home, only to realize that time hadn't stood still for anyone while I was chasing my dream. My parents had gotten older. The reality of their aging hit me like a cold wind, unexpected and unwelcome, piercing through the protective bubble I had built around my dreams. I never considered that. The home I knew, the roles we played, had all changed. I was no longer the child coming home to be cared for—I was the adult who had to figure out how to support my mom as she cared for my dad. The weight of that responsibility settled heavily on my shoulders, a burden I wasn't sure I was prepared to carry.

As I continue driving, my thoughts drift to my grandma, the one person who always made Chicago feel like home, no matter where we were. Her memory wraps around me like a warm blanket, offering comfort in the midst of my swirling thoughts. If my parents were my anchors in the world, she was the bedrock. Her presence was unwavering, a source of strength I drew on more times than I can count. Her house, the big eight-bedroom place in Bronzeville on Chicago's South Side, was the family headquarters. The creak of the old wooden floors, the faint smell of her cooking wafting from the kitchen, and the sound of her laughter echoing through the halls are etched into my memory like the lines of a throwback song. It was where we all gathered, where stories were told, and where laughter filled the rooms. The walls of that house had absorbed decades of love, loss, and everything in between, making it more than just a building; it was the heartbeat of our family. My grandma was its heart. Without her, the house was just bricks and mortar, but with her, it was home.

"You heard of Bay Bay's kids? Well, those are Say Say's kids." My grandma's voice plays back in my mind, spoken with that mix of signifying and love that she could pull off. She was the kind of woman who could make you feel like you were the most special person in the world, even as she teased you. My cousin Tiffany still brings up those family-famous words from our matriarch whenever she gets the chance, and every time she does, it brings a smile to my face, even now.

I have six children—three boys and three girls. At the time of my grandma's passing, my youngest was just a baby, not even a month old. He's the only one of my children she never met, and that thought still tugs at me. I didn't make it to Chicago from Madison in time to share him with her before she transitioned. But somewhere in my naive, overly optimistic mind, I like to believe that as she was transitioning out and he was transitioning in, they met somewhere in the in-between, had their ancestor-to-descendant moment, and then kept moving on opposite paths. That would explain why he, my last child, is such an old soul. My grandma must have left him a little bit of herself to carry back to us. It sounds good, right? It gives me comfort to think that way, even if it's just a story I tell myself.

She was ninety-four when she left us. I had convinced myself that she would live to be one hundred, at least, so her death came as a surprise to a lot of us. But even though it caught me off guard, I was able to make peace with it because I had spent the last six months of her life traveling from Madison to Chicago, sitting on the edge of her bed, recording her story. It became our ritual, our thing. From December until June, I made that trip every month, gathering her history, her memories, and her wisdom.

Sometimes, my younger cousins, my children, aunts, and uncles would join us, crowding around the bed to listen as she recounted stories from a life that had spanned almost a century. Other times, it was just the two of us, sitting alone, me with my "Grandmother's Book," a book similar to a baby's book, and her with quick mind and hilarity. I asked her about everything. "Grandma, tell me about the day you and Granddaddy got married."

"Well, we took the EL to ..." she remembered.

Wait, did they have the EL train back then? Wow, I thought to myself, astonished at the sophistication of Chicago's transportation system, even in the 1940s.

I asked more questions.

"Grandma, how are me and my mom alike? How are we different?" Each time, she would smile, sometimes laugh, and dive into the stories, giving me pieces of a past that had shaped us all.

Listening to my grandmother share her journey both grounded and filled me up. It gave me a sense of belonging. I had come from someplace. But it also made me not just see her as a grandma but as a woman who had to make decisions and compromises, who had cried in her life, and who had been afraid of things as much as she had been fearless. I was able to see that whatever I was going through in love, family, or maybe even some other aspects of my life, she had probably gone through.

But now, I realize that much of what she shared with me has faded from my memory. The elders, her children, had secured that book long before I arrived in Chicago to collect it. And I'm okay with that because, at the time, they needed those stories more than I did. I remember sitting there, hearing one of them say, "I never knew that about Mother."

Another said, "Mommy never shared that with me." A part of me wanted to judge them for not knowing and not asking, but I kept those thoughts to myself.

I can't say those things out loud because it would be disrespectful, hurtful, and judgmental. It would also be ignorant of me to pretend I don't understand how mother-child relationships work. We take for granted that our mothers will always be there, so history never seems to matter until it's too late. We, as daughters, get so caught up in our own resentment over how we believe our mothers fell short that taking the time to understand their stories feels beyond our capacity. And as Black women dealing with our own wounds from microaggressions, sexism, and emotional and mental violence, it's hard to imagine what our moms carried, not just because we see them as invincible, but because they don't make it a habit to be vulnerable. That's just not what Black women from her generation did—they kept their business close, kept up a good front, and didn't show too much emotion.

I don't remember everything because I never had the chance to revisit our conversations in their entirety. On Father's Day of 2014, we completed the book. A month later, she was gone. And the book we created together? I haven't seen it since. I do have the memories of those trips back and forth to the family house, collecting my grandmother's story in what would be her final days.

Uncle Reverend Socks took over her room, and in a way, he's become the traveling heart of the family. His presence is always felt before you see him—the sound of his boots clomping on the porch. He's always popping up at his sisters' houses, making his presence known with a loud greeting, a booming laugh, and the clatter of whatever tool he's brought along, whether he's dumping their garbage, shoveling their snow, or cutting the grass. And, of course, there are always a few missing cans of pop from the fridge when he's around, evidence of his visits as sure as the freshly shoveled walkway.

Whereas everyone used to come to headquarters to visit Grandma, Uncle Reverend Socks now brings a little bit of 618 to everyone else. As he makes his rounds, you can almost hear the echoes of Grandma's old house—the creak of the door, the shuffle of her slippers on the hardwood floor—woven into the fabric of his visits. He's the ambassador of the family, carrying with him the warmth and familiarity of 618, spreading it wherever he goes.

But to visit 618 now is to find the heart of the home locked away, its warmth dimmed by the absence of Grandma's ever-present light.

Without my grandma, the house no longer feels like the warm, welcoming refuge it once was. For me, that sense of stability and belonging has faded, and instead, each visit feels more like an intrusion. It is as if, without her there, my children and I have become bulls in a china shop. Our presence disrupts the careful balance my mom and aunts had worked so hard to maintain in their homes.

When we arrived at my mom's house, it didn't take long for the reminders to begin. "Well, that TV doesn't work because your kids destroyed it." "This TV had a remote, but your kids destroyed that too." "I used to have a really nice chair right here, but ..." On and on that tour would go, pointing out the damages accumulated over time, as if each broken item was a marker of our visits.

In my aunt Word's home, we never stayed long enough to create that record. Aunt Word always welcomed us with food, treats, and a steady flow of God's message. Not much technology, not much entertainment—just good food and a whole lot of Bible. It was a different kind of sanctuary, one where the focus was on spiritual nourishment rather than material comforts.

"Here y'all go, Boom Boom," Aunt Word would say, calling me by the nickname she gave me, as she set bowls of one of her famous soups on the counter. "And don't forget to say your blessings."

Then, there was my grandma's house, which had now become fiercely protected by Aunt Charm. She wore bright red lips and a reddish-brown afro, neatly secured in place by one of her various head wraps. Unlike my grandma, who had welcomed us with open arms despite the chaos we brought, Aunt Charm didn't play. Under her rule, there was no lingering or hanging out without a purpose. You did what you came to do, and then you left.

"How long are y'all going to be here?" she'd ask the moment we stepped inside, as if we all understood what the question meant. There would be no bulls lingering too long in her china shop. Although not my friendliest aunt, she's a caregiver, looking after the small children of her daughter who had left this earth way too young, watching over a partner who was dealing with the lasting effects of a stroke, and taking care of my brother, who was blind. She was protective of that house, not just because it needed guarding but because that's who she was.

The final space belonged to Aunt Baby, who had recently purchased and renovated a home she planned to use as an Airbnb. She lived in Texas but kept this home in Chicago. At one point, I was talking with her about renting her Chicago home so that I could be closer to my parents and help my mom care for my dad with dementia. She was so supportive. But I could also see that she loved her new home. Before my grandma passed, when she'd come to visit, she'd sleep in the bed with her. Now that Grandma's gone, Aunt Baby sleeps in the living room of the home she grew up in. Even though Aunt Guardian had carved out a space for her, making it private, I'm sure it's not the same. I wonder if she feels like a guest in the home she once lived in. And now she has her own space? Why would I interrupt that?

Even if she didn't mind, sleeping in the living room was not the same as sleeping in the bed with your mom ... but she's not here anymore. And for someone who has been independent for so long, it's nothing like sleeping in her own bed, but she didn't have one here. So as much as she said it was okay for us to be in her nice, newly renovated home, I realized that there was a good chance we would both regret it later. She would regret it because, for the first time, she owned her own space in the city she grew up in, a space she hadn't yet discovered she might be very protective over and may want to be a little selfish about. And I would regret it because I would find myself dealing with her resentment. Not to mention, you know, bulls in the china shop—Say Say's kids. We have this history, and I didn't want to take the credit for being the first people to destroy her walls or damage her belongings. I didn't trust us.

The truth is, whatever my aunts and mother have, it's theirs. Their homes, filled with the warmth of carefully chosen furnishings and the smells of meals cooked with love, are sacred spaces built over lifetimes of hard work, sacrifice, and dedication. They have spent lifetimes building, growing, and amassing. Each room holds echoes of their struggles and triumphs, a testament to the lives they've created. They didn't need me and my kids crashing and taking up space in their hard-earned sanctuaries in the name of being family and "showing up." The thought of imposing on their carefully maintained peace filled me with guilt, a nagging sense that my presence might have upset the delicate balance they'd worked so hard to maintain. In the words of Dr. Hazel Symonette, if I was going to offer help, let it be "helpful help." I was going to have to find a way to be present without adding to their stress or raising their anxieties. No more bulls in the china shop, knocking over the things they'd spent years putting in place.

But what was I going to do? The question weighed heavily on my mind, a constant companion as I tried to navigate the growing challenges. My parents needed me, including my mom, who would never admit it. She was overwhelmed by the responsibility of caring for my dad. Dementia had stolen large chunks of the man we once knew, leaving behind an occasional stranger who sometimes frightened her with his outbursts. My fiercely independent mom had always been clear about what she could and couldn't tolerate in a relationship.

"In relationships, you gotta know what you can deal with," she'd say. "Now, Ike, he's argumentative and has his women. But that doesn't bother me. What I can't deal with is a man who fights. And he can't deal with a woman who cheats. We know what works for us. And we keep folks out of our business." Her words were always delivered with a confidence that made you believe she had everything under control, and for the most part, she did.

But with dementia, he began to show aggression, something new and terrifying. The sharpness in his voice, the unpredictable outbursts—it was like watching a storm gather in a once calm sky. My dad started having problems with bodily functions, urinating and defecating on himself. The smell of antiseptic and soiled linens became a regular part of the household, a constant reminder of how much had changed. My mom struggled to reconcile this new reality with the man she had known for so long.

"Ike has always been a con man his entire life. Now he thinks I'm his maid, walking through the house, shitting on himself, and there I am walking behind him, cleaning it up," she'd say, a mix of frustration and fear in her voice. Her words carried a raw edge. "I don't mind wiping up his shit. He eats eight times a day and doesn't eat the same meal twice. I don't mind that either. But when he falls on the ground and wants me to pull his old ass up, that's too much. Hell, I'm old, too. If I'm helping him up when he falls, who the fuck is going to help my old ass? He knows how to get up." Her love was laced with frustration and fear—a fear she wouldn't dare admit but couldn't hide. The lines on her face, the weariness in her eyes, all spoke of a woman stretched to her limits yet still holding on.

Determined to support my parents, in 2018, I devised a plan to send my children to Chicago to help care for their granddad as part of their homeschool curriculum. The idea was born out of desperation and a deep desire to connect my children with their roots. I wanted them to experience the connection to extended family that I had growing up, to learn their family's history from those who lived it, and to feel a sense of responsibility toward older generations.

But I was also thinking about something else. While raising me, my mom had been so committed to relying on no one that she didn't teach me how to show up for her. Her independence was like armor, protecting her from the world but also keeping others at a distance. She always said, "People always want to be there for you until you need them the most, and then they disappoint you. Now, me, I take care of myself. I don't need anyone to take care of me, and I pay my own way. But I don't depend on nobody, and I don't ask anyone for anything." Her words were a mantra, repeated so often that they became ingrained in me, shaping how I approached the world.

Over the years, to avoid feeling rejected (and because I was spoiled and lazy), I didn't offer much support, even when I saw that she would have benefited from it. Regret gnawed at me, a bitter taste in my mouth as I remembered all the times I could have done more. One day, while visiting her in Chicago, I took her to Jewel-Osco, a grocery store she had shopped at throughout my childhood. For this particular run, I stayed in the car as she went inside to make her purchases. When she came back, I was on the phone, laughing and talking to a friend or a relative. I opened the van door and watched as she struggled to balance managing her cane and putting her bags in the vehicle. The sight of her struggling, her hands full and her movements slow, hit me like a punch to the gut.

Even though I saw she was having a hard time, getting out to help wasn't my first instinct. Instead, I sat there, frozen in my own selfishness, letting her struggle. I kept talking and watching until, finally, I felt convicted. *So you're just going to sit here and watch her go through this?* a voice in my head said. The guilt washed over me, heavy and undeniable, pushing me into action. I ended the call, ignored her protests, and got out to help. The relief in her eyes was fleeting, but I caught a brief flicker of gratitude that she quickly masked with her usual toughness. I could tell from her body language that my choice mattered to her.

For my children, I wanted it to be their first instinct to serve the elders around them. I wanted them to have the empathy and awareness that had taken me years to learn. I didn't want them to hesitate. I wanted that to be a part of their worldview from childhood into adulthood. I envisioned a future where helping family wasn't a choice but a natural response, as automatic as breathing. Selfishly, I wanted it to be so normal that when my time came to be cared for, the transition from caretaker to receiver of care would be seamless and unbroken. The thought of being vulnerable, of needing help, scared me, but I wanted my children to be ready when that time came. Clear about where I stood on this issue, I sent my fourth and fifth children to Chicago first, and when their time ended, I sent my oldest son.

My parents and children enjoyed their time together, and they grew to have a very tight bond. The house came alive with the sound of children's laughter, shared stories, and the joy of rediscovered connections. And as much as we all loved the arrangement, it wasn't sustainable. The strain of daily caregiving began to show in small ways—exhaustion creeping into their voices, tension rising over small misunderstandings. Part of the problem was that my mom still worked. This meant the kids would be left alone with my dad for entire workdays, which worked in the past when he was himself. When my older kids were smaller, especially my two oldest girls, they would spend summers with him. He was a rock back then, full of life and wisdom, teaching them the old ways—how to play with a yo-yo, how to cook a meal from scratch, how to listen to the stories that only he could tell. While the younger children were having fun with their granddad, listening to his stories and laughing at his jokes, they were starting to experience a different version of him—one who would tell them stories about how he was waiting on his mom to pick him up or who would suddenly burst into tears, crying about how much he missed his brother, who had died almost a decade ago. The shifts in his behavior were jarring, a reminder of the relentless progression of his illness. It became clear to us that he would need a different kind of support from me and my children, one that would include him spending more time with me. The realization was bittersweet, a mix of acceptance and sadness as we adjusted to the new reality of our lives.

In 2019, after another extended hospital stay, my mom and I decided it would be best if my dad came to stay with me for a while. Having no luggage of his own, my mom filled a garbage bag with clothes, handed me his medicine and a portable urine container, and sent us off from Chicago back to Madison.

On the ride, I played the songs and artists I knew he loved: "Can You Stand the Rain" by New Edition, K'Jon's "On the Ocean," and anything by Patti LaBelle or the Temptations. Several times, he used his little handheld urinal. It was a nice ride. Over the months, we'd make that trip back and forth a few more times until COVID-19 ended them. Although we said very little, I knew my dad enjoyed the ride. It made the two-and-a-half to three-hour journey bearable as long as the playlist was good.

My dad was impatient and hated any kind of traffic congestion. We made it a point to travel late at night, leaving Chicago around ten o'clock and often reaching our destination around one o'clock in the morning. This time was no different.

And like that night, Chicago's traffic was still being itself.

I was so excited to have Diddy (that's what I called him) at home with us. He had at least twelve children, but out of all of them, I was the only one who had been consistent in his life. It was very clear to me that the day would come when I'd have to take on the responsibility of caring for him. I just didn't think that the time would come so soon. I thought I had at least ten or fifteen more years, or if I'm honest, I imagined we wouldn't be here until I became much more financially stable. As I imagined it, my business would've matured a little more, and I would've had a lot more dollars in the bank. God had other plans, apparently. And it was okay because despite our history—one in which I had to develop a hard shell on the outside to protect myself from the pain and hurt that came with a dad living with drug addiction—I still loved my daddy.

He was the first man I'd ever loved and admired and had fun with. He gave me my name. He used to read the dictionary when he was in jail. And he ran across the word *sagacious*, meaning wise, shrewd, and calculating. It was right across from the word *salacious*, which means pornographic. There is only one letter difference between the two words. And I always thought that one letter was the difference between me working on the pole or at the podium. Given our family history with sex work, I believe that his quiet but very intentional way encouraged this part of the tree to grow in a different direction. He taught me the value of names. He taught me how to make pancakes, crush pecan shells, cook lobster, and he often talked to me about life.

As a child, I walked down the streets with him, singing and laughing. Seeing us together made strangers smile. We had a bond so intense that when I was in danger, he sensed it, and vice versa. Once, when I was a very young child, I woke up out of my sleep crying because I dreamed he was in a casket. My mom and I took the EL, traveling all the way to the North Side of Chicago to where he was living to check on him because the dream had left me shook. When we reached him, he was both surprised and happy to see us, explaining that he had been in trouble. Dealing with the aftermath of a fight one of his stepchildren had been involved with, he had been in a situation where a group of kids had been throwing rocks at him and the house they lived in. Typing this now, as an adult who scrolls through the internet and reads about school shootings, human trafficking, women dying at the hands of their lovers, and Black women and men dying from police brutality, his bout with the angry teens with rocks sounds so trivial. But back then, it felt as big as a nuclear war. It felt dangerous and deadly. And to hear him tell my mom about it, well, it was worth traveling across the world just to be near him.

I hadn't felt that kind of connection with him for a while. The years had built some walls between us, walls made of time, distance, and unspoken words. Having him home with me allowed us to form a new bond. A part of me longed to be his little girl again, even if that meant doing so as his caretaker. I looked forward to serving him, even though I didn't quite understand what I was taking on.

Within twenty-four hours of arriving, my dad disappeared. Panic shot through me like ice water in my veins, the calm of the previous day shattered in an instant. I was upstairs, getting ready for a work event. The smell of my perfume lingered in the air, mixing with the tension that suddenly filled the room. With my makeup on and the back of my dress needing to be zipped, I came downstairs to ask my son to fasten it for me and noticed that my dad wasn't there. The space where he had been sitting was empty, and the quiet in the house suddenly felt ominous.

"Cho, where is Ike?" I asked, trying to keep my voice calm.

"I thought he was upstairs with you," Cho said, confused.

"No, Cho, he wasn't with me. He was downstairs watching television," I said, the fear rising in my chest.

Frantically, I searched our building, knocking on doors, checking elevators, and walking from floor to floor. I called 911 and then canceled my event. The police arrived, and within a short time, they found him sitting in a red car, a shade similar to my van. When they brought him back, he was disoriented, rubbing his head as he walked toward me. I was overwhelmed with relief. As the officers explained where they found him, my eyes filled with tears, imagining all the ways things could have gone terribly wrong. I thought about someone shooting him, thinking he was trying to steal items from their car. I imagined him being arrested or beaten because, to someone who didn't know him, his Black body—as old and compromised as it was—might have been read as a threat or seen as criminal.

Seeing the worry etched into my face, my dad looked at me with a vulnerability I wasn't used to seeing in him. "Say, girl. You do love me," he said, his voice tinged with a mix of surprise and realization, as if that was the thing that mattered most in that moment.

I was confused. "Of course—what? What are you even talking about right now?" I was so confused. It baffled me that the parent who always called to check on me and who was always warning me about the dangers of the world wasn't registering the gravity of this moment in his mind. I was stuck. That was when it started to make sense to me that we're not in Kansas anymore, Toto. Dementia had placed us in a whole new world.

Everything about that ordeal made me understand that the man before me was not the one I once knew. My job was to protect him, my family, and myself. That meant I would have to put alarms on the doors so that we could hear them when they opened and closed.

But that wasn't all. To ensure his quality of life was good with us, I bought underwear, t-shirts, and jogging pants for him. I protected the mattress he slept on by purchasing a waterproof cover. I got him house shoes so he would have something comfortable on his feet as he took his daily walks down our building's hallways, with one of my children accompanying him. And while the initial investment in him was unexpected and more than I could afford, I felt honored to do so. I was proud to be doing my part.

Every time I helped him bathe or made sure his clothes were freshly laundered, it wasn't just about dignity—it was about fighting the sense of loss that was creeping in, one small, insistent step at a time. But more than that, I felt that the key to making any of this work was to make the situation as comfortable as possible for everybody. I didn't know what he understood or how he was able to see the world through his devolving mental state, but I knew that he had always been a clean man who cared about his appearance. As someone who lived with addiction, he always looked dignified. I wanted to keep that going. I also wanted to keep him organized in appearance as a way of trying to keep us all organized in our minds.

There were parts I struggled with and didn't seem to have an answer to. For example, we didn't have a washer and dryer in my apartment that worked well, so we used the one in the building. Every day, I paid to wash clothes that had been "peed out" or "pooped out." While with me, he had a few more hospital scares. One of which gave him the official diagnosis of dementia. Before that, he didn't know what to call his bad memory, confusion, wandering, and angry outbursts. We didn't know how to explain the wallet full of "air money" that he passed out to different family members, proudly announcing that he was giving us $100 bills, as he put his balled-up fist into open hands, only to release nothing into them.

One doctor explained to me that his years of drug use had most likely contributed to his dementia. When they asked him whether he had a history of drug and alcohol abuse, he answered honestly.

"I don't drink no alcohol. But I do get high. I've been doing that for a long time now."

During his hospital stay, we met with representatives from different parts of the medical industry. These included occupational therapy and physical therapy. Both made arrangements with me to visit my dad at my apartment. The former was coming to help him regain his ability to do the activities he had been accustomed to doing: brushing his teeth (though he had no teeth), putting on his clothes, etc. The latter was to help him move his body parts. Between these visits and his ambulance expense, my mom and I determined that with the insurance he had, it was not sustainable for him to continue receiving care in Madison, as his insurance didn't cover his treatment in Wisconsin.

We also faced another issue: While my dad couldn't remember a lot of things, he remembered his check. One thing's for sure, and two things for certain, my daddy was not about to forget that check. Neither dementia nor Alzheimer's nor anything else that could afflict him was gonna make him forget his money. He received his government check at the beginning of the month and was determined to make it back to Chicago to cash it. There was no way we could convince him to take that long trip back and forth over and over each month. Without moving his checks and insurance to Madison, it would be very difficult to care for my dad outside of Chicago.

Unfortunately, we didn't have much time to consider and explore how we were going to resolve this issue because COVID-19 hit. With a few very short exceptions, I didn't see my parents for almost two years. By Christmas of 2020, we planned a three-month stay in Chicago to support my parents, especially my dad. However, the reality was far from ideal.

When we arrived, I came bearing all the gifts we had discussed: a new television, a Ninja Foodi, and grapes—straight from a Wisconsin supermarket. But these were just the beginning. My mom watched me and my children proudly bring in box after box and lug in a large, gray, three-foot-long cooler filled with food. Just as I brought in the last of it, feeling proud that I had finally accomplished something that could benefit her, she pulled out a note from management and read it aloud in her most professional voice.

"The City of Chicago prohibits the entrance of visitors during this time of COVID," she announced, letting me know that no matter what I had brought or what I planned to do, I was still a guest in her home—an unwelcome one at that.

The plan was to stay for three months. I didn't last two weeks, which is why the kids and I are on the road, driving back from Chicago to Madison. I'm driving the speed limit, but my mind is racing one thousand miles an hour.

"Do I need to start thinking about buying a house?" I ask myself out loud. "If so, how?" I continue down that line of thinking.

As a child, I imagined I'd inherit my grandma's home. For some reason, I had the audacity to believe that, somehow, ownership of the family house would skip a generation, bypassing her children—my aunts and uncles—and then skip over all their children—my cousins—and come to me. I assumed it would land in my lap. In my mind, none of them cared about it as much as I did. My aunts, uncles, and cousins weren't discussing the history or sharing the memories. In my mind, those were the things that a house represented. That's why you would want to own a family home, to create new stories, and to pass them on.

It never fully dawned on me that a house offered security and wealth. I never looked at 618, the address to "headquarters," as real estate, especially as a child. Those concepts were foreign to me as a kid, outside my vocabulary and worldview. Although some of the most significant parts of my life were lived out on property that either my maternal grandparents or paternal grandparents owned, by the time I began thinking about my place in the world and carving out a space of my own, the only vocabulary around housing I was comfortable with was Section 8, low-income, and renting. I wasn't alone. I had watched the older girls around me have children and get their apartment in the housing complex where their mothers had raised them. None of us was talking about buying houses.

I don't remember anyone intentionally planning to get pregnant so that they could "get their place." Not once could I recount hearing any girl in my age group or the ones before it saying, "When the time comes, I'm going to be a young mom—a teen mom, maybe—and get my apartment." Instead, many of us dreamed of going to college or getting married; some may not have dreamed at all. Dreaming is a risky business. It's much easier not to get our hopes up too high, to live in the present, and to let tomorrow take care of itself. Even the Bible tells us that. And before we know it, we're pregnant, not always because we wanted to have children, but as Dorothy Roberts puts it, because "we don't have enough reason not to."

People often turn their noses up at women like us, women who have lived in low-income housing for generations. But this is the closest thing to an "inheritance" many of us will ever have. Our parents weren't in a position to buy us a home or leave us one. The legacy they can offer is Section 8. Because they managed to beat out the thousands of people who weren't able to make it onto the list or who are still on the list, they and their children on their lease have an opportunity—if they are lucky, like my mom and I were—to live in a safe, clean, well-maintained housing complex that gives them the space and stability to change it all and dream, whether for them or their children. In some cases, safe and clean housing is the dream. And making it into that housing complex is the promised land.

But I gave up my Section 8 in Chicago a long time ago. I traded it for a shot at becoming a doctor, earning a PhD from the University of Wisconsin–Madison.

While some Section 8s can travel with you, mine was project-based, specific to the housing complex that had granted it to me. Unless the whole complex—bricks, people, and all—would pick up and move to Madison, Wisconsin, with me, I would have to leave it all behind. Start over in a new city and take my chances with this strange and scary thing called "market rent"—rent without the restrictions of subsidies, no Section 8. And I did. For years, I lived in campus housing, paying what I believed to be market rent. I was paying over $1,100 per month, a major change from living in an apartment complex that paid you to live there. At least, that's how I understood the "utility check" I received every month while living in Chicago. It was meant to cover a portion of our gas or light bill. And while I used it for that, it still felt like a personal investment in me. Anyhow, there would be none of that in the place I moved to in Madison, Wisconsin.

The next place I moved into was filled with the scent of spices and cooking by people from all over the world. I qualified for a middle-income subsidy, but there were still no utility checks. Rent was slightly higher than before, but I also had more room. The townhouse apartment included four bedrooms and two bathrooms—enough space for most of my children to comfortably fit two in a room. My youngest and I shared one of the smaller rooms in the home. For thirteen years, I "thugged it out" there in Madison with me and my babies.

I didn't do it alone. I had the help of my department, a teacher from my children's school, principals, community programs, one or two partners, and my closest friends and family. Even though most of what I did was legit, on the "up and up," it always felt like I was finagling, finessing, hustling, and trying to make everything work. It always felt like my head was down, always at the mercy of someone or some program—even though I was fighting for what I believed was a good cause: to raise myself out of poverty and to give my children, their children, and grandchildren extraordinary lives.

Even with that mission, there is something that feels so demeaning and lowly about having to depend on everyone else to help you accomplish the goal. It's not the people who support you—even though it can be—it's more about the processes and structures you have to go through. Even when the gatekeepers try to treat you with as much dignity as possible, you're still aware of the stereotype and how you may be perceived. "Welfare queen." "Unfit mom." "Breeder." "Baby maker." "Hood baby." "Stain." "Promiscuous." "Ill repute."

By the time I had completed my PhD, I had been able to define myself for myself.

I'd taken all the help and support that had come my way and mobilized them to create a life on my terms, to build a mothering practice that honored the needs and realities of my children and myself. So much of that work was also about building a life so that I could bring something back to my parents. I hadn't really thought about what that something would be. Maybe it was traveling around the world, or flowers on holidays, or pop-up Sunday brunches. I don't know. What I do know is that I had finally had "Doctor" in front of my name, or PhD behind it—whichever you prefer.

The years had passed, and I had finally done it, just to arrive back home to discover that my parents—still spunky and funny and alive—had gotten older. I hadn't accounted for that in my dreams. In my dreams, they would be the same age as they were when I left, with the same energy, as if I had pressed pause on their lives—while I went away for ten or fifteen years to do this thing, to bring back something uncertain, in addition to "Doctor" in front of my name or PhD behind it.

During this time, my dad—who has always been healthy—has managed to have several brushes with death, including a heart attack, maybe a stroke, and now he has dementia. My mom, who is still fiery and quick-witted, still rising and working, saving everyone's homes, is now walking with a cane and is much smaller than she once was, even though her hair is still as red as ever.

A proud woman and a couple fixed in their ways, how do I offer them "helpful help"? There will be no traveling, as I imagined, and while flowers are appreciated, I think something more is needed.

Yeah, I need to start thinking about buying a house. Whatever that's going to mean, I think as I drive. *But, hell, my credit score is about 490, maybe 500, and with no connections in Chicago, shiiiiiiiid, I have a better chance of buying a home in Madison. At least there, I know people. It may be easier for me to buy a house there than to rent in Chicago.* I laugh at the thought. And then I wondered, *Wait. Can I buy a house in Madison?*

As the headlights light up the dark highway, I can't help but feel a sense of both loss and possibility. My parents, children, and I are all transitioning, each navigating new roles and realities. And during all that change, I am starting to see that maybe, just maybe, it is time for me to create a home of my own—a place where all of us can belong, together yet separate, a new kind of family headquarters for a new chapter in our lives. While I am not yet completely sold, the seed is at least taking root.

CHAPTER 3

FELONS CAN'T RENT

JANUARY 2021

These six months have been heavenly. The chocolates and dinners, the sexy emails and flirty calls—the "I love yous." I haven't been this happy since … well, I don't think I've ever been this happy in love, not as an adult. On the one hand, it's all so dreamy. I want to stay in the dream because reality is complicated. For example, I love the idea of him coming home. I can dream about that all day. But in reality, home is a place I've yet to define for us. With its thin walls, judgmental neighbors, and the clause about felons not being able to rent here, my apartment isn't an option. I need to find a space where we can rebuild, away from the whispers and sideways glances. I need to find a place where it's safe and legal for us all to live freely. And as someone who has lived in subsidized housing most of my life, I have no idea what that looks like.

Now, don't get me wrong, I thank God for subsidized housing. Without it, in my early twenties, I would have stayed dependent on a partner who put a rope around my neck and left me for dead in my own urine. It was because of Section 8, low-income housing, student housing, and then middle-income housing, that I completed my bachelor's degree, master's degree, and PhD, respectively, while raising all six of my children as a single mom. That central pillar of stability gave me a fighting chance to address all the other chaos and uncertainties in my life. It gave me a "safe" space to retreat and strategize on how to get out of poverty and build wealth. It gave my children somewhere consistent to lay their heads down at night, even if that meant lying on the floor because there were moments when we didn't have beds. It gave us a starting point that would serve as the foundation of so much more. At the same time, I still struggle with some of its practices and policies. Inspection is one of them.

Inspection day in low-income housing is a clear memory for me. That's the day management visited a person's home to check over the property, surveyed for damage, monitored for cleanliness, and made sure there were no extra bodies in the house. By "extra," I mean no one living there who isn't on the lease. But we always had someone living there. And by "we," I mean the majority of the women in that housing complex. We had boyfriends, children, parents, cousins, nieces, nephews, and friends. We didn't do this out of spite or rebellion against authority. Some of us did it because we needed help with our kids. Others did it because we were trying to keep our families together. Quite a few of us did it for love. We wanted companionship, needed to care for an elder, etc.

I think about this, and my mind wanders back to the night before one of the many inspections I had in the complex I grew up in. I had my first three children, and the house was a mess. All my other friends, the ones who were not in school and who didn't work, were looking forward to the day management came in and viewed their nice, pristine apartments with their beautiful furniture. But I was a nervous wreck. It was clear outside, but my head was foggy.

What the fuck, Sagashus? What are you gonna do? What are you gonna do? What are you gonna do? I think to myself as I pace back and forth. Looking at the mess all around me, I am panicking. My chest is getting tight; I'm hyperventilating.

"Fuck, fuck, fuck, fuck, fuck, fuck, fuck, fuck, fuck. FUCK!" I scream out loud, still pacing.

I see kids outside, enjoying themselves, eating ice cream, jumping double dutch. The sight of it triggers even more anxiety.

What's wrong with you? Had you started on time, you would've been done by now. But here you are, with your last-minute ass, just now getting started. That's what you get. I think to myself about the panic attack that is coming on. *With your procrastinating ass, now you don't know what to do. Don't even know where to start. You can start by putting his fucking shoes in the trunk of your car, along with the rest of his shit.* Another part of my mind takes over and starts running the show.

"Good idea. Got it." I say to myself.

"Okay, now how about you call over Matt, our nephew, and pay him a pretty penny to help you keep this roof over your head," I suggest, more like demand. "I mean, you might as well just do the shit yourself because you're going to have to tell him where to put everything." I taunt myself. "But at least you won't get put out."

When it was time for inspection, we hid and erased all signs of those other bodies. We put away the men's boots and clothes and told our "visitors" they had to leave until the inspection was over. While we understood the rationale behind this practice—one that also happens in other places around the world—it also made it difficult to keep families living in poverty together and whole. It made it challenging to be a unit with dignity. It created a culture of shame, fear, and secrecy. It doesn't matter whether I'm a child or an adult in this memory; that feeling around inspection day is still the same for me.

Just like we housed people for many reasons, we kept those people a secret for even more reasons. Sometimes, we didn't tell because the person staying with us was just passing through—a temporary visitor staying too long not to be considered a resident but too short to warrant the paperwork that comes with "reporting a new member of the household." The second reason we often didn't tell was because it meant reporting the other person's income, which could mean a rent increase. The problem for many of us wasn't the fear of paying but of not being able to pay. The rules weren't always clear or available to us. What were the income guidelines? What were the cutoffs? Was it one dollar over? Was it a penny? I can't tell you how many times I heard about moms of two, three, four, or five reaching for and wanting better jobs, applying and getting accepted, just to turn down the offer because they were afraid that making just a little bit more money could upend their stability, leaving them homeless.

I'm considering all this as I imagine where we will live when my fiancé, the Quiet One, comes home. He is in federal prison and has been there for almost ten years now. Although we had stopped dealing with each other long before he got locked up, recently—with the breakup between me and Prodigal, one of my other children's dads—he and I have rekindled. This all sounds so messy. I know. And yet, here we are.

It's January 2021, and from the looks of things, he will be released in 2023. The problem is this: I distinctly remember my lease saying no felons allowed. Those weren't the exact words, but that was the exact message. And I remember it because, when I moved into this place, I was with Prodigal, who was for sure a felon. If I had allowed him to live with us and keep our family whole, that would've been one thing. It would've meant sneaking him in and out of the apartment. It would've meant not including his name on the mailbox. It would've meant staying as quiet as I could during arguments so they could end sooner, minimizing the chances of neighbors or management hearing us. But with the Quiet One, I imagined it would mean something completely different. Because he will be on house arrest when he comes home and then on parole, I imagined that it would mean having to ask management's permission for him to be there. It meant not keeping it a secret. And based on what I understood from the lease—no felons allowed—it meant finding a new place for us all to live.

I have to stress "us all" because he has an older sister who has made it very clear that wherever he is, she will be. If she had her way, he'd come live with her. We've already had one nice nasty Facebook run-in where she wrote, in front of God and everybody, "You're not his wife, yet," marking her claim as someone who still has priority over me. And as much as I wanted to be angry with her, I couldn't be because my first encounter made an impression.

I visited him at the Cook County jail when I was nineteen. As I sat in the waiting area, the previous set of visitors returned from seeing their loved ones. A very pretty, light-skinned girl locked eyes with me and said, "You're here to see the Quiet One, aren't you?"

"Yeah," I answered honestly, caught off guard. I didn't think to lie, which would've been the safest choice. To the extent she looked pretty was also the extent that she sounded and acted rough. In fact, in both her mannerisms and sound, she was the female version of him.

She started falling apart right then and there.

"See, this is what I'm talking about. I'm sick of this shit," she said, fighting back tears, going into a full-on meltdown.

Afraid for my life, I watched this woman he was also involved with fall apart, wondering when she'd turn all that hurt onto me. But before that happened, the Quiet One's sister, who had been there all along with another woman, interrupted.

"Trina. Trina. Calm down," she said. She was equally as pretty, if not more, as the girl she was consoling. But she had an old spirit. "We're not gonna do this right now. Okay?"

The other girl pulled herself together and, like magic, walked away and left me to my visit. My first encounter with the Quiet One's sister was that of a woman beyond her years, saving me from getting my ass whipped. I don't have any real beef with her. How could I? Even though she doesn't remember that encounter with me, I will always remember her and that moment. And now, because of that history, I show her the respect of saying nothing.

Instead, I pick at him about it.

"So, your sister has me wondering whether or not I even need to look for a place to live. Are you going to live with her, or what?" I deliver this question nonchalantly, teasing him.

"Man, what are you talking about?" He asks, sounding as if my question came out of nowhere, and as far as he's concerned, it did.

"I mean, are you going to go live with her? That's the question," I add as carefree as I began the discussion. *Your sister wants you to come live with her. She wants to iron your clothes and cook your meals.* I want to say, *She wants to be your woman, your wife. She wants to be me.* But I don't say that. Instead, I say, "So, your sister ... she wants to wash your underwear and cook for you. What do you want?"

"Sex."

We both laugh. I push a little more.

"Okay. And then what?"

His response makes me feel a little more secure. *Is that all he wants?* I wonder. I know he loves me and wants to be with me. And yet, what if ...

"My point is this. I work. I work a lot. I know you're used to women who cook pot roast for you and bake you German chocolate cake, nieces who ensure your clothes are ironed and cleaned, and a sister who still treats you like a baby. But will I be enough for you?" As much as I'm joking about his sister, I wonder if he really wants a woman who will clean his drawers and cook for him all day.

He listens intently, understanding my insecurity and the reassurance I need.

"I know how to cook," he says.

At that moment, I get it. With the Quiet One, I've learned to listen for what's not said as much as for what is. And he's saying this: I knew who I asked to marry me before I asked. I know what comes with that ask, and I'm good with it.

"So, does that mean you don't want to stay with your sister?"

He gets quiet in the way that he does when he's already answered a question and doesn't intend to answer it again. Understanding the statement in his silence, I change the subject. But changing the subject doesn't solve our housing issue. Where are we going to live? That question looms over my head.

A thought occurs to me. We could live in one of the Quiet One's houses. Before getting locked up or becoming "justice-involved," as Nyra Jordan's TED Talk refers to people who have been through the prison system, the Quiet One owned two homes. Exploring our options, I ask my mom, the housing counselor, to look up the status of the first home. What she turns up is unclear to all of us, including him. Someone who thinks they're a family member has been covering the cost of the house he was living in when he got arrested. He knows that to get it back, he's going to have to pay thousands of dollars in back costs to that person if it's who and what he thinks it is. The idea doesn't appeal to him, so we look into the second home. This one is completely paid for, the one he tried to give to me years ago, when he first moved in, to avoid losing everything. But back then, I couldn't afford to pay for a paid-for home. Let me explain.

In 2016, the Quiet One, who by that time had become the father of two of my children, offered to give me a home he had already paid for. He was in federal prison, fighting a drug trafficking case, and that home was one of the last pieces of property he had owned, if not the last piece. Everything else had been seized and was in custody as possible evidence or had been stolen by girlfriends, picked apart, and distributed by loved ones. This piece of property was all that remained. He was renovating it at the time of his arrest. I was able to see the potential of this place, which I had never seen before, as he talked about the jacuzzi tub, expensive toilet, and appliances he had placed in it. He talked about this beautiful thing and that beautiful thing. He was proud, and my only job was to finish the vision he had already begun to complete in this paid-for home—that and to pay the $5,000 in back taxes.

When he made the offer, I was both excited and a little skeptical—maybe a lot. First of all, the house wasn't in his name. How do I take ownership of a house from someone whose name is not on the deed? Second of all, the neighborhood was "sketch." It was in Chicago, on the South Side, in Roseland, an area known for shootouts, murders, and violence. Third, the home next to the one I would be taking over was connected with someone I was always suspicious of, a friend of my children's dad. He was known for being disrespectful, reckless with women, and violent.

Once I reached the property, a new set of concerns cropped up. Nothing about it said partially renovated. Instead, the building screamed abandoned and condemned. The grass was overgrown, and the staircase steps were missing. After entering the house, all of the things he had told me were there weren't. Had I heard him wrong? There was no jacuzzi, fancy toilets, fixtures, or appliances. Hell, I think pieces of the floor were missing. The house was nothing he had described. Had he exaggerated? The next time I spoke with him, I described my experience. And I heard the heartbreak in his voice.

"Man, somebody broke in that house and stole all my shit. And I 'bout know who did it."

It was all good, though, because we had a plan. I called my uncle Degree—even though I had never seen him fix any home—to look at and assess the place, just so that a man could put his eyes on it as if being a man means you are born knowing how to renovate what appears to be a condemned and abandoned house. The conditioning runs deep. But I digress.

So, as soon as the Quiet One told me about the house, I retrieved the keys from his brother and brought my uncle to check out the place. It wasn't that I expected him to know what to do; I really just needed his approval and blessing. I needed him to be proud of me for becoming a homeowner, no matter how I got the home. Besides, if I didn't get his approval, I wouldn't get anyone's, as he is an eternal optimist and a seasoned diplomat, always trying to keep the peace. Subconsciously, I guess I was wondering, *Is this house in such bad shape that even he would have to disagree about me taking it on?*

He walked up with a look of measured concern, as if trying to fix both his face and his mind to figure out how this was going to work. How was his niece going to fix this house? How were her Wisconsinite children going to live in Roseland? Was this house even worth the trouble? Seeming as if he had to muster up a way to process it all, with hesitancy, my uncle, the diplomat, gave us his blessing. With that, he waited outside while all six of my children and I joined hands and prayed together in that house. I can't remember the exact words, but I remember the thoughts and hopes. I imagine that our prayer went something like this: "Lord, bless us. Bless this house. Bless this family. Watch over us. If you see it fit for us to own this house, remove barriers. If you see fit for us to renovate this home, send us a construction team. If you see fit for us to rent it out to a mom looking for a home with her children, show us how. Daddy, I want to buy up this entire block and make it a community for our clients. Show me how … if it's your will. Amen."

It's always a risk to end a prayer with "if it's your will" because there is a good chance it's not His will. That means that whatever I'm working on can just slip through my hands, a relationship can end, or a loved one can pass. Ending a prayer with "if it's your will" means that I have surrendered my authority, and the final say-so is not mine. It means that I have given up my right to power through a situation that may not be good for me. I have given up my right to make a bad situation worse. It means that I have chosen to not take things upon myself and go forward without the covering and backup to do so. "If it's your will" understands that the outcome may not be what I want it to be and makes peace with that reality.

Within three to six months, that house was no longer an option for me. From prison, my children's dad was dating a woman in Chicago who was obsessed and controlling over him in a way that seemed like love to him and dangerous to everyone else. She had a shrine of him in her room and a picture of him pinned to her car's dashboard. She made t-shirts with his face on them. She changed her social media from her name to "his wife." And so, I could hear the edge in her voice when she'd say things like, "Yeah, so, that's good he gave you a house. I mean, women like us deserve those things. His ex didn't." I heard the desperation in her voice when she told me about how the federal judge complimented me at his sentencing, saying in his decades of being on the bench, he had never seen such a well-orchestrated and organized show of support for a defendant.

Here's the quick and dirty backstory. Because his conviction was based on hearsay from co-defendants with very long rap sheets, I knew it was very important that the judge understood who he was outside of their testimonies. And so, I started a petition that collected hundreds of signatures in his defense. We had doctors, judges, and other notable pillars of the community write letters of support. We also collected letters of support from each of his family members. I called his brother, met with his son, and transcribed letters from my children and me. We coordinated a caravan of his family members and friends to arrive in court on the day of his sentencing with white t-shirts and black words that expressed how he made a difference in each person's life. "He shows up to my track meets." "He helps me with my homework." "He's my superhero." "He listens when I have no one to talk to." "He is my heart." I wasn't there that weekend, and neither were my two children with him. That was April 2016.

That same month, my cousin had just passed away, and the next month, I was supposed to defend my dissertation. Between supporting my cousin, as I was her only blood family in this city (outside of her children), launching my brand, and helping the Quiet One not get twenty-five years in prison as a first-time offender, I had let my dissertation fall by the wayside. With the time I had left, it was damn near impossible to complete the dissertation in time for me to walk across the stage and graduate. And so, while I was the brain behind how we advocated for him in court that day, my children and I weren't physically there to hear the judge's compliment. But my children's dad's woman at the time was, and she was triggered.

"Yeah, the judge said that about you, but she said I was the dedicated wife." This was the lie she told me. Others have contradicted her story. But anyway, I digress.

Shortly after that, my children's dad would call me about discussions that she and I had shared. She had found a way to twist them up and take them out of context enough that what had once been a great relationship between him and me turned into months of us not speaking. I decided to give up my hopes of following through with that house and left it up to him and her. The house seemed to be what this was all about in the first place, and she wanted it.

All of that aside, I wasn't confident that I could pay off the $5,000 in back taxes and more than $20,000 in renovation costs. While I had always been good at raising dollars for different causes—personal and professional—the Quiet One didn't have that experience with me, and he didn't seem to have the confidence. In his eyes, I was just a schoolgirl. The whole time he'd known me, I'd been broke. I wasn't like the go-getters and hustling women he was accustomed to. I wasn't a nurse who worked long hours like some of his family members and previous partners. I didn't deal in credit card scams and sell drugs like other women he might've known. Nothing about my life suggested to him that I would be able to do anything with his remaining property. I didn't want to add to his disappointment. So I gave back the keys to a home I never owned. And I was happy to let it go. By the time I spoke to him again, the woman and the house were gone. I guess "if it's your will" applied to him, too. That was in 2016.

In early 2021, we were weighing all our options, including that one. While in Chicago for winter break, I went to visit that old house I had walked away from five years ago. It looked even worse than it had before. The lawn was overgrown with weeds. Its windows were broken. Even with all of this, I still held on to hope. I asked my mom to do some research. I wanted to know if someone purchased it, or if the city had taken it because of the back taxes. After a few days, we discovered that some LLC in California owned it, with only a P.O. Box. Something about the LLC's distance and impersonal nature made me decide it was time to move on. Besides, the Quiet One had made it very clear that he wanted a fresh start in a different city and state. So with no real options, I started dreaming about our futures.

At this point, I had been imagining my dream home for some time. I hadn't thought about the inside or outside aesthetic of the home. Instead, I was thinking about the space—the number of rooms we needed, the cooking space, the number of bathrooms, dedicated areas for the business, etc. In addition to these, I needed enough land and real estate to accommodate my two "mothers-in-law," the mom of one of my exes and my soon-to-be husband's mom. I also needed space for my mother, father, and Aunt Word. I had made up my mind that these were the elders I'd care for and keep close to me. My Sierra Leonean mother-in-law, my ex's mom, inspired the idea. Years ago, she told me that African parents' children are their 401k. When the parents retire or are unable to care for themselves, their children provide for them. I loved the idea of that. So, as I journeyed toward my own financial goals, I thought about the elders I wanted to provide for. I thought about what kind of space I wanted them to have. At the time, I didn't have the words for it, but the more I prayed, journaled, and researched, the clearer things became. I was looking to either purchase or build a compound. I would have a main home and three smaller ones surrounding it. That was the vision.

I started Googling and searching for "compound properties," "compound estates," "compound homes," etc. My search results showed me beautiful luxury spaces in Texas and other southern cities. I began collecting screenshots, bookmarking internet pages, and printing images. I started sending links to the elders and images to the Quiet One, telling them about my dreams. To my surprise, everyone was quiet. Excitedly, I presented my vision, texting the information while on the phone, and the conversations would turn awkward and uncomfortable. One of the mothers-in-law cheered me on, kind of like a parent cheers on their child when they are telling them something that feels make-believe or when they have presented art that is basic and maybe even ugly. Because they don't want to discourage the kid, they tell them, "Good job! You can do it!" in a voice that sounds encouraging to children but condescending to adults.

"Uh-huh," she said. "Well, okay, baby. You go right ahead, and you do it. That is such a beautiful property. You go right on and get that for us."

I told my mother about it, and she said, "You know, I'm still dreaming, too. And I'm going to build me a house right there on 41st Street next to Mother's house. We still own land down there. And I'm going to build a home for the seniors and the disabled. But I'm not going to have a mortgage. And it's going to be fixed income." Never mind what I had just presented. She had her own dreams, and I had to honor her vision and respect her dreams if I wanted mine to be respected. So I never mentioned it to her again.

I told Aunt Word about it. She listened, fascinated, as if I was telling her about some kind of adventure. I couldn't tell if she liked the idea and enjoyed dreaming with me or if she believed it was possible. Either way, she encouraged me.

"Aw, the Boom, the Boom," that's the nickname that only she called me, "I love this." I felt the joy and curiosity in her voice as she spoke. "Tell me more."

Finally, I shared my vision with my soon-to-be husband's mom. At first, she said things like, "Oh my God, Sagashus, this is beautiful." For weeks, I sat on the phone with her in what I imagined was a safe space and talked about my plans. One day, after she had a few drinks, she and I sat on the phone, and she said to me, "I think you're greedy. You're aiming too high and getting people's hopes all up. God don't like that, baby. Why don't you just be happy with what you got? And stop feeding my son all of those dreams. Just let him do his time without getting his hopes too high." I was stunned. Disappointed, somewhat embarrassed, and ashamed, I stopped talking about the compound altogether, deciding that whatever I do, it's best I come up with a plan on my own.

Letting go of my discussions about compounds and communal spaces for our family, I had no idea what my next steps were. Renting didn't feel like an option, not with his background as a felon and our very large family. There's this book called *Evicted: Poverty and Profit in the American City* by Matthew Desmond. In it, the author said that "Black men are locked up, and Black women are locked out." He was talking about men going to prison and the reality that Black women struggle to keep roofs over their children's heads while also living with poverty. He was talking about unfair eviction practices and other discriminatory actions from landlords toward Black moms. I knew that the odds were against us when it came to renting, but I was confident that I could buy what I wanted, what I had imagined for me and my family.

As I sit here, grappling with the realities of our future together, I can't help but think about how deeply entwined our personal struggles are with the broader, systemic issues that plague this country. The lease that forbids felons from renting is not just a line in a contract; it's a manifestation of a much larger, more insidious system. It's the prison industrial complex continuing to exert control over the lives of those who have already served their time, ensuring that even after release, individuals like the Quiet One remain entangled in a web of restrictions that dictate where they can live, who they can live with, and how they can rebuild their lives.

I'm no sociologist, but casual research reveals studies that have shown that nearly 79 percent of formerly incarcerated people are denied housing due to their criminal records. This isn't just a statistic; it's a reality that millions of families face, a reality that I am now living as I try to create a home for us. As I write this chapter, the federal government says they understand the issue and are working to address it. And while that is great, and I look forward to those changes, my reality is now. And the issue is pressing.

Historically, these barriers are rooted in policies deliberately crafted to marginalize and control. The war on drugs, mass incarceration, and the subsequent criminalization of Black and brown communities have all contributed to the current state of housing discrimination. Policies like the "One Strike" rule in public housing, which allows for eviction based on criminal activity—even if the crime occurred off the premises or a guest committed it—were implemented under the guise of safety but have instead destabilized vulnerable communities further.

As I navigate this maze, I'm acutely aware that this isn't just my struggle. This is the struggle of every person who has been touched by the criminal justice system, of every family that has been fractured by incarceration, of every child who has watched a parent disappear behind bars, only to find that, even upon release, they are still not truly free. The Quiet One and I are up against a housing issue that is much bigger than us.

If I were the type to go on my soapbox and rant, I'd say this system is relentless. It forces people like me, who are just trying to build a life, to confront impossible choices: stay in a place where we are not welcome or take a financial leap that could lead to ruin. These are the kinds of choices that the prison industrial complex forces upon people long after they have supposedly "paid their debt to society." It's a debt that keeps accruing, with interest, demanding more and more from those who can least afford it.

But despite these obstacles, I am determined. The Quiet One and I will find a way through this, not just for ourselves, but as a form of resistance. By creating a home where we can both feel secure and build our future, we are defying a system that often proves that it doesn't care about the poor or people who make decisions based on their poverty. This is not just about buying a house; this is about reclaiming our right to live freely and fully despite the prison that still looms over us, even on the outside.

The challenge is monumental, but so are my heart and hustle. As much as the system tries to box us in, to dictate our options, to limit our horizons, I will find a way. This journey isn't just about surviving; it's about thriving, about carving out a space where love, hope, and dignity can flourish.

I don't know yet where we'll land, but I do know that renting is looking less and less like an option. We need a space where we can build our lives without fear, shame, or the constant reminder of a past that we are working so hard to leave behind. Thinking about my parents and now the Quiet One, the need for a home is starting to feel more urgent.

CHAPTER 4
POVERTY DOES SHIT TO YOU
JANUARY 2021

I'm washing piles of clothes in the laundry room, trying to clear my head and think about my next move. Where are we going to live? How can I make my business more profitable? Thoughts race a thousand miles a minute as I work alone in this cozy space.

There are only two washers and two dryers in it, but this laundry room in my building is my getaway. It's my excuse to leave the apartment without leaving the building, so I am absent and present simultaneously. Taking up space with my laundry baskets and clothes spread out everywhere, the message is clear: I'll be at this for a while. Washing, drying, and folding is an all-day job. I often multitask, catching up on missed calls or listening to audiobooks. But this day, I find myself washing, drying, folding, and thinking.

The hum of the washing machine fills the small laundry room, a steady, monotonous sound that usually helps to quiet my thoughts. But today, it is drowned out by the relentless uneasiness in my mind. I reach into the dryer, pulling out a warm, soft towel. I fold it effortlessly like I have done thousands of times before. There is no need to put my thoughts into what I am doing. I have advanced degrees and over 10,000 hours of experience in laundry. I am a master. The more I move—washing, drying, folding ... washing, drying, folding—I feel a sense of calm come over me. Here, I am not questioning myself. I am not caught in another wild learning curve. I am just being. My hands are guided by muscle memory—washing, drying, folding...washing, drying, folding. My heart stopped racing, slowing to a calm beat. Washing, drying, folding. I was moving as if someone had set me on autopilot. Now, with the anxiety out of my body, my mind calmed, organizing one million thoughts into a coherent question, "What am I going to do about this living situation? Am I renewing my lease, or am I moving somewhere else?" Washing, drying, folding ...

Without warning, my mind drifts to another time I felt this sense of ease, like I was moving without thinking. It was during a walk I was taking with my girls.

In 2016, I took a rare walk to the grocery store with my oldest daughters, Dianna and Yemi. Usually, I'd drive—rushing from one task to the next, always pressed for time. But that day, the warm sun and the promise of a slow, unhurried walk with my girls convinced me to leave the car keys behind.

Dianna and Yemi walked a step ahead of me, caught up in their world, chatting about whatever was happening in their summer programs. I trailed behind, enjoying the sound of their voices and the ease of the afternoon. It was one of those simple moments where everything felt right—until Yemi's voice cut through the air with a line that stopped me.

"Because, you know, poverty does shit to you," she said, her tone as casual as if she were commenting on the weather.

I couldn't believe what I'd just heard. My fifteen-year-old daughter, Yemi, who knew better than to swear in front of me, had just let that sentence roll off her tongue "like talking 'bout it." Dianna's reaction was immediate. Her eyes widened in shock, quickly followed by a look of sheer horror, and then she burst into laughter. It was that kind of laughter that was impossible to hold back and made your sides hurt.

Yemi, oblivious at first, quickly caught on. She froze, looking at her sister, then at me, as if trying to figure out what was so funny. And when she finally realized what she'd said, her hand flew to her mouth, her eyes wide with embarrassment.

I just stood there for a moment, trying to process it all.

"So, poverty does shit to you, huh?" I murmured, trying to keep a straight face, fighting the urge to laugh. "Tell me, what has it done to y'all?"

The girls exchanged a look, still giggling, but they could tell from my voice that I wasn't angry—I was genuinely curious. And in that moment, I knew this conversation was about more than just a slip of the tongue. It was about the realities we were all living, the truths they were beginning to understand, and the ways we tried to make sense of our world.

As a mom, a large part of my mothering practice was marked by shame, fear, and a lot of insecurity. J. K. Rowling, the author of the Harry Potter series, once wrote this: "People very often say to me, 'How did you do it? How did you raise a baby and write a book?' And the answer is—I didn't do housework for four years. I am not a superwoman. And um, living in squalor, that was the answer."

Like her and her child, we lived in squalor. But my friend group wasn't marked by a bunch of J. K. Rowlings, not early on, at least. I wasn't surrounded by people who understood the "hard" choice between keeping a nice and respectable (there's that word again) home and pursuing my dreams or investing time in creating the kind of life that would make a difference in my children's future. And so they talked, gossiped, and judged me for not having the tidiest kids or an immaculate apartment. But it was never just about cleanliness. They were judging me for not being feminine enough, a lady, and for not being domestic enough.

Those ugly feelings affected the way that I parented my children—what and who I allowed and didn't allow into their childhood experiences. For example, I didn't let my children have company. I didn't have company. Their childhood didn't include fun sleepovers, and my early days as a mother didn't include girls' nights.

We didn't have barbecues and evenings filled with movies and games—at least not with people outside our home. I was ashamed and afraid of what would happen if I let outsiders in. Would that judgment lead to accusations of neglect? Could I lose my kids because in trying to build a future for them, people would think their present was dangerous at worst and subpar at best? What was the fine line? And where was the crossing point?

There were too many unknowns, and the stakes were too high to risk. So, I played it safe by keeping everyone else out and locking us in. Fear kept us isolated, and isolation kept the fear alive.

I also played it safe by appeasing children to calm tantrums—to the best of my ability. I couldn't risk the noise for our safety and to keep a roof over our heads.

When I first moved into an apartment in Madison, I had an experience that made me so paranoid that if my children breathed wrong, I was on them. The fear of eviction was a constant, gnawing worry at the back of my mind. It was a terror that seemed to control how I parented.

When I first moved into my second apartment in Madison, I knew I had to do something about it. I had six kids to think about. The last thing I wanted was to be locked out, as the lesson from *Evicted* kept reminding me: "Black men are locked up. Black women are locked out." I'd never experienced homelessness, and I was determined to keep it that way.

So, with my fear as my motivation, I decided to be proactive. I'd knock on every door of every neighbor who lived on my floor and wing of the building. Maybe if they knew me, if they knew my children, they'd come to me first if there were any problems instead of going straight to management. Maybe then, I wouldn't have to worry so much about that looming threat of eviction. And if I took care of that, then I would be able to mother my children with less fear.

The hallway carpet was ugly—gray and industrial. The doors were old, wooden, and creaky. But I walked and knocked anyway, introducing myself like I was campaigning for office.

Knock, knock, knock. The first door creaked open, and I offered a smile. "Hi! My name is Sagashus. I just wanted to let you know that I moved into apartment 114 with my babies. I have six of them, ranging from a toddler to a high schooler, so you know. I'm a grad student juggling a lot, and I really depend on my village. So, if for any reason you need me, don't hesitate to come by. And if you have any questions or concerns about me and my children, I am happy to talk. Here's my information, and I look forward to connecting with you."

Some conversations ended right there, with a polite, "Welcome to the neighborhood." Others lasted a little longer, where we exchanged pleasantries and talked about the building. I walked away from most doors with the impression that I'd made a real connection, that people understood I was approachable, and that they would come to me first if there were a problem.

But then, one day, I came home and saw a notice tacked to my creaky, wooden door. A noise complaint. My heart sank. Why hadn't they come to me first?

The complaint came from the elder who lived right across from me. She had spoken to my oldest son, Cho, about not bouncing his basketball in the building. But when she heard the sound again, she didn't bother to talk to him again. She went straight to management.

Management and I discussed the complaint, and eventually, it became clear that the bouncing ball she heard hadn't even come from my apartment—it was from another neighbor's place. But in my head, Ms. Ainsley Anxiety, as I like to call her, kept whispering that this was just a warning. Under the right conditions, that complaint could quickly turn into a family of nine—me, my six kids, Prodigal, and my bonus daughter, Nari—living on the street. And then what? What would I do with six kids? Where would we go? Who would rent to a woman with six children and an eviction on her record?

The thought of it haunted me, a constant reminder that no matter how many doors I knocked on or how many connections I made, the fear of being locked out was always just a breath away.

So I was careful about how I disciplined my children and to what extent I held them accountable. More often than I'm proud to admit, I didn't always hold them to the highest standards because I was afraid that if I pushed too hard, they'd push back and rebel, scream, or test boundaries the way that strong-willed, hurt, or traumatized children often do. Instead, I hushed and shushed them when they needed consistency and structure. At times, without saying it, I was silently pleading, *Please, be quiet. Or you're gonna get all of us put out.* Other times, I just flat out said it because when you're a single parent living in a space where you share a wall with strangers who may or may not file a complaint against you or your children for being too loud—a complaint that can lead to a thirty-day notice that, in turn, leaves a whole family of seven, eight, and sometimes nine unhoused— the stakes are always high. The fear of losing what little we had was a constant presence. So yes, in my own family, amongst my children, I shrank and played it small, parenting safely, even when it didn't serve them.

And yet, even through all that fear, I tried to build a family culture that promoted good values—our family values—because values shape the way we live just as much as money does, if not more. I tried to make places that often felt like cages feel less like places that confined us and more like our homes. The idea had come from the time I spent with a therapist. He told me that if I wanted to unify my household, I had to build a culture rooted in ideas and beliefs that mattered to us. I had to get my children to buy into a set of thoughts and practices we could all live by and rally around.

Because I was afraid to discipline my children, I started going to therapy. There, my therapist told me that instead of obsessing over disciplining my children, I should turn my attention to creating a family culture where both the expectations and consequences were clear. The kids should know what to expect at all times. I know he might've meant one thing, but I took that idea and ran with it. I remember coming home and calling one of our family meetings while still living in campus housing. My oldest child couldn't have been more than twelve, and the youngest at the time was no more than two years old.

"Family Meeeeetiiiiin'," I yelled.

A bunch of little voices echoed behind me, "Momma said it's a family meeting." "Family meeting, y'all." "It's a family meeeeeeting. Come on!"

We gathered around the table.

"All right, you all," I said. "Here's the deal. I know we all have different last names. And we're not going to change that. But what if we created an acronym that combined all our last names together? That way, we can have one family name."

"What's an acronym?" Cho asked.

"An acronym is when you take letters, usually the first letter of a bunch of words, and form one word," I explained. "If we were to take the first letter of each of our names and create one word, what would it be?" Eagerly, they got to work. With pens and paper in hand, they started to work on different combinations.

"But wait, before you get too far," I interrupted, "come up with a word that means something. It has to be a name that makes us proud."

For weeks, we met, exploring different ways we could combine our names to create one that would be strong enough to lead us for years to come, and then, finally, we came up with one.

"H.E.L.M." What do you all think about the word *helm?*" I asked them.

No one seemed to like it at first. Some of the kids scrunched their faces, and others flat-out said they didn't like it.

"Dianna, look it up for me, please," I said, eagerly waiting for the big reveal.

Googling the word, she read, "Helm: a tiller or wheel and any associated equipment for steering a ship or boat." Everyone looked underwhelmed and confused, including Dianna.

"Okay," I said to her. "Now read the next definition."

Quickly going back to the page she was on, she repeated the word again and then went right into the definition: "A position of leadership."

I repeated the words, "A position of leadership." Feeling a sense of pride come over me, I looked at everyone at the table. "That's who we are, a family that leads. And never forget that. We are going to lead ourselves, our extended family, and our community, by living a lifestyle rooted in values. We're going to live with intention, and we're going to live in the present with our futures in mind. Pick up your pens and paper, and list all the things you love about our family, all the things you want to change, and how you want the world to see each of us and all of us. From there, we're going to start building our family culture."

"Wait, Mommy, what?" Yemi said, looking confused. I looked around and noticed that everyone else was struggling to understand, too.

"My fault, y'all. Let me slow down," I said, laughing at myself and realizing I was talking to my toddlers and teenagers like I was talking to my college students.

When Layden was born, we went through the same process, adding a W to our name and changing it to W.H.E.L.M, which means "an act or instance of flowing or heaping up abundantly; a surge." With this new addition, our family identity evolved, but the core message remained: Our family was a force, united and driven by purpose. W.H.E.L.M. wasn't just a name; it was a declaration of who we were and aspired to be. Every day, I tried to instill this belief in my children, reminding them that we were more than our circumstances—we were builders of our future.

This belief was encapsulated in the vision statement that has guided our journey:

W.H.E.L.M. Vision 2039

- Date, partner, and marry intentionally.
- Parent responsibly, lovingly, and purposely.
- Embrace family.
- Love, respect, and care for each other, including extended family.
- Be kind.
- Take care of mental health through awareness, medicine, and therapy.
- Respect everyone.

By 2039, my youngest child will be twenty-five. My hope is that by offering this vision to them and creating with them, it will usher each one of them into adulthood with a sense of direction, purpose, and inspiration. One of the main pillars of my vision is for us to heal and create a healthy line for generations to come.

In our dirty, unkempt home, I had speakers installed so that my children and I could listen to audiobooks—stories that celebrated resilience and kindness—hoping to instill a sense of worth that no external judgment could diminish. In the spaces that often felt like cages, I introduced family retreats (because we couldn't afford to go to resorts and getaways), where we enjoyed good food and extended time together, delving into the ideas that would ultimately become our foundation. These small, intentional acts were my way of planting seeds of hope and resilience in my children. Our home became a sanctuary, not just from the outside world's harsh views but from the creeping doubts that sometimes settled within.

And in that sanctuary, we laughed—a lot. Cho could always be counted on for his impulsive and shady comments. He's the kid who says what everyone else is thinking but knows better than to voice out loud—my politically incorrect one. We'll just leave it at that. Then there's Ryland, with his endless "back in my day" stories: "Back in my day when I was a baseball player, I had more home runs than anyone. But the paparazzi were on me too hard, so I quit and became an astronaut." The stories would go on from there.

When it wasn't Cho's off-color jokes or Ryland's fantastical tales about a life he was too young to have lived, it was Layden's backhanded compliments: "Mom, you are so hot, fat, and miserable, but I just love you." In his defense, he was only repeating my own words back to me. And then there were all the kids playing the dozens, roasting each other, and talking about each other's dads. "That's why your dad ..." "So. I ain't even about to start talking about your dad with his ..."

When it wasn't that, it was the kids imitating me and everyone else. "Aye, aye, Brooklyn. Who is this?" Imitating my tone and mannerisms perfectly, they begin a sentence with, "You know ..." Everyone, including me, would be falling out with laughter. Because if we didn't have a dime, we had plenty of imagination. And that kept us all entertained as we lived in our little bubble of poverty, strategizing and laughing our way to a better life.

Through it all, I clung to the belief that our values, laughter, and plan would be the bedrock upon which my children could stand tall and proud, no matter what came our way. And as a mother who had often felt crushed by shame and fear, I dared to dream bigger, not just for myself but for my children.

I was so bold that I dared to believe that I, along with my children, could break generational poverty, build generational wealth, and find joy in the process because we had each other. The dream of purchasing a home was the cornerstone of that vision. While doing so doesn't erase the shame and embarrassment, it creates a sense of pride that squeezes a lot of those ugly feelings out.

And if I dream big enough and have faith big enough to set my sights on the right kind of home, then we can have the kind of space that would allow us to live clutter-free in a home that we could invite others over to, hosting events without fear or shame. This dream wasn't just about bricks and mortar; it was about creating a legacy, a place where my children could feel safe, loved, and valued.

But equally important, having space with walls that were detached from our neighbors would give my children the freedom to express their emotions—scream, yell, cry, and release the anxiety, fear, and hurt they carry in their bodies in ways that make sense to them at the time. It would also allow me the freedom to respond to and guide them in a way that meets them where they are, without the fear of judgment influencing my response. In a way, this home would be our healing space, a place where we could grow and mend the wounds that poverty had inflicted. I'm convinced that such an environment would foster emotional resilience and a deeper connection between us, helping them navigate their feelings in a healthy and supportive space. Buying a home for my children would mean having a safe space for us to live and grow and heal from a lot of the shit that poverty has done to my babies.

I think about this as I wash, dry, and fold clothes in the building's laundry room. And then another thought takes over. My children are the bulls in the china shop, so they couldn't go to Chicago if something happened to me. And while Dianna may be able to watch over them, now that she has moved out and gone to college, she is no longer on my lease. Where would she house them? What would happen to my children if I were no longer on this earth? If something were to happen to me, where would they go? I want them to stay together and have a home that anchors them even if I'm no longer there. In a world where we've always been outsiders, I want them to have something truly theirs—a place they can always return to, a sanctuary offering shelter, security, and the love they need to heal and move forward.

It's time that I buy a house. Between the pressing needs of my parents, my man, and my babies, it's time for us to claim the space we deserve—a place we can finally call home.

CHAPTER 5

CINDY TRIMM

FEBRUARY 2021

Christmas of 2020 had come and gone, and as much as January dragged on, it left, too. My children and I celebrated the New Year in Chicago with my parents, and within the first week of 2021, we were gone. With some distance between me, my mom, and the whole situation, I was able to see things more clearly.

The tension between my mom and me had gotten so thick that being there was unbearable. I admit I was ignorant. Never having dealt with a wife caring for a husband with dementia, it didn't dawn on me that she didn't want my help. She needed respite—time for her own self-care or space to focus on her work without worrying about her husband's outbursts. She didn't need my help—he did. She needed a break. But the more I was there, the less I affirmed that reality.

When he soiled himself, I cleaned him. When he was hungry, I fed him. When he needed his hair cut, I (or one of my sons) took care of that, too. Whatever he needed, my kids and I handled. But we didn't stress to her that she didn't need us—he did—and she needed that distinction to be made clear. As much as she loved me and her grandchildren, she resented my being there because I didn't announce that I wasn't there to help her. Her pride needed me to know that I knew that she wasn't the one who needed me. But I had totally missed the point.

It was crazy that I made that mistake because I knew better. I was disappointed in myself because I knew better. Most of the women in my family are proud. And we'd rather pick a fight and make you feel small than admit that we need your help. And when it comes to that, my mom is the worst of all. But I knew that already. I just dropped the ball.

As I drove back home to Madison in search of a stimulus check I never received because my account was levied for failure to pay state income taxes, I had time to think about all of that. I had exhausted all the funds I brought to Chicago, and it was time to replenish my account. I told my mom I needed to go back to Wisconsin, and despite the tensions between us, we agreed I would return within a few days. But when I got back to Madison, things were not what I had anticipated. The financial situation was a mess, and there was no way I'd be going back to Chicago broke.

Fuck. I didn't see that shit coming. Quiet One needs commissary this week, and I have to get back to Chicago. Shit! How the fuck am I going to do this? I panicked to myself, feeling the weight of the situation.

The longer I stayed in Madison and reflected on my experience with my mom, the more determined I became to buy a home. I was desperate for a real sanctuary where I didn't have to worry about the lease terms or whether my kids were too loud. A place where my parents could find peace, where my fiancé could come home to after a decade away, and where I could build the life I'd been fighting for. The idea of a home—a stable, permanent place where all of us could breathe—became more than just a goal. It became a necessity, a non-negotiable. If doing so for my children and my parents wasn't enough, I would do it for the women who follow the Infamous Mothers brand, the company I founded.

Back in September 2020, we started a one-year program focused on building health alongside wealth. Because of COVID, women were pivoting their businesses, struggling with their own fears of dying in the pandemic while also trying to figure out how they were going to maintain their livelihood. I had been doing some research on the wealth gap and learned that without the strains of a pandemic, entrepreneurs are at higher risk for mental health challenges. I already knew about Black women and maternal mortality rates: Black women are three times as likely to die birthing children as white women. I wanted to change those numbers within what I call the IMverse (Infamous Mothers Universe). I was interested in closing the wealth gap in the IMverse, but I wanted to create a culture that did that without sacrificing our well-being. That's how Covet, our health alongside wealth program, began.

It's now February, and I am about to start a session with the women of our first Covet cohort.

As everyone begins to log on, I notice that Tanisha's beautiful, deep brown skin glows, and her curly natural hair is well hydrated, as she settles into the Zoom call from Detroit. "Hey, Sis," she greets us in a serious voice, the exhaustion from everything she's juggling evident in her tone. Despite her weariness, she's here, showing up just like she always does.

A moment later, Aunt Business pops up on the screen, relaxed as usual, dressed comfortably in a t-shirt. She's at home in Dallas, her backdrop a warm yellow wall with a window and an abstract painting hanging just behind her.

Qiana and I both log in from Madison, and my screen fills with the sight of her playful grin as she waves at us. "What's up, ladies?" she chimes, her energy a welcome contrast to the weight we're all carrying.

We've been meeting like this for five months now, and the rhythm of our sessions has become as familiar as the faces on the screen. Tonight, we start with our usual check-in on the week's workout sessions with Gretchen, our online fitness coach for this Covet cohort.

Tanisha jumps in first, recounting how she powered through a particularly tough session despite wanting to quit halfway. "I'm Petty Betty," she jokes, her voice laced with determination. "Y'all know I wasn't quitting until the last one of us tapped out. I had to keep pushing."

Aunt Business nods approvingly, her expression one of understanding and respect. "I hear you, Tanisha, girl. I had to meet myself where I was this week. Did what I could, and then I had to sit down, chile. But I jumped back in when I could, shoot."

Qiana, focusing on her goal of drinking half her body weight in water, adds with a bit of a sigh, "I don't know, y'all. I still don't like water like that."

Tanisha pulls out her sleek water bottle and waves it in front of the camera. "I drink water that's a little more expensive as a way of embedding luxury into my routine," she says with a knowing smile.

We all pause, impressed by her perspective. It's one of those moments where someone says something simple yet profound, and we all look at each other on the screen, nodding in agreement.

"That's brilliant," I finally say, voicing what we're all thinking. We start discussing how we could all elevate our routines by incorporating little luxuries, even in something as basic as drinking water.

The conversation shifts to meal prep, and we all admit we could be doing better. "No matter how much we work out," I remind them, "we can eat our way out of the benefits of any workout routine."

The reminder is met with a chorus of agreement, each of us reflecting on how our eating habits can either support or sabotage the hard work we put in at the gym. The conversation flows naturally, filled with laughter, mutual encouragement, and the shared understanding that we're all in this together.

Once the serious discussions wind down, I take a deep breath and smile at the camera. "Alright, ladies. I've got something new for us tonight. It's not finished, but I want to test it out—Books, Bullets, and Babies."

I hold up the eight-sided die, its symbols glinting in the light. Everyone's eyes widen with curiosity.

"So here's how it works," I explain. "I'll roll the die, and whatever it lands on, you'll pick a card from the corresponding deck—Books for wealth, Bullets for anything from sex to health, and Babies for mothering. The card will have a reflection question for you to answer."

"Sounds intriguing," Tanisha says, leaning forward with interest.

"Tanisha, you're up first," I announce, rolling the die. We all watch as it bounces around before finally landing on the Book icon. I reach for the card, feeling the group's anticipation.

"The question is," I read aloud, "Who is your favorite guru, and what makes you trust this person? Why do you follow them?"

Tanisha pauses, considering her response. "I'd have to say Dr. Cindy Trimm," she begins. "I follow her because I can see the fruit of her teachings in her life, in how she lives."

Curious, I lean forward and ask, "Can you elaborate on that, Tanisha?"

She nods thoughtfully. "It's her home," she explains. "For me, Dr. Trimm's home is a symbol of success. It's proof that she knows what she's talking about. When I see the life she's built—the peace, the order, the beauty of her surroundings—it shows me that she's living the principles she teaches. That makes her worthy of my following."

Her words hang in the air for a moment, each of us reflecting on the idea of tangible evidence of success. It sparks a deeper discussion about the mentors we admire and the symbols of their teachings that resonate with us personally.

I think about her words.

Once again, I find myself thinking about the value of homeownership. This time, it's within a work context.

While I understand the financial case for renting—even wealth experts shy away from owning where they live—I also understand that homeownership has been a dream and a means of protection for many of my women. It isn't just about having a roof over our heads; it is about creating a sanctuary, a safe space that is ours, where we can close the door to the chaos outside and find peace within.

If I am going to make a difference in their lives, I think, *this is one way to gain the credibility I need.*

In that same pilot, we were all reading *Rich Dad Poor Dad*. In it, author Robert Kiyosaki made it very clear that homeownership is a liability unless it's bringing in income. A tall order just got taller. On top of my other "delusional" idea of purchasing a home big enough for me and my six children to each have our rooms, a space for my parents, and an office to run my business, now I was adding to the mix that it had to be income property as well.

Why not? If I'm going to dream, I'm going to dream so big that it makes me blush; otherwise, I feel like I'm not doing it right, I reflected with a smile. *I have to dream so big that it makes me run and hide. My dreams have to take up space, and they have to feel impossible for me to know I'm playing in the right arena; otherwise, I feel like I'm playing in God's face. My dreams have to be so big and so bright that they feel like nothing less than a miracle. This is that kind of dream. I'm already looking at it and knowing that somewhere on this journey, I'm going to tap out, and God is going to have to tap completely in.*

I picked up the phone to call my real estate agent, thinking, *Ruby's with the shits*, meaning, in this context, she's not running from a tough case or an "impossible" situation. *So if you wake up that unicorn and her magic wand, you better be ready because she's going to find what you're looking for—sooner or later. Are you ready for this?* I debated with myself as I dialed, my heart racing.

I tried to purchase the paid-for house in Roseland.

The second time I tried to purchase a home was in 2017, the year we published our first book, *Infamous Mothers: Women Who've Gone through the Belly of Hell and Brought Something Good Back*. That year, I met Ruby at a gathering to support Senator LaTonya Johnson for her senate run. The event was hosted by a woman who supported Planned Parenthood and women's rights. Her home was filled with "fancy" women, most of them white—maybe all of them white, except for me and Senator Johnson. I don't remember their faces, but I do remember the feeling. They felt like the kind of women who wore cardigans and pearls and had political power, if for no other reason than they were willing to put in the work and the dollars to support their candidate. Needless to say, LaTonya Johnson won the seat, and I believe the women at that gathering played a role in that.

The house was warm, with a cozy atmosphere that belied the influence held by the women inside. Wealth here didn't flaunt itself with pearls or designer suits. Yes, there were cardigans, but yoga pants were just as common. These women were powerful in a quiet, understated way, sipping wine and discussing matters that could shape outcomes well beyond the room we were in.

Ruby was introduced to me near the door. Although it wasn't open yet, I could tell she was already disengaged. She spoke politely, but her attention was clearly divided as if she had just remembered that her carriage was about to turn into a pumpkin or that she had left a pot on the stove. Either way, mentally, she was already across town dealing with another matter. Even as she shook my hand, her eyes were distant, her mind seemingly in two places at once. We spoke about the book, exchanged info, and then she was gone.

"This lady is odd, and she doesn't like me," I muttered defensively, feeling some kind of way because I needed this lifeline, and she blew in and out. The way she moved, I figured, "There's no way she's interested, and she's not going to get back to me." Clearly, that says more about me than about her because she not only connected with me, she became invested in my journey.

Fast forward a few months from that initial encounter, Ruby and I were in a building. I don't remember how we connected after the night of the gathering. I don't even remember how I got to the building. But I do remember she worked there with a program for women in recovery. I met some of the other staff, some of the women. I learned that Ruby was a writer who won an Emmy for a children's show. And she was really a fun and interesting person. She had funny stories about traveling to foreign places, using sketchy services. She was adventurous and down-to-earth, and she was quirky in all the best ways.

Ruby and I quickly became friends, and she soon became something of a mentor to me, guiding me through my journey toward homeownership. I was terrified of banks, though. I am afraid of going to a bank in the same way I am afraid of going to barbershops.

Years ago, after I did the big chop, I was lost. Because I didn't have much hair on my head, I was unsure about what to do next. I didn't have enough hair to go to the beauty salon, so my cousin recommended that I get it shaped up by her barber, a guy named Trell. I went to his shop one night, hoping he could just "fix it"—fix my hair, fix the way I saw myself as a Black woman with strong African features, fix my awkwardness and insecurity. As I sat in the chair, I could feel the eyes of the men in the shop on me, assessing, judging.

I remember Trell talking with another guy in the shop about a pregnant woman who wore a catsuit. They laughed and joked about how beautiful and shapely she was, their words making it clear they found her desirable. My stomach twisted into knots as I listened, feeling more and more out of place with each word they exchanged. I had just had my first child. Not before, during, or after that pregnancy did I have the kind of body that men would praise for wearing a catsuit. I felt invisible, irrelevant—like I didn't belong in that chair or even in that shop.

I could sense Trell's frustration as he worked on my hair, blowing out my coarse, thick, now "virgin" hair. The comb caught on a tangle, and with a loud snap, it broke in his hand. Trell and the other guy erupted into laughter, and I felt the blood rush to my face. I wanted to sink into the floor, disappear, or at least run out of the shop with my face covered in shame. Their laughter wasn't malicious, but it didn't matter. In that moment, I felt small, inadequate, and completely out of place.

Over the years, I'd grow my hair back and then cut it off again, repeating the cycle. I'd experience more encounters like that—male-dominated spaces that either made me feel laughed at, small, or like a pitiful case that no one knew "how to handle." My hair was too unruly, my personality too awkward, my features too African, my body not "sexy enough." So I avoided barbershops until I finally found a brother-sister-owned salon that felt right, with a barber who made me feel at home. He didn't just see my hair—he saw me.

Banks felt like all those other barbershops. They felt condescending, predatory, and like I didn't belong in them. I didn't feel safe. In this case, it wasn't because I didn't have the right kind of body. They were interested in a different set of "assets." I had no money, bad credit, and no collateral. In the same way I felt homely sitting in that chair as they talked about the pregnant woman in the catsuit, I felt even more homely just thinking about walking into a bank. There was nothing enticing about me that would make a banker want to think twice. In fact, on paper, I was quite laughable.

Reflecting on all those years, in 2017, I told Ruby that I didn't think I'd qualify for a bank loan and that I didn't want to even bother. That's when she introduced me to the idea of a community bank. Ruby explained to me that community banks exist to help the community. They don't require you to check all the boxes like larger banks do. They have a more flexible way of doing things to meet the community where they are.

I've never heard of a community bank. I'm intrigued, and I want to learn more, I thought, feeling nosey. I was not inspired yet, but I was curious.

By this time, Ruby had fed me, taken me to her home, driven me around the city, and told me about her exploits. I trusted her. And if this woman, who was something like my fairy godmother in housing, believed that she knew a wizard named Kelli who could make it happen for me and my family, then to hell with it. We were off to see her.

What do I have to lose? I thought as we drove off, the city blurring past us.

That day, Ruby picked me up from campus housing, where I lived with my six children and partner. I got in her car, a sporty older Saab, I believe. She and her husband, Chris, had more than one car, and I had been in both. This time, I believe it was the gray one, the Saab that she'd end up lending to me when my own car stopped working, when it seemed like everything in my life had become broken, not just my car. But that's a story for another time. The point is, I believed it was the Saab because that's the car that seemed to make the most difference in my life. And that day may have been no different.

The drive felt like an hour, even though it might have been about thirty minutes. We were going through places I had never seen to meet a woman I didn't know at an institution I didn't trust. It wasn't her institution, per se. It was all banks. I can't remember the conversation Ruby and I had along the way. But knowing us, it was probably something about her travels. I loved hearing those stories. Maybe they were an overview of what I should expect. We also discussed kids, food, and writing. (Ruby's a natural teacher.)

In what felt like the middle of nowhere, our drive came to an end. We were pulling into a parking lot in front of a beautiful structure. I could see that it was a bank, but it felt different, kinder. We walked through the doors into what looked like a meeting room with a large wooden table and several comfortable swivel chairs. I don't remember how Kelli got there—whether she met us at the door or joined us in the room—but I remember her and her legal pad. Her voice was very friendly. Her presence, the way she walked and carried herself, wasn't intimidating or scary. She was a mom with a large family, similar to mine. I could relate to her. She was dressed professionally—maybe a sweater and slacks—but nothing that suggested too much of a difference between us.

She seems ... normal, I observed, feeling my shoulders relax a bit.

I remember sitting at the table with her. She offered us each a bottle of water, an experience I had yet to have at a bank. Then before we knew it, we were in "it"—into my hopes and dreams, the projected numbers, my real numbers, and that credit score. She had my entire story played out in numbers. And in Kelli's hands, for the first time in my life, I didn't feel ashamed or less than as I shared my truth inside a bank.

So, choose a bank with real people in it. Noted, I thought, surprised at the comfort I felt in that moment.

In recent years, I had been working with a financial coach I absolutely loved—another mom named Aiden. But she was located at a credit union. Working with her within the context of a credit union had become one step in the process of healing my relationship with financial institutions. She made me feel seen, and she felt like an advocate, like someone who would fight for me, and over the years, when she'd climb higher in that credit union, she did fight for me. Because of my experience with Aiden, the mom who loved to talk about her boys and their baseball, I had come to love that credit union. As long as she was there, it felt safe. Now, Kelli was creating the same experience within a place that I had never thought capable of welcoming someone like me.

That day, Ruby and I left Kelli's bank feeling inspired. We went straight to a local grocery store and stood in line at the kiosk-style bank within it. Ruby did everything but hold my hand while trying to put me on the path to homeownership. And this was part of that effort. One of the things Kelli stressed was that I needed to improve my credit score. To do so, Ruby had brought me to this bank-in-a-store setup to open an account for a product that was designed specifically to help increase credit. They extended me $1,000 in credit, and I would make monthly payments on that loan until it was paid off, except—and here's the smart part, at least I thought it was a smart plan—I wouldn't withdraw the money. I'd leave it in the account and use it to make my monthly payments. Genius, right? I essentially borrowed their money and used it to pay them back as a way of showing that I could make on-time payments. I was surely on my way to homeownership.

At the same time I was connecting with Ruby, I was also working to build my business. Remember, the whole point of meeting with Ruby was that I was convinced that my brand was going to be so successful that I could buy a home outright, paying $300,000 in not cold but warm and heartfelt, hard-earned cash. And because Ruby believed in me, she was willing to put me on that homeownership path while I built my company.

The first step was to sell thousands of copies of our new book. In my mind, I could already see it: stacks of books flying off the shelves, the pages turning in eager hands, the words of our stories resonating deeply with readers across the nation. We were about to publish our first book, and in my mind, it was going to sweep the nation. I imagined people sitting in their favorite reading spots, inspired by the stories within, laughing and crying, feeling connected to the women we call Infamous Mothers. From there, we were going to launch a series of workshops and classes. The excitement of those future gatherings buzzed in my mind—the buzz of conversations, the exchange of ideas, the collective energy of a room full of people united by a common cause. The brand would be fully activated, with an updated website and our own stock photography. I pictured sleek, professional images that captured the essence of our movement, each one telling its own powerful story. I would travel around the world speaking and create an Infamous Mothers headquarters for our new team because we had to create jobs and offer safe spaces. The vision was crystal clear, a beacon of hope and purpose that I clung to in the face of every challenge.

That was the dream, but hardly the reality. We launched a crowdfunding campaign that never got off the ground—quite the opposite of our first campaign, which had received support all the way from Germany. The excitement we had felt before was replaced with the sinking feeling of watching numbers barely move, the stark contrast cutting deep. We raised maybe $5,000. In hindsight, I believe that we could have done everything we had hoped to do, except we had one major problem—marketing. The realization hit like a cold splash of water: No one outside of our initial supporters even knew we existed. And we had already run that well dry with the $25,000 we had raised not too long before we had come back with the new request. The memory of that first success was bittersweet, a reminder of how far we had fallen this time. Those initial dollars were to complete the book: pay our photographers, designers, makeup artists, travel, and room and board expenses, etc. It was a coffee table book, and we wanted the women photographed to feel beautiful, powerful, and regal, so I hired a friend from high school, Krystyn Johnson, who is now a celebrity makeup artist, to give these women an experience. And she did just that. It was beautiful. The next dollars were to print the book. From there, we were going to sell them and activate a movement. The dream had been so vibrant, so full of life, but in reality, it felt like chasing shadows. Like I said, that was the dream … hardly the reality.

The flop of our 10,000 books campaign was the biggest embarrassment of my entrepreneurial career; the sting of failure was sharp and unforgiving, a public reminder of my misstep. There were more to come. In one way or another, we needed to get these books printed, which meant until then, my hopes of launching our classes and workshops, hiring people, and creating a safe space were going to have to be put on hold. It was like watching pieces of my dream crumble, one by one, leaving only the most essential elements standing. It meant I couldn't focus on a speaking career, nor could I put my energy into buying a home. The idea of a home, once so clear and inviting in my mind, faded into the background, replaced by the urgent need to keep this project alive.

It wouldn't be long before I would withdraw from and essentially sabotage my credit-building effort. The thought of building credit now felt like a distant, almost absurd notion, like something out of reach for someone in my position. I didn't need credit, and I didn't need to be having my head in the clouds, doing "white people" things, acting as if I was something I wasn't. The frustration boiled up, making me reject everything that didn't feel raw, real, and immediate. I was a hustler. Everything about me was grassroots, on the ground, in the trenches, eat what I hunt, "just gotta make it." The grit and grind of survival were where I felt most at home, even if it meant rejecting the very tools that could have made things easier. And people like me didn't think about credit and bank loans. At best, we had a checking and savings account—if we were "fancy." But pre-paid cards, phones, and payday loans were good enough. The practicality of these choices felt like armor against the judgment of the world, a way to stay true to who I was. I didn't have time to be who I wasn't. I had to hit the ground and raise the dollars and do the work. The urgency of survival drowned out everything else, narrowing my focus to what needed to be done right now. And I did just that. With the support of a group of women from around Wisconsin, specifically Green Bay, we raised an additional $25,000. The relief was tangible, a small victory in a series of battles that were far from over.

I had the audacity to believe we could do it. And now look at me, having the nerve to be surprised, I thought, still shocked at what we'd accomplished.

With the little bit of credit I had mustered up over that time, I used it to practically steal a rental car and set off on a whirlwind, impromptu book tour across the Midwest, guerrilla-style. The car smelled like fast food and feet, a mix of desperation and determination. I had no book to sell, just a manuscript of the stories I carried with me like a precious secret. I drove to Chicago, Minnesota, Green Bay, Milwaukee, Iowa—the miles blurring together as I sped down highways, the sun rising and setting through the dusty windshield. The car rental place was blowing up my phone. The incessant buzzing in the cup holder was a constant reminder that I had agreed to bring it back days before. But I wasn't going to return it until I had my $25,000, and I didn't have the money to extend my contract. The pressure was on, and I was just beginning.

Fortunately, Amy, my friend and business coach at the time, did have the means. Amy, with her wild ideas, understood my madness in a way few others did. She was just as crazy as I was. She understood what I was trying to do, what I needed to do for me, my family, and the community of women who had grown to love our brand. They saw it as a source of inspiration and said it made them feel seen. There was a fire in her eyes, a mix of concern and intrigue, as she watched me navigate the edge of disaster. With just the right mix of both, Amy watched me take control of my fate and decided she'd fuel the fire by going to the car rental place and extending my rental for a month—paid in full. She called me with that news. I could feel her smile through the phone. It was one of both encouragement and warning like she was throwing gasoline on a fire she couldn't quite control.

I continued this one-woman tour, driving to places like domestic abuse shelters, high schools for pregnant teen mothers, the housing complex where I was raised and where my mother still lives. The car became my office, my sanctuary. The hum of the engine and the rhythm of the road were the sounds that grounded me. I would do live readings from the manuscript, my voice echoing in small, dimly lit rooms, answer questions, and take pre-orders, sharing pictures of our journey along each stop. The goal was to raise the money, still through crowdfunding. Every time I stood in front of a group, I could feel the weight of expectation pressing down on me, the unspoken hope that this would be the moment everything clicked. *It's all or nothing*, I reminded myself. The words echoed in my mind like a mantra, a constant reminder of the stakes.

While it raised awareness, we still didn't raise the dollars. The disappointment settled in like a cold fog, creeping into my bones. But we did capture the attention of a statewide organization that would ultimately solve our problems. They would contract with us to create and offer courses to women who are survivors of domestic abuse, using our book as the central text for their course. They would cover the cost of programming and materials up to $25,000. The relief was visible, a sudden lifting of the weight that had been dragging me down. With their help and the help of other individual sponsors, we were finally able to print our coffee table book. Holding that first printed copy in my hands was like cradling a newborn, the culmination of so much hope and hard work. It didn't matter that I still lived in campus housing and that I struggled to pay my bills. We had a win.

A year would go by before I would consider purchasing a home again. The idea hovered in the back of my mind like a distant dream, one I couldn't quite bring myself to chase. And I only dared to do so then because it didn't include a bank, and it would be to help support a friend in the middle of a life transition. It felt like a safe bet, a way to tiptoe back into the idea of stability without fully committing. But that fell through. Once again, I couldn't produce the capital. The familiar sting of failure permeated my body, a reminder that I was still tethered to a reality I couldn't escape.

Three more years would go by, bringing us to 2021, and this same friend would be selling her second home. This time around, I had the capital, but something told me to wait. It was a gut feeling, a whisper in the back of my mind that urged caution, even as my heart longed to leap forward. My friend was going out of the country to be with her family during another transition. We'd talk about moving forward once she returned, but something in my spirit told me to wait on Ruby, the unicorn with the wand. I could see her in my mind, the image of her waving that wand, bringing something magical to life. I had already told her what I wanted, and while I expected it to take her years to find it, something just told me to be still and wait.

Waiting felt like surrendering control over my destiny. It was a slow, painful process, like watching a flower bloom in slow motion, knowing you can't rush nature. It tested my patience and forced me to confront the deep-seated fear that maybe I wasn't meant to achieve this dream. Doubt gnawed at the edges of my resolve, whispering that I was wasting time, letting opportunities slip through my fingers. But at the same time, I felt a pregnancy in the wait. There was a quiet fullness in the stillness, a sense that something was growing beneath the surface, something beautiful and inevitable. I felt the wait had something full and beautiful to offer me if I just sat still. So I did.

During my friend's time away, Ruby found a home that met all the requirements of my dreams, and seeing it configured the way it was—well, it took my breath away. I had never imagined this finished product. The first glimpse of the place sent a shiver down my spine, that kind of feeling when something clicks perfectly into place. The irony is that I didn't expect Ruby to find what I was looking for so soon. As much as I was itching to move forward, deep down, I had resigned myself to a long wait, picturing years of searching, of false starts and near misses. I thought it would take her at least three years because what I was looking for was so unique, so specific that it didn't seem to exist in the Madison market. The idea of it felt like trying to find a needle in a haystack—a dream that was almost too good to be true.

And, if I'm being super honest, I didn't want her to find it for another three years. That's how long I thought it would take for me to get myself ready to be a homeowner—to fix my credit and secure enough dollars. I imagined that I would send Ruby on this goose chase, and while people asked me what was taking so long, instead of admitting that I was scared or that my finances weren't together or that my credit was still messed up, I could just say Ruby hadn't found a home that suited us yet. But God had other plans, plans that unfolded in the most unexpected ways.

A woman and her husband, who had their own dreams, designed a home that was residential on one side and commercial on the other, where she ran her acupuncture business. The design was elegant and purposeful, with a seamless flow between the spaces that made it clear this home was more than just a building—it was a vision brought to life. And while we had very different businesses, we had remarkably similar visions for what we would want and need inside this hybrid property. Walking through it in my mind, I could almost hear the quiet activity in the commercial space, balanced by the warmth and tranquility of the residential side, where every detail seemed to welcome you in.

It was time to revisit Kelli. The anticipation built like a rising tide, mingling with a deep sense of peace that spread through me. The thought of seeing that home, of stepping into a space that felt like it was meant for me, filled me with a sense of anticipation and calm, as if all the waiting had led me exactly where I needed to be. The air seemed to be full with possibility, and as I imagined walking through the doors, the scent of fresh wood and clean air filled my senses, grounding me in the reality that this wasn't just a dream anymore—it was my future.

But this wouldn't be my second encounter with Kelli this year—it would be the third. Ruby and I had first met with her at the start of the year to explore possibilities. That initial meeting felt much like our very first sit-down with Kelli. Except this time, the outlandish idea wasn't about raising capital.

Before the pandemic, I had moved my Infamous Mothers brand completely online. I made the shift for the women I serve, but the transition brought an unexpected advantage: When the world shut down, we were ready. Our established online presence became our lifeline. People knew us, trusted us, and that familiarity helped us thrive during a time of uncertainty. The surge in revenue meant that, this time around, money wasn't the biggest hurdle.

Now, the real challenge was finding the perfect home to fit both my vision and my family size. It was about repairing my credit and slowing down long enough to clean up my books—to prove that the income was there.

"This time, I need to do it right," I resolved, determined to make this work.

So, I know y'all see this thing snowballing, right? For shits and giggles—and for the sake of clarity—let's recap. First, there's my parents. My dad's dementia is worsening, and my mom, who won't admit it, needs help and respite. The tension between us is thick, like the air before a storm, and it only grows heavier each day. Then, there's my "justice-involved" fiancé, who's about to come home after doing a ten-year bid, but he can't stay in my current apartment because the lease says no felons allowed. The thought of him coming home only to be turned away terrifies me. Add to that, my six children are literally walking down the street saying, "Poverty does shit to you," and they're not wrong. Their words hang in the air like a huge question mark, as if asking, "Well, Mom, what are you going to do about this shit?" I've been letting them get away with all kinds of things because I'm terrified we'll get put out if they breathe too loud. I can't afford any tantrums.

And now, to top it all off, the women of the IMverse are telling me that credibility for them is looking at the fruits of God's blessings in how we live, both spiritually and physically. Tanisha's words echo in my mind, a reminder that I'm not just leading with words—I'm leading by example. I mean, I get it. If I'm going to lead, I need to show that I'm living what I preach. It's not just about saying the right things; it's about living them. And living them, for me, means buying this house.

This house isn't just a want; it's a need. It's a sanctuary for my parents, a stable home for my fiancé and children, and a testament to the women of the IMverse that dreams—no matter how impossible they seem—can be achieved. Every piece of this puzzle has come together, clicking into place with a sense of inevitability that feels both terrifying and exhilarating. This isn't just a purchase; it's a declaration. It's me saying, "Yes, I've been through hell, but I'm still standing, and I'm building something solid for myself and for those who believe in me."

CHAPTER 6

INCONCEIVABLE

MARCH 2021

There was a time when I couldn't imagine who I wanted to be when I grew up. I mean, I literally couldn't see myself in a career or profession. Whenever someone asked what I wanted to do or who I wanted to become, my mind would go completely blank. The idea of dreaming about a future tied to work or purpose felt foreign—almost impossible.

But while I couldn't picture myself in a job or career, I could dream about love. I spent hours imagining my crush—whoever he was at the time—loving me or "saving" me from what, I never really knew. Even as a young girl, I craved that kind of rescue. My imagination could run wild when it came to romance and being chosen, but when it came to seeing myself in the world as someone with ambition or direction, there was nothing.

It's a strange thing, that void, that blackness. That's all I would see. At some point, I settled on becoming a construction worker. I imagined myself standing on a scaffold with a hard hat, whistling at the men. You know what's crazy about that? I'm afraid of heights, and I can't whistle.

I didn't know it then, but I was surrounded by people who couldn't imagine futures for themselves. They were people who didn't expect to live past eighteen or twenty-one. For some, the issue was less about their own deaths and more about someone else's—their children's father, best friend, wife, or mother. Even though they managed to survive this or that tragedy—like recovering from their wounds after getting shot right alongside their person—they stopped living the moment their person died. Yes, they'd continue to care for their children, clean their homes, and go to work.

In some cases, women would even go on to have more children, partner with new people, and grow older. They'd laugh, cry, make love, and pay bills. In other words, they performed life, existing years beyond the incident. Still, they had stopped truly living ten, fifteen, or twenty years ago. Some people were shells of themselves, their bodies going through the motions. At the same time, their spirits were left behind, weeping at their loved one's gravesite. They never found a way to be whole again after the car accident, the stabbing, the drive-by, or the disease that everyone was so hush-hush about.

For so many people I knew, life became the graveyard of their dreams. Men who had once been NFL prospects or were on track to become medical doctors, and women who had envisioned themselves as college professors, CIA employees, or famous artists, all found themselves at unexpected crossroads. They faced impossible choices: Pursue their dreams or care for a family member? Drop out of school because of an unplanned pregnancy or keep going against the odds? Accept a once-in-a-lifetime career opportunity in another state or stay behind to care for an ailing parent who refused to relocate? Go back to school to become a registered nurse or hold onto a dead-end nine-to-five that offered just enough money and schedule flexibility to keep paying lawyers to help a son, daughter, husband, or parent fight a case?

My own story wasn't so different. In the world of my youth, dreams were often deferred. Like broken beer bottles, used condoms, and crack bags, they littered the streets for miles in every direction—remnants of what could have been, scattered and forgotten.

When I went to boarding school, I tried to dream again. The energy and enthusiasm of my peers were contagious, and before long, I was bitten by the college bug. I applied to seventeen schools, hoping to major in something between math—because I was told that as a Black woman, I should pursue it, even though I didn't like it—and writing. I got accepted into fifteen, including Spelman. But I couldn't attend any because I didn't know I was supposed to apply for financial aid or scholarships. That's the risk of dreaming—you can miss a step or two. So, I graduated from my fancy boarding school and returned home to the South Side of Chicago, where I attended the University of Illinois at Chicago (UIC) and gave birth to my first three children. For the next ten years, I was there fighting, arguing, learning to sleep through gunshots, turning my head as people I cared about made drug transactions, and bonding with girlfriends over stories about cheating men and baby daddies trying to figure out how to be fathers when many of them never had one.

While attending UIC, I was accepted into the Ronald E. McNair Post-Baccalaureate Achievement Program. Amongst ourselves, we just called it McNair. It was designed to pipeline first-generation students and people of color into doctoral programs. The irony? I was terrified of research. The only "D" I'd ever earned was in Research Methods. But when I saw the flyer, I cared more about the $3,000 stipend that came with being a scholar than I was afraid of research. I had just given birth to my first child and had no money. I was desperate, more afraid of failing my baby than anything that program could throw at me. So, I applied.

I remember my advisor cringing through my first presentation as I struggled to string together ideas, form a research question, and communicate big thoughts in simple ways. I was embarrassed and uncomfortable, standing there with my afro and some homely outfit, trying to figure out this scholar thing, this parent thing, this adult thing. But even with all those ugly, uncomfortable feelings, I pushed through. Someone who couldn't take care of herself depended on me to make it happen.

About two years into the program, all the McNair scholars from around the country gathered for a conference in Puerto Rico. I was the only one from the humanities in my cohort at UIC, so while my colleagues prepared poster presentations, I gave an oral presentation. The pressure was intense. I didn't want to embarrass my university or myself by fumbling through my talk as I had in front of my advisor a few semesters before. So, instead of touring the island, tasting the food, or joining my peers in some "what happens in Puerto Rico stays in Puerto Rico" fun, I locked myself in my hotel room and lost myself in the work.

My paper was on Gayl Jones's *Corregidora*. I can't remember exactly what I argued, but I know it was related to sex and blues. Again, I watched advisors cringe as I delivered my talk. But this time, it wasn't because I was fumbling through my ideas or struggling. I knew my work, inside and out. And I delivered it with confidence. This time, they cringed because I had chosen a provocative text filled with sex, cussing, and incest, and I didn't shrink from it. I quoted and analyzed the work, using equally bold and colorful language. By the end of my talk, one of the McNair advisors was beet red, but I didn't care. I had given it my all and delivered the most authentic, heartfelt, and well-researched work I could offer.

When I finished, the room erupted in applause. My UIC colleagues and people from around the country stood up, cheering and clapping. That was the first time I saw what I wanted to do for the rest of my life.

I got back to Chicago, and life returned to normal—relationship drama, poverty, struggle, fighting, arguing. But for the first time in my adult life, I felt different. That feeling became my North Star, a compass guiding me toward the right path. I searched for it when I wrote my papers and when people asked me what I wanted to do with my life. I knew I was on the right track if I felt close to it. If I felt distant, something was wrong. I relied on that feeling after I graduated in 2004, stepping away from the structure college had provided.

A few months after I walked across the stage, my mom went out of town and left me in charge of her home. A family member who had been struggling with addiction was angry that she left me in charge instead of him. So, he broke into her house and attacked me in front of my children. I remember tussling with him at the edge of her bed. He couldn't see me reaching for the lamp behind us. I imagined myself beating him over the head. Before I knew it, I slid to the ground and ran out of the house, leaving my three children behind, huddled together on the stairs as I left. He attacked me, but I knew him well enough to know he wouldn't harm them.

Somehow, I found myself back on UIC's campus, sitting in the McNair office. Whether I drove or took the bus, I honestly can't recall—but what mattered was that I was there.

Chasing that feeling again, I pushed past my fear and started applying to graduate school. First, I got a fee waiver for the Graduate Record Examination (GRE) and the GRE subject tests. Then, I applied to the University of Iowa and the University of Wisconsin–Madison.

This time, I got into both with full funding. Madison offered a slightly better package, so before long, I was moving to campus housing with my three children, twenty-five dollars to my name, and whatever broken-down furniture I had hauled from my apartment in Chicago.

It was 2006. About a month after moving into our new apartment, my kids and I were sitting on the floor watching *Akeelah and the Bee*, a movie about a young Black girl in South Los Angeles who dreamed of going to the Scripps National Spelling Bee despite her mother's objections. As she faced the odds, her mentor shared these words by Marianne Williamson: "Our deepest fear is not that we are inadequate. Our deepest fear is that we are powerful beyond measure. It is our light, not our darkness, that most frightens us. We ask ourselves, who am I to be brilliant, gorgeous, talented, and fabulous? Actually, who are you not to be? You are a child of God. Your playing small doesn't serve the world. There's nothing enlightened about shrinking so others won't feel insecure around you. We were born to make manifest the glory of God that is within us. It's not just in some of us; it's in everyone. And as we let our own light shine, we unconsciously give other people permission to do the same ..."

The truth is, I was afraid of my light and my power. Until then, I had been flirting with greatness but never boldly stepped into it. I'd poke at it, tease it, then run back to the other side of the street—back to mediocrity, to safety. Mediocre was familiar. It let me straddle the fence between greatness and danger. I could go to school, show up now and then, and mess around with some guy who'd make me cry later. I could gossip, get lost in the drama, then return to writing my paper or preparing for a conference. Mediocre let me do just enough to set me apart in one world while letting people see my potential in another, but never enough to really convert that potential into power. Mediocre allowed me to revisit a dangerous place—the past—because the present required too much focus and structure, and the future was way too uncertain. But then there was that North Star, and now, this new reality: I was afraid of my own greatness. Hearing those words gave me something to hold on to.

But it was reading Rick Warren's *The Purpose Driven Life* that sealed the deal, giving me the confidence to be a single mom of three kids while pursuing a doctorate. I can't quote him exactly, but I remember something like, "Your parents may not have planned for you, but God did." I always knew my parents wanted me, but I never felt like I belonged. I always felt awkward and out of place, like I didn't fit in my extended family, in school, or in the community. Reading those words made it okay that I didn't fit, because I wasn't an accident. God had a larger plan for me. No matter how awkward or invisible I felt, it would all make sense someday. I existed for a reason, right? And my awkwardness had to mean something in the grand scheme of things, right? I took that optimism and excitement into my first year of graduate school.

I'll never forget those early seminars where my peers discussed literary theory and criticism like everyday conversation. It was English, but it might as well have been Sanskrit. My head still aches thinking about the "translations" I had to make, the mental acrobatics required. There was Nietzsche's *On Truth and Lies in a Nonmoral Sense*, Derrida with his cryptic concepts, Kant, Descartes—so many names, so many theories, all in English, except it didn't feel like it. These theorists pushed the boundaries of language, expanding concepts and giving words new meanings. I was way out of my league.

Like the others that year, that class wasn't something you could fake your way through. In college, I'd been the kind of smart person who could miss weeks of classes, listen to one discussion, and piece it all together. Graduate school didn't work like that. Becoming a doctor didn't work like that. Decoding this "English" meant reading, studying, and poring over paragraphs for hours, cross-referencing sentences with books and articles until it made sense. There was no disappearing and winging it. I had to be present and fully engaged.

By the end of my first year, I was ready to sabotage myself. Too proud to quit but too uncomfortable to stay in this new world, I searched for something familiar, something that felt safe. I searched for the Quiet One. It was 2007, and I was grappling with something that felt uncontrollable, something I couldn't quite grasp.

I met the Quiet One in 1996, the summer I graduated from high school. The air was thick with the warm scent of freshly cut grass and the faint aroma of barbecue drifting from nearby yards. The sun was setting, casting a golden hue over everything, making the cracked pavement shimmer underfoot as I strolled down the street with some of the other girls from the housing complex. I wore a crisp white Western Michigan University jersey with gold letters stitched in brown, the fabric soft against my skin. My hair was in the short, sleek style that was all the rage in the nineties—think Halle Berry, Malinda Williams—the edges sharp and precise, still slightly damp from the gel I'd used to smooth it down that morning.

I was much thinner then, my figure more delicate. People often stopped me in grocery stores or gas stations, their curious eyes scanning my face as they asked if anyone had ever told me I looked like Nia Long. Something about that comparison made me stand a little taller, the corners of my lips curling into a smile as I graciously accepted the compliment. While he never said it, I'm sure it was the haircut that caught the Quiet One's attention that evening, his gaze lingering a moment longer than it should have as we passed by.

Back then, I was dating a guy named Jamel, who drove an electric blue Regal that purred like a cat when he revved the engine. He'd told me he'd be out of touch for a while, visiting family in another state. People communicated through beepers in those days—little devices tucked into waistbands or clipped onto belts—and reaching someone on the road wasn't easy. I believed him without question. But when I saw a candy apple red Thunderbird cruising down the street, its paint job gleaming under the streetlights like liquid fire, I was paralyzed with shock. My heart pounded in my chest, the rhythm erratic, as my mind raced to make sense of what I saw. I knew it was him.

Determined not to be caught off guard again, I stalked that street every day, waiting for the car to appear. The days felt long as I hung out "on the gate" with my friends, the metal fence cool against my back while we idly chatted and laughed. Finally, after a few days, the candy apple red Thunderbird slid by again, and I was ready. I stared intently at it, waiting for the driver to explain himself. I was thrown off because, unlike the previous car, this one had tinted windows so dark they looked like they were covered in black velvet, concealing everything inside.

The car eased down the street, and I stared at it. The driver must've been staring at me, too, because the car slowed to a stop. The window came down, and in a drawl that sounded like a mix between Chicago and New Orleans, the driver said, "Since you're all up in my car, check it out." It wasn't Jamel, but I was intrigued by his audacity, calling me out like that. He was right—I had been "all up in his car," watching. But the moment I heard his voice, it was like everything around me faded into the background. The distant sounds of children playing, the bass from the music, and even the laughter of my friends, all became white noise. From that moment on, he had my full attention, his presence magnetic and impossible to ignore.

A few months after meeting the Quiet One, I enrolled in school. My first semester was in the winter of 1997, the air cold and biting, with snow crunching underfoot as I made my way to classes. Though I had one or two serious relationships during that time—including ones that led to three children—he and I hooked up on and off throughout my undergraduate years. Sometimes, we dated during our relationships with other people, sometimes in between them. Our encounters were always charged with a kind of intensity that was both thrilling and unsettling, like walking a tightrope between passion and danger. We were on and off for years, hanging out for six months, then parting ways for another six. Over time, he became my constant—the one thing I understood and could predict, no matter what.

Ten years later, I was still seeking that comfort, his familiar scent—a mixture of weed and leather—lingering in my mind like a haunting memory. But it wasn't from him on Chicago's South Side this time. It was from Madison, Wisconsin, as a first-year graduate student. The sharp smell of books and fresh ink in the library was a stark contrast to the warm, comforting familiarity of his world. Before long, I found myself looking for him again, for the safety of our world so I could run from mine. I looked for him so I could chase him, be dismissed by him, or even be disrespected. That familiar chaos was the distraction I needed to avoid the discomfort, shame, and guilt of being unable to focus long enough to read or write like a serious scholar.

Chasing him and enduring that familiar humiliation was easier than struggling with new concepts and readings. The tension in my shoulders would melt away in his presence, replaced by a different kind of tension that felt like home. At least he was predictable—that discomfort was predictable. And now, years later, as a graduate student, I was looking for that same familiarity. I was looking to get involved with him again to escape the deer-in-headlights experience of graduate school.

I went to Chicago looking for him. The cold, crisp air bit at my cheeks as I stood outside his door, anticipation and anxiety swirling in my stomach like a storm. From a friend of his, I discovered that he was in Minnesota, so I went there. He then came to Madison. We went to Chicago. For months, we bounced between the three places, the miles slipping away under the tires of our cars, until finally, in the summer of 2007, I ended up pregnant with my fourth child. The perfect sabotage. Surely, the university wouldn't tolerate this. To add insult to injury, I was behind on my rent in student housing. The weight of my decisions pressed down on me like a physical burden, my steps heavy as I walked to the housing office. When they asked why, I told them, "I gave all my money to my drug-dealing boyfriend so he could flip it." The words tasted bitter in my mouth, the lie both desperate and foolish. Whether it was true or not didn't matter. I wanted to scare them. I wanted them to be so intimidated by me, my scary boyfriend, and this unborn baby that they'd send me home.

But no. The housing people just looked at me and said, "Sounds like you don't need to go back to Chicago. We're putting you on a payment plan." Their voices were calm, almost soothing, like they were talking to a child throwing a tantrum. Not only had I failed at sabotaging myself, but I had also made an already challenging situation worse by adding another child and putting myself further into debt. The realization hit me like a punch to the gut, the air leaving my lungs in a rush as I walked out of that office, the weight of my actions pressing down on me even harder.

I often tell that story and credit the housing people for where I am today. That moment was a fork in the road, a defining point in my life. Had they sent me home, I'm almost certain I would never have looked back. I would've closed that chapter and settled into a new one back home, not becoming a doctor, not starting a business, not writing books. I would've settled for what made sense, choosing a relationship over my dreams, a nine-to-five that fed my family but didn't fulfill me. But they didn't send me home. And now, I'm everything I wouldn't have become. I still credit them, but in writing this, I realize I have to credit myself, too, for being here and for reaching my goal of earning the highest degree possible. I had to be here to try and sabotage it.

Radical honesty is another important lesson from this experience. I was trying to sabotage myself because I felt out of place. And I felt out of place because I didn't understand the work. And I felt I didn't understand the work because maybe I didn't do enough reading in undergrad. I was busy making babies and living a chaotic life. I must've missed all the lessons on theory and criticism. And it showed in the classroom. On a typical day, I would show up late to class and slide into the seat closest to the door, hoping not to draw attention. But their English felt like French or Sanskrit to me. The professor, a tall man with a wild beard, was fun and eccentric, scattered but kind. He asked a question, and the student beside me jumped in with an answer. Her words rolled off her tongue like she'd been born understanding this language of theory and criticism. I could only sit there, a spectator in a ninety-minute game of tennis, watching as ideas were batted back and forth, leaving me clueless and lost.

How do they know this shit? And why can't I catch on? I've done the reading. This is some bullshit, I thought to myself as I suffered through another class, my mind spiraling into frustration and self-doubt.

But something inside me snapped that day. *I can't keep living like this*, I declared in my mind. *As soon as office hours start, I have questions. And if I have to live there, then that's what it is. But I'm going to get this shit, too, just like everybody else.*

And that was it. I wasn't going to be a spectator anymore. If it meant spending every spare minute in office hours, dissecting every word until it made sense, then so be it. I was done with feeling lost. I was done with feeling less than. I was going to make this world my own, even if it killed me.

I was out of my league, but I couldn't fake it until I made it. Culturally, it wasn't in me. And yet, faking it is how everyone else coped with being new graduate students. But I couldn't do that. So, I went to my professor and confessed that I didn't understand the material and that I wasn't like my classmates.

"I'm lost," I admitted after class, sitting in his office. "I didn't go to Harvard, I haven't spent a summer in Cambridge, and this theory stuff feels like a foreign language to me."

He listened, nodding thoughtfully. "Your classmates don't get it either—they're just posturing," he said, almost smiling.

"Posturing?" I asked. "What is that?"

"It's pretending you understand everything, even when you don't. It's a part of the culture here," he explained. "But you don't have to do that. It's okay to ask questions and admit when you're struggling."

His words were a relief. My truth was all I had, and now, I felt it was enough.

By 2009, I was writing a master's thesis that included a discussion on Nietzsche's *On Truth and Lies in a Nonmoral Sense*, a long way from the girl who got a "D" in Research Methods. I was becoming a scholar. At the same time, I was raising five children alone in a strange city. I was away from my family for the first time, struggling to balance school, parenting, and the isolation of being a single mom in graduate school.

My relationship with my mom was changing, too. As I delved deeper into my studies, my conversations with her became less frequent. I began to expect too much when she visited, policing her interactions with my children, trying to create a "perfect" environment. But her visits became less and less frequent until they stopped altogether.

One day, frustrated and tired, I asked her, "Mom, why don't you help me more with my kids? Why aren't you there for me?"

There was a silence, and then she responded clearly, effortlessly, and very matter-of-factly. "I had two children, fourteen years apart, because that's what I could handle. I figured you had the number of kids you could handle."

I was stunned. But what could I say? She was right. Just because I had birthed so many children, why was it her obligation to take on more than she could handle? That was unfair of me, and I had to figure it out.

But before that conversation, she and I had another talk that changed my perspective forever. I was in the thick of being a graduate student. My funding had run out. I was struggling so badly financially. The kids were unkempt; the house was filled with dirty clothes and flies. I couldn't afford to pay my rent. And I remember feeling so overwhelmed. I called my mom. I needed her help. I needed her. I was so broken on the inside. I was scared, and I felt like I was sinking. I was desperate.

I don't recall all the words or what we discussed, but I do remember feeling as if I was sobbing on the inside, begging and pleading with her, trying to convict her for sending me to a place that she had raised me to be in and prepared me to go to, just for me to be alone in a strange land. I recall her standing strong, holding her ground against all my uncertainty, fear, and long-suffering.

Although I don't remember her exact words, I recall the revelation that came from them: *This woman threw you from a burning building so that you could have a better chance at life, so that your kids could have a better chance, and now you are calling her—the woman who sent you forward from the burning building, the woman who is still in that burning building—seeking what? She did her part. Anything else is a bonus.*

So what do I mean when I say that she threw me from a burning building so that I could have a better chance at life? I meant in all the chaos, violence, and dysfunction that surrounded us, she raised me to choose a better environment, even if she refused to choose one for herself.

And while she was not physically in Madison, she did so much from Chicago— sending money when she could, always answering the phone when I called, always fighting for me when I needed an ally. I was on my path, going down a journey that she couldn't accompany me on because she was on her own walk. If I were going to succeed, I had to stand up, as a woman, like she had, and figure it all out.

At the same time, I was coming to terms with my position in my immediate family. I had come to Madison to study Black love and men in prison. After one year of being here, I had been exposed to James Baldwin's *If Beale Street Could Talk*, the text that transitioned me from what I came to do to what I would end up doing. Written in 1974, *Beale Street* is about a young man named Fonny who is imprisoned for a crime he didn't commit. The story is told primarily through the eyes of Tish, his pregnant girlfriend. She is the one traveling back and forth to visit her partner. She's the one fighting for his freedom. This book, along with other things I had been reading, sent me down the path of studying motherhood and led me to a branch of feminism called motherhood studies. There I'd be exposed to a world better than any candy shop.

One of the sweetest pieces I'd find was one I'd discover by the time I fully transitioned from the master's program in African American Studies into the PhD program in English in 2009. It was an article that talked about women faking motherhood like we fake orgasms. Reading that would change the way that I parent forever. It made me ask a question I never thought about or was too afraid to ask myself: *Was I satisfied as a mother?* For years, I had been unhappy and resentful about raising my children. I was angry on the inside, but I couldn't show it. And so, I performed mothering for the first years I lived in Madison. I combed my girls' hair, dressed them nicely, and kept Cho up. I worked hard to keep my house clean and cook Sunday dinners as a good mother should. And I was miserable, stressed, overwhelmed. I didn't have time to be a perfect mom. I didn't have the resources or the support to cook these Sunday dinners and comb my girls' hair. I didn't have time to clean my house.

Some of my most embarrassing moments had been the reactions I had gotten from announcing I was pregnant. Rarely did I get that joyful excitement that you see on television. Over the years, I would hear things like, "I don't think my baby momma would like that. She and I are talking about getting back together. You're gonna have to abort it." "If you have that baby, I'm gonna push you and it down some stairs." "You're pregnant? Maybe you should get to know who you're having kids with before you have kids with them," says the man who had given me the babies. "You're pregnant and you have chlamydia? Well, I gave you chlamydia, but I didn't give you no baby."

There was so much trauma and pain surrounding the babies that I didn't have (pregnancies that didn't make it to full term), as much as surrounded the ones that I did have. I had to provide for the ones I did, primarily alone, and to do so, I had to get through this program. And so I ignored my trauma and suppressed all the feelings that came with it. I kept performing until I encountered that article. After reading it, still reeling from the revelation that I may just be faking motherhood, I dared to face myself, even if only for a second. And I asked myself, despite my fear of the answer, *Well, shit, Sagashus, are you faking motherhood? Do you hate your kids?* I sat there, eyes wide open, but inside, it felt like there was another version of me, cringing with eyes shut tight as if by hiding from what I could see, I could also block out what I might hear. As if by closing off my sight, I could somehow stop the thoughts that were sure to come next. On the outside, I appeared calm, but inside, I was desperately trying to hide from it all.

But all of that felt like it was for nothing. Without hesitation, I heard the most sincere and honest voice inside me respond, *I don't hate my kids. I don't hate being a mother. I love both. What I hate are the circumstances in which I am a mother. I hate mothering in poverty. I hate mothering without the benefit of a partner. I hate mothering without my extended family around me.*

While I couldn't change two of those situations, I realized I had some control over the third one.

One of the first things that occurred to me was that if I wanted the benefits of an extended family, I had to create one. I did that by telling my story and sharing the stories of my children. People would see me walking into one meeting all disheveled or arriving at another with my crew of children, and it was clear we were struggling. But instead of leaning into the struggle, I leaned into the vision. I'd say, "Listen, me and my kids came here with twenty-five dollars to our name so I could become a doctor and give them a better life. We left everything we knew back in Chicago, including our family. I was raised with all my cousins, aunts, uncles, and grandparents around me. I want my kids to have that, too. And I'm hoping we can build that with you."

Over the years at UW, I said that a lot because each semester brought a new opportunity for me and my children to grow our village.

So many Black graduate students in Madison came from places like New Orleans, the Bay Area, Chicago, South Carolina, Michigan, Georgia, Mississippi, Florida, the Bahamas, Nigeria, and beyond. Like me, they were used to a large family network—accustomed to nieces, nephews, aunts, and uncles. And so, we became family for them, and they became family for us. When I was overwhelmed, my friend Sharon, who, like me, was from Chicago and lived in campus housing, would come by and take Ryland and Brooklyn (my fourth and fifth children) into her red wagon and pull them on a walk to Target. Chris, from D.C., would play soccer with Cho (my oldest son). And Tezeta, from California, would take Dianna and Yemi (my first and second children, my oldest daughters) on self-care days and trips to the movies.

Renaldo was a dapper dresser, always in sharp suits, collegiate sweaters, and those fun socks—the kind with cartoon characters and quirky designs that made you smile. He always had a pair of stylish glasses perched on his nose, looking like he had just stepped out of *GQ* magazine. Renaldo was our very own Fonzworth Bentley, the epitome of class and charm.

Coming from somewhere in Georgia, with the warmth of the South still in his voice, and an alum of at least one HBCU, Renaldo had that older sibling energy. He was the eldest of several, after all. He knew how to jump right in with us with no hesitation. He was the one who'd buy my daughters' swimsuits for their summer camps, always thinking ahead, always thoughtful. When I would disappear from Madison, lost in one of my many attempts at self-sabotage, it was Renaldo who'd come looking for me in Chicago, determined to bring me back. He was the one I'd pour my heart out to about all my heartbreaks, listening with the patience and wisdom of someone who had seen it all.

Renaldo wasn't just a friend; he was the first new family member I found when we both arrived at the university as part of the same cohort, though in different departments. Over time, our little family grew as more members joined us. We'd hang out, share secrets, eat each other's food, go grocery shopping together, console one another, and be the support system we all needed. Renaldo was at the heart of it all, the glue that held us together, making our bond feel like home.

These additional family members were crucial if we were going to make it out of our institution alive. No matter how much we wanted our original families to understand our experience, they couldn't, especially since many of us were first-generation graduate students.

The hardest thing about this new family was that people left. Graduate school is transitory. No one is supposed to stay there permanently. We do our time—two years, three years, seven years, twelve years—whatever it may be, and we leave. Some people leave because they've graduated, while others leave because they can't take it anymore. I saw both kinds of departures. Each time someone left, it felt like a part of my support system was being chipped away. I had to prepare myself for the inevitable—either I'd have to be okay with them leaving, or I'd have to be the one to leave first.

But leaving wasn't an option for me. I had committed myself to this journey, and my children were counting on me. I was determined to finish what I started, even if it meant facing these struggles alone. The extended family I had created in Madison was crucial, but it wasn't a complete solution. I still had to rely on myself, on my own strength and resilience, to make it through.

By 2010, I had learned how to navigate the academic terrain. I had found my voice in the classroom and my place in the scholarly community. I was no longer the lost girl who felt out of place in her seminars. I had become a mother, a scholar, a woman who could hold her own in a world that once felt so foreign. But the journey was far from over. Every day presented new challenges, new reasons to question my path, and new reasons to keep going.

The community I had built, both in and outside the classroom, was a testament to the power of connection and support. My children were growing up in an environment where they were surrounded by love, even if it wasn't from their biological relatives. They had a village of people who cared for them, helped me raise them, and were there for us when we needed it most.

And through it all, I never lost sight of my North Star. That feeling I had discovered years ago in Puerto Rico, the one that told me I was on the right path, continued to guide me. It wasn't always easy to follow, and there were many times when I wanted to give up, but I knew I couldn't. I had come too far, and I had too much at stake.

My journey wasn't just about me; it was about my children, my family, and everyone who had supported me along the way. It was about proving to myself that I could achieve my dreams, no matter how impossible they seemed. It was about reclaiming the dreams I had once been too afraid to have and making them a reality.

Looking back, I realize that every step of this journey has been about growth—growing into my role as a mother, scholar, and woman who could stand on her own two feet. I had to learn to trust myself, trust the process, and trust that I was exactly where I needed to be, even when it didn't feel that way.

And now, as I stand at the threshold of the next chapter of my life, I am reminded of the words I heard in *Akeelah and the Bee*: "Our deepest fear is not that we are inadequate. Our deepest fear is that we are powerful beyond measure." Those words have stayed with me, guiding me through the darkest moments, reminding me that I am powerful and have the light within me to overcome any obstacle.

I'm no longer afraid of that light. I've embraced it, let it guide me, and used it to create the life I once thought was impossible. And as I move forward, I carry with me the lessons I've learned, the strength I've gained, and the unwavering belief that I am exactly where I am supposed to be.

CHAPTER 7

NOTHING'S WASTED

MARCH 2021

We're in the middle of one of our virtual weekend retreats, a group of women from around the country gathered online. Their faces fill the screen—a patchwork of worlds that collide and intersect in this shared space. Each woman is here with a purpose, bringing her whole self into the room, expecting something big, something transformative.

The quiet ping of notifications echoes softly and picks up pace as more women join. The room fills with a quiet yet powerful energy. Some women lean into the camera, their spaces giving glimpses into their lives. SheBossLA, for example, sits in front of a bright wall lined with custom Callie Decor, hip-hop lyrics woven into tapestries. A candle flickers on her desk, a warm, steady light beside a mug that reads "[IN]FAMOUS." The smell of lavender and eucalyptus probably fills her room, matching the calm strength in her presence.

OrganicSoulMama, in contrast, has vibrant plants hanging behind her, a jungle of greens softening her space. She sips water from a tall glass, her hair loosely tied back in a scarf that blends beautifully with the tapestry behind her. There's a serene energy about her, but her eyes reveal the exhaustion of managing three little ones at home.

From another screen, I catch sight of CEOinHeels, her backdrop pure luxury—a sharp contrast to the more earthy tones. She's polished, poised, and sipping orange juice from a sleek glass. She sits in front of a minimalist setup—leather-bound notebooks, high-end pens, and the occasional hint of her multi-million-dollar corporate office. Yet, there's a quiet hunger in her eyes, as if she's still chasing the next level.

And then there's JazzyQueenzChi, full of fire. She has a Chicago skyline behind her, framed by the faint hum of city noise. A soft jazz beat plays in the background, spilling into the space between us. Her nails, bold and bright, tap against her coffee cup, her energy crackling through the screen like static before a storm.

I sip my tea, the warmth of the mug reminding me of the mantra that's guided me through the toughest times—*Nothing's Wasted*—boldly printed on the side. It's grounding, reminding me that every challenge, every pivot, every heartache has become fuel for the journey.

A woman from New Jersey raises her hand. "How did you start your company? What was the moment that made you say, 'Yep. It's time'?"

I pause, feeling the tea warm my palms. It's a great question, but the answer isn't as simple as she might think. I could tell her the easy version: "There was a hiring freeze, and I saw an opportunity." But that's not the whole story. The truth is, there wasn't just one defining moment—it was a series of moments. Each one pushed me closer to the edge until I finally took the leap.

I lean toward the camera and say, "It's funny you ask that because there was more than one moment that made me start Infamous Mothers. Each one pushed me closer to saying, 'I'm done waiting. I'm doing this on my own terms.'"

They listen closely, their screens still, their eyes locked onto mine. So, I dive in.

It was 2010. I was sitting in a cramped, windowless room at the university, surrounded by my fellow graduate students. The stale air smelled faintly of chalk and old books, the kind of academic musk that sinks into your clothes. The fluorescent lights buzzed overhead, casting a sickly glow that made everything feel colder. I could hear the rustling of papers and the tapping of pens against the metal chairs, as if everyone was trying to distract themselves from what was coming.

The professor up front, who clearly gave a damn, looked like the life had been sucked out of him. His voice cracked slightly as he delivered the news like a hammer to the chest: the academic job market had collapsed, and universities across the country were freezing new hires. He advised us to stay on as teaching assistants until things got better, his eyes flickering downward, avoiding our shocked faces.

The room felt like it was closing in. The murmurs grew louder, buzzing like flies trapped in a jar. I could feel the collective panic, the tightness in my chest. It was like the air had been sucked out of the room, leaving only fear. It felt like we were all lined up in a slaughterhouse, branded and tagged, waiting for the inevitable. No one dared question the process. They just accepted it, moving closer to the door, even though we all knew what awaited us on the other side—uncertainty, rejection, nothing.

People turned to me. "Sagashus, you'll be fine," they said. "You're a Black woman. Your research is sexy. You'll be a hit on the job market."

I nodded, but inside, the weight of their words pressed down on me. I loved academia. I loved my colleagues and professors. We were tight. But the institution wasn't built for women like me—Black women with six kids. I was juggling school, life, and special needs with a future that was crumbling. Academia might have wanted me, but it wasn't designed to support me. It wasn't built for us. I didn't want to wait in line to be slaughtered.

But there was another reason I had to leave. My son, my brilliant boy, was dyslexic. While I was buried in the pursuit of a PhD in English, he was struggling to read at grade level. It felt like a cruel twist—the mother chasing academic excellence while her son wrestled with something as fundamental as words. At night, I'd lie awake, the weight of everything pressing down on me like a physical burden. Six kids depended on me. My son's dyslexia kept me up the most. I couldn't escape the image of him at my PhD graduation, standing there in front of the crowd, his voice echoing in my head: "Shame on you, Momma! Here you are getting a PhD in English, and I can't even read!"

That imagined voice, laced with pain and frustration, haunted me. It was like a knot in my stomach that refused to untangle.

I'd watch him try to read sometimes, his fingers tracing the words on the page, his brow furrowed in concentration. His eyes would well up with frustration, and that pain? It was a mirror. His struggle reflected my own fears and failings. I couldn't sit back and wait for academia to fix things. It wasn't just my career on the line but his future.

And then there was the money. When I imagined becoming a professor, I thought about the prestige, the salary. I thought $80,000 sounded like a million bucks. But by the time I was deep into my program, I realized that $80,000 wouldn't even be enough to cover what I needed to support my large family. I had six kids. I knew my older two could have a shot at getting their college tuition covered through the Precollege Enrichment Opportunity Program for Learning Excellence (PEOPLE) program if they got into UW–Madison, but what about the rest? I started to realize that academia wasn't going to give me the life I wanted for my family. The cost of living outside low-income housing and food stamps was climbing, and I couldn't see how staying in academia would provide enough.

There was also a deeper reason for leaving. I had to confront a hard truth: The women I was researching who had lived through struggles and challenges that mirrored my own—weren't in the ivory towers. The people who would benefit most from my research weren't sitting in classrooms or attending conferences. They were out in the world, living real lives, facing real issues.

I remember one of my professors, Michael Thornton, on an ethics panel I organized. He said something that stuck with me: "Often, we make a living, put our kids through college, and buy houses off research that may or may not benefit the people at the center of that work." His words sat heavy on my chest. I didn't want to be someone who made a living by writing about women like me without giving anything back to them.

"When I finally left academia," I tell the women, "it felt like breaking free. I was stepping out of line. The process felt like I was sneaking away on the Underground Railroad."

I see the confusion on their faces, so I explain. "Strange, right? Here I am, a free woman in a free world, and yet, I felt like I was escaping in the middle of the night with my life. If I got caught, there would be severe consequences, amputations, whippings, and hobbling. This is all figurative, of course. That was the psychological trauma that I was dealing with. And people, like my business coach, helped me quietly sneak out. Leaving academia wasn't a decision I made lightly. People had invested in me—mentors, colleagues, the McNair Program. They wanted me to succeed in the ivory tower, to bring my Black body and my research into spaces that had historically excluded us. They had high hopes for me, and I felt the weight of their expectations every single day."

I pause, letting the memory settle in the room. I can still feel the tension in my stomach from back then, a knot of worry that never seemed to go away.

"It wasn't just about leaving academia," I continue. "It was about breaking free from a system that wasn't designed for me. I had to sneak away, had to run toward something else—something I couldn't fully explain at the time but that I knew was mine. Leaving felt like a betrayal of everything they thought I stood for, but staying would have been a betrayal to myself."

Another woman, this time from Baton Rouge, raises her hand. Her voice is soft but determined. She sits in a room with walls lined with framed quotes and artwork—bold colors against dark wood. There's a low hum of music in the background, like she's set the mood for deep thinking. "What do you think about business partners?" she asks, her voice steady but curious. "Do you have one? Did you start with one?"

A pang of shame fills my stomach. I take a deep breath before answering. "Yeah, the answer to this isn't one that I'm proud of. So, when I started in 2015–2016, I had a business partner; at least, she was there early on. I had the vision and the research, but I didn't have the capital. A friend of mine, an anesthesiologist, had the money but couldn't dedicate the time. She was willing to pay the $25,000 needed to cover all expenses associated with creating and publishing the *Infamous Mothers* coffee table book. To me, it was the perfect partnership."

I could feel the tension building as I continued. "But when my mentor from Doyenne found out, she asked me how much my friend was getting from the deal. I told her 50 percent of everything. She challenged me, saying, 'I know that $25,000 sounds like a lot to you, but let me ask you this: If Harvard came knocking on your door and told you they'd give your child a free education if you signed over half of her life to them, what would you say?'"

As the virtual retreat continues, I am also navigating another battle. The Quiet One, my fiancé, has been in prison for eight years, and I have been fighting to get him out under the First Step Act.

We started the legal process in December 2020, and now, during this retreat, I constantly check my emails, waiting for the lawyer's update. The women on the call have no idea I am balancing all of this—their questions about building a business and my own emotions about the Quiet One's possible release.

Then the email comes. My heart pounds as I open it, praying for good news, but what I read hits me like a punch to the gut.

"The Quiet One's sentence does not appear to have been enhanced under any of the above provisions. As such, the First Step Act does not assist him."

That is it. No early release. No reunion. Just more waiting. I feel deflated, like all the air has been sucked out of me. But I can't show it. I have to keep going.

A woman from North Carolina raises her hand. "What's the first thing you did to get started?" Her space is different from the others. Hers has a small altar in the background with candles lit. Though we can't smell it through the screen, I'm sure there is the unmistakable scent of incense in the air. There's a tapestry on the wall with the words of a Nina Simone song stitched into the fabric. A calm, centered energy radiates from her.

I smile, knowing this is a pivotal moment to share. "The first thing I did was build a brand, even before I had a product. I created a logo. I remember the night it happened. I was on a date, heading to see the movie *Chi-Raq*. As we walked into the theater, I suddenly had a vision of what I wanted the logo to look like. Right there, I dug into my messy purse, found a chewed-up pencil and a scrap of paper, and sketched it out on the spot. It was wild."

I pause, feeling the energy of that moment. "I shared the concept with Chris Charles, who I hired to bring my rough sketch to life. Chris is brilliant— an all-around creative force. He's a photographer, graphic and web designer, an architecture enthusiast, an army veteran, and so much more. He's also my mentor when it comes to marketing and design."

I see heads nodding on the screen, and I continue. "I'll never forget what Chris told me. He said, 'The biggest mistake I see is when clients try to make their logo encompass their entire brand, instead of letting their brand represent the logo.'"

The audience leans in, and I elaborate. "Chris explained that it's the brand that sells—the product, the vision, the marketing, and the presentation. The logo doesn't do the heavy lifting. The brand has to be 'dope,' connected, and stand for everything great you're doing. The logo reflects that, but it's not the selling point."

The woman smiles, and I sense the gears turning in her mind. This is the moment when everything clicks, and she starts to see her own vision taking shape.

I sip from my mug, the warmth grounding me. My mind shifts to the news I'd just received about the Quiet One. I think about the horrors he's seen in jail—how inmates were left in rooms with piles of dead bodies because the prison system was overwhelmed by COVID-19, unprepared for the outbreak in overcrowded spaces. I picture him and other men being transferred from one prison to another, only to end up in an abandoned building, ceilings caved in, asbestos hanging from what was left. It reminds me that jail is designed for punishment—to make people pay, over and over again. I'm sad, heartbroken. I want to break down right here in the middle of this retreat.

Then I glance down at the words on my mug: *Nothing's Wasted*. I can't see it now, but somehow, this news has to become fuel. Every setback, every pivot, every disappointment—it's all fuel for something greater. I wonder what this will turn into.

Without prompting, I start speaking to the women in the retreat. "Being in academia wasn't wasted. It taught me how to build a brand, how to research, how to stand in my own power. Getting my PhD in English gave me the critical thinking skills I needed to run a business, so that experience still counts—because I say it does. Homeschooling my kids wasn't wasted either. It taught me how to balance chaos and responsibility, how to create something that worked for my family."

I pause, thinking to myself, *Even this pain with the Quiet One is not wasted. It's all part of the journey*.

"This is the mantra I live by," I tell them. "Nothing's wasted. Every failure is fuel. Every challenge is a stepping stone. Every setback is a setup for something greater—if we choose to see it that way."

As I finish explaining the "Nothing's Wasted" mantra, I glance at the screen and see the chat box suddenly light up. Messages start pouring in, the small pings creating a rhythm in the background like raindrops tapping against a window.

BrittanyHustles: "Sis, this is everything! How do you stay motivated? I feel like giving up sometimes, especially when the money ain't coming in like I thought."

CEOinHeels: "Girl, YES. What's your advice for women like me trying to break into male-dominated industries? Do you change your approach or stay the course?"

OrganicSoulMama: "How do you balance all this without losing yourself? I've got three kids under five, and it feels impossible some days. Any tips for avoiding burnout?"

JazzyQueenzChi: "You ever feel like people only respect you when they see you 'making it'? How do you deal with folks who didn't believe in you before but want to ride with you now?"

GrindandShineATL: "Do you think it's necessary to have investors, or should I stay solo for as long as I can? I don't wanna give up control, but I feel like I'm hitting a wall financially."

The questions keep coming, fast and sharp, filling the chat with the real, raw concerns of women hustling to make their mark. I can feel their energy reaching through the screen, a palpable hunger for answers. It's not just about business. It's about survival, about thriving in spaces not meant for us, about taking back power in a world designed to limit it.

PlantMamaQueens: "Love that 'Nothing's Wasted' mantra. How do you stay true to yourself when everything feels like it's falling apart?"

SheBossLA: "Any advice for dealing with imposter syndrome? I have days where I feel like I don't deserve any of the success I'm getting."

MsVisionary: "I'm curious—what do you do when your 'why' changes? Like, what drives you today isn't the same thing that got you started. How do you pivot without feeling lost?"

Each question hits differently. Some are about the grind, some are about the mental toll, but all of them are laced with a deep desire for connection, for growth. The chat box becomes a living, breathing thing, the heartbeat of the retreat pulsing with the collective energy of women refusing to stay small.

I take a breath, letting the weight of their words settle on me. These are the women I've built this space for—the ones whose journeys mirror mine in a thousand ways. They're out there fighting for their dreams, balancing the weight of their worlds on their shoulders, and navigating spaces that weren't designed for them.

This is the work. This is the reason I left academia, the reason I built Infamous Mothers from the ground up. These women. Their stories. Their hustle. Their pain and triumph. It's all connected.

I smile, knowing that, just like me, they'll turn their challenges into fuel. They'll find a way. Because when you understand that nothing's wasted, every step you take—even the painful ones—moves you closer to greatness.

CHAPTER 8

TIGHT IN A BUD

APRIL 2021

The soft hum of the Quiet Storm R&B playlist drifts through the room, soothing the edges of my racing thoughts. The scent of vanilla caramel from the plug-in diffuses throughout, adding a warm, inviting atmosphere. A soft, golden light from the bedside lamp stretches shadows across the unmade bed, its rumpled comforter evidence of my restless pacing. The teetering stack of dog-eared books on the nightstand mirrors the chaos swirling in my mind, and the light pressure of the pen between my fingers brings me a familiar, grounding feeling.

Has it been months or years that I've been at this? Mothering my children, building my business, trying to create a future with the Quiet One, and trying to find a way to put a house I own around all that. This whole thing is wild. The fact that I am even trying to add one more thing to the mix is insane, and yet, if I accomplish it ... what a game-changer.

I reach for my journal, the worn leather cover grounding me, heavy and thick, like I'm holding the book of life. I flip it open and let the pen hover, knowing the battle that's about to unfold between the parts of me that always seem at war. Rya, the adventurer, lives for the thrill of seizing the moment. Then there's Penny, the conservative one, always careful, always cautious, afraid of disrupting the balance. And here I am, Sagashus, balancing them both.

Other voices linger within me too—Ainsley, who carries the weight of anxiety and OCD tendencies, and Temperance, the boundary-keeper. But tonight, they are silent. Temperance rolls over in her corner, saying, "Whatever mess you all make, I'll deal with it in the morning."

It's up to Rya, Penny, and Sagashus now.

"Okay, let's do this," I whisper into the stillness.

As soon as the pen touches the paper, Rya rushes in, loud and insistent, filling my mind with her excitement. I write quickly, my hand slanting with the speed of my thoughts.

"Look, Penny, you're tripping," I scribble, the ink bleeding into the page as Rya's energy surges. "This house represents freedom, adventure, living life on our terms. Why should we let fear or doubt hold us back? YOLO, right?"

My heart races with Rya's fire. She's bold, fearless, always ready to leap without thinking about the consequences. But just as quickly, Penny's voice creeps in, quiet and measured, slowing the pen as if anchoring me back to reality.

"But Rya," I write slowly, "this isn't just about seizing the moment. What will people think? Are we doing too much? What if they see us as greedy or disconnected from the struggle? What if we can't handle it?"

Penny's words weigh me down, the air in the room growing colder, heavier. I feel the tension build in my shoulders as doubt settles in like a weight pressing against my chest.

But Rya fights back, the pen speeding up again.

"Greedy for buying a house big enough for our family? Seriously? And what image are we worried about here? That we're good strugglers? Peaceful in poverty? We've earned this."

Sagashus steps in, my hand calming the storm of thoughts. "I hear both of you," I write, each stroke now measured, my tone softening. "Penny, I get it. You're worried about what this means, about whether we're moving too fast. But Rya, you're right. We've worked hard and deserve this. Still, the space in between—where we hesitate—is filled with tension and fear."

I pause, the weight of the decision settling in my chest, the pen growing still. The question of whether I deserve this house feels too familiar. Suddenly, I'm back—seven months pregnant, caught in chaos I couldn't escape.

It wasn't just him I was fighting. His whole family had turned against me. His mother's voice still echoes in my mind, dripping with venom.

"I'm going to send my nieces over there to kick yo' ass."

Confused, hurt, but young and full of pride, I shot back, "Fuck you and your bitch-ass nieces. Send 'em."

That comeback would come with consequences, and I knew it was disrespectful. But back then, I was full of youth, too naive to understand the power of vulnerability.

Frustrated that I had disrespected their aunt, his cousins were ready to kick my ass. And so was he. I had just cussed out his momma. The weight of my swollen belly felt heavier that day—not just physically but emotionally. I was carrying his child, but it felt like I was carrying the weight of a collapsing world.

Desperate, I called my brother. His voice was calm but always a little slick, always ready for whatever came his way.

"What's going on, baby sister?"

"Hey, Bobby," I said, my voice trembling. "His family is trying to jump on me. His mom is threatening me. His cousins say they're going to jump me, and I'm pregnant. Seven months. And he's ready to jump too."

"Whoa, whoa, slow down, Big Bang,"—his nickname for me. "Tell me what's going on, from the beginning." I calmed down and explained everything to him. He listened patiently. There was a long pause. I knew my brother was weighing his words carefully.

"Let me ask you something," he finally said, his tone softer, deliberate. "Are you so hard up for an apartment that you're gonna let this nigga and his family beat yo' head in?"

His words hit hard. I wanted to say no. I wanted to be stronger. But deep down, I knew the truth: I was holding on to the illusion of stability, even in the middle of chaos. I didn't want to go back to Chicago and be just another woman with a baby and no man living with her parents. I wasn't ready for that truth.

So I chose the chaos because it was the only thing that still felt like mine.

I put pen to paper, and the memories flood in—the chaos, the fights, the love that seemed to burn so hot but never lasted long enough to hold us together.

Sagashus: "Was the drama between us really all ours? Or was there something bigger at play? Something old, something passed down?"

Rya jumps in, sharp and impatient. "You're overthinking it, Sagashus. You stayed because you wanted to. It's not some ancient force pulling the strings."

I hesitate. Rya's right, at least partly. I chose to stay. We were crazy about each other, but love wasn't enough. And I can't help but wonder, the drama, the hurt—it never stopped. Was it all really just ours?

Penny: "Maybe it wasn't. Look at everyone we knew. How many of them had stable families? Maybe we didn't have the tools either."

I think of the pattern—a script we all seemed to follow without knowing. For centuries, our ancestors weren't allowed to build families. They were forced apart, moved like cattle. Is that trauma still shaping us?

Rya: "Come on, you can't blame slavery for staying in a bad situation. That was your choice."

I write. "Maybe Rya's right. But how can I ignore the patterns of broken families passed down through generations?"

Penny: "It's not about making excuses. It's about understanding why we fall into these cycles."

I scribble faster now. "Slavery didn't just break our bodies; it broke our families. Maybe that brokenness is why we stay in chaos—because it's the only thing we know."

Rya: "You're making it sound like we're trapped by history."

I pause. "No, we have choices. But understanding where the chaos comes from helps us stop repeating it."

As I sit with those thoughts, another memory surfaces from 1996 when I was in boarding school. I had been eager to prove myself even then, to show that I was worthy, despite what the world kept telling me.

My cousin brought his friend to visit. The friend saw Carson and was immediately smitten. "Aye, hook me up with your girl," he said to me in a hushed voice. But I wasn't interested in setting him up with Carson Moon—the petite, light-skinned girl everyone adored. I wanted him to see me, to choose me.

Instead, I shot my shot. We spent months hanging out, talking on the phone late into the night. And before long, I was in bed with him, taking his virginity. For a moment, I thought I had won him over.

But then, one day, the truth slipped out, casual and cutting.

"You're perfect," he said, his tone matter-of-fact. "I just wish you were packaged differently."

His words hit hard, not just because of him but because of what they represented. It wasn't just about Carson Moon. It was about everything I wasn't. I wasn't petite. I wasn't light-skinned. I wasn't what the world wanted me to be.

Another boy, Reggie, had once told me, "You're built for hard labor." It sounded like a compliment, but it felt like a sentence, trapping me in the same box my family had always been in—one of struggle, not growth.

Babies, work, drama. That was the rhythm of my life. And I never questioned it.

It's 2004. I remember sitting in Professor Nancy's office, my palms sweaty as I built up the courage to tell her about my dreams. I had fallen in love with her work and teachings so much that I decided I wanted to go to graduate school. I wanted to get a PhD in English. I wanted to do more.

"I'm thinking about graduate school," I said, my voice tentative. "I want to study women throughout the Diaspora."

I expected her to understand. Instead, she chuckled softly and shook her head. "Come on, kid. Stop kidding yourself. You're a single mother of three. Just become a high school English teacher. Stay in your lane."

Her words stung. I had spent so long building up my confidence, and in an instant, she shattered it. I laughed it off, masking the hurt. But deep down, her words lingered.

Stay in your lane.

Even after I proved her wrong—after I got accepted into one of the best programs in the country—her voice stayed with me. Every time I reached for more, her doubt was there, whispering that maybe she was right. Maybe I should stay small.

But I'm done with shrinking. The box I've been living in no longer fits the woman I'm becoming. I write steadily, my hand sure now: It's time to be bold and thoughtful. Growth is painful, but staying small is unbearable.

I close the journal and lean back, its weight resting in my lap. I think about all the voices that have told me to stay small. My brother's question, my cousin's friend's cutting words, and Professor Nancy's doubt all echo in my mind, reminders of every moment I've been asked to shrink. To stay in my lane.

But I'm ready to expand. I'm ready to stretch this box and make it big enough to hold all of me—all the messy, complex parts that have been shaped by history, by trauma, by love. I'm ready to claim my space, no matter how uncomfortable it might feel.

To be clear, I'm not trying to escape the box. I'm trying to make it big enough to contain all of me—and in doing so, make it big enough to contain all of us. The box I was born into taught me loyalty, resilience, and survival, but it wasn't designed for growth. Now, I'm learning to expand it, to push against its walls and make space for my dreams, my ambition, my contradictions.

But expanding this box isn't just for me. It's for every Black woman who has been told she's built for hard labor. It's for every single mother who has been told to stay in her lane. It's for every one of us who has been asked to shrink, to hide, to conform to a version of ourselves that doesn't fit who we really are.

This expansion is about creating space for all of us to thrive, to blossom, to take up space unapologetically. It's about reclaiming the right to define who we are on our own terms, without the weight of the past dictating our future.

The room feels different now, less oppressive, and the air is clearer. The conversation within myself winds down, and I'm left with a sense of peace, however temporary it might be.

Rya speaks up, satisfied. "See? This is what happens when you trust yourself. You expand. You take up space. You're ready."

Penny, though quieter, admits, "I guess we made it through. But it's still scary. Every step is risky."

Sagashus settles between the two. "It's always risky when you're expanding. But this isn't about abandoning who we are. It's about stretching—making the box big enough to hold all of us."

And now, with my closed journal resting on my lap, I'm thinking about identity and how mine is changing. As my mind drifts, The Stylistics come on. I hear the words to "You Are Everything": *You are everything and everything is you.* They begin to fade as my own words start to form in my mind. My journal may be closed, but the conversation continues.

"To break into a new box, one that would offer me options, freedom, and the ability to stand taller, I had to face the reality that the box I've been in is too small. But I didn't want to leave it behind. My Blackness, my connection to my roots, and the values that shaped me are integral to who I am. I wasn't interested in abandoning them. But I do need a space big enough to accommodate all of me— my dreams, my successes, my vulnerabilities, my contradictions."

Rya agrees. "Why should you have to leave parts of yourself behind just to move forward?"

I reply, "You know what I always say. Nothing's wasted. Everything can be recycled or serve as fuel. But I don't need to amputate pieces of myself to fit into someone else's box. Instead, I'd rather do some repurposing and redirecting. That's what expansion can look like for us."

Penny nods, though still hesitant. "But expanding comes with responsibilities, too. We were raised with a code: 'Don't forget where you come from.' 'Keep it real.' 'Family over everything.' What happens when those rules start to feel confining?"

I pause, reflecting. "Growing up in poverty, those rules defined what it meant to be Black and poor. But I have begun to understand that those rules didn't have to confine me; they could be the starting point for something greater."

As I sought upward mobility, the messaging shifted: "Lift as you climb." "Don't sell out." And the weight of these new commandments began to sit heavily on me. To question them felt sacrilegious. But fitting into that box meant sacrificing parts of myself—my dreams, my voice, my right to define my own identity.

Rya asserts, "Why should you have to choose between where you came from and where you're going? You are both, and I don't care what anyone says; we are here today because of what we've gone through yesterday—good, bad, or indifferent. We ain't running from that. And we're not shrinking. Don't let people make us shrink because of our pasts."

I accept her words. "Yeah, nah. I'm not choosing. I'm stretching, making my box bigger and roomier until it can hold the full spectrum of my identity."

Penny finally concedes. "You're right. But what happens to the people who stay in their boxes?"

Rya, ever defiant, says, "Maybe your expansion will show them what's possible."

Since the conversation in my head seems to need more space, I grab my journal once again, and I begin to write, "Growth isn't just about me; it's about creating space for those around me, allowing them to rethink the pieces of themselves they've been forced to bury, who they once were, and who they are. Instead, they can recognize that they are who they are because of who they once were. And that's a beautiful thing."

I reflect on how my success—this house, this next step—isn't just about me. It's about challenging the boundaries of the boxes that others are living in.

"If I buy this house, new questions will arise for everyone. 'Who is she now?' 'What does her success mean for us?' All of our identities are up in the air now, and all of our boxes are being disturbed, tested, and expanded."

Carl Thomas's "Emotional" plays in the background, taking me back to the South Side of Chicago. *I'm emotional, and I can't let go. I'm trying to hold on to you.* I smile as the music fades, and my thoughts settle again.

Recently, my sister-cousin Mistee asked me what it feels like to be on the verge of becoming a millionaire. Her daughters were listening, so I paused, wanting to offer a thoughtful response. "It feels like I'm finally ready," I said. "But it wasn't always that way."

Rya chimes in. "This is about taking up space. You're sitting at the table now."

I reflect further. "Living with poverty is like living with an abusive partner. Over time, you believe that the scraps are all you're worth. But now, I'm prepared to take my place at the table I built. I'm going to eat from it."

I continue, "This isn't just about financial success; it's about reclaiming my right to abundance. For years, I've been trained to serve others while standing on the sidelines, but now I understand that I deserve to sit at the table too."

Dr. Venus Opal Reese says that becoming a Black woman millionaire is a revolutionary act. But the biggest revolution is the one happening in my mind—the revolution that made me risk blossoming because staying tight in a bud had become too painful to bear.

Penny admits, "It's scary to expand. But you're ready."

Rya is more excited. "This isn't just about you. It's about every woman who's been told she's too much or not enough."

I conclude, "The revolution is realizing that the table I built isn't just for others. It's for me, too. I'm ready to take up space, to sit at the table, and stop apologizing for wanting more."

This expansion isn't just a personal victory. It's a revolutionary act—a declaration that I will no longer be confined to the margins and content with scraps. I'm here to thrive, to take up space, to blossom, and to do so unapologetically.

The music fades, and the weight of the journey settles over me. This box I'm expanding isn't just for me; it's for my children, my family, and everyone who's walked this path with me.

CHAPTER 9

DEAR GOD

APRIL 2021

It's three in the morning. I wake up to use the bathroom. I'm tired, and I don't want to cross the distance from my room to the bathroom. The distance feels like it's days away when, in reality, I'm just going right outside my room. I slide my feet into my worn-out house shoes, pausing on the side of the bed to gather myself for the journey ahead.

"If I don't get up now, I'm going to pee on myself," I mumble out loud.

Then, suddenly, another voice rises up inside me — not mine exactly, but one that sounds like somebody's momma: firm, no-nonsense, and tired of excuses.

"Don't lay back down, Sagashus."

"You can do this."

I hear it, clear as day. Not soft or sweet, but strong — like a woman who's raised kids through storms and doesn't have time for whining. And in that moment, I listen.

Reluctantly, I stand, and then, as if an external force is pushing me, I drag myself to the toilet, feet heavy against the floor. In the words of Shug Avery, I "do my business." And instead of getting back up to cross what feels like miles and miles of carpet, I sit there thinking about the journaling session that closed my night. It's funny how that works. Three hours ago was not only a different day but an entirely different month. Wow. What a difference 181 minutes can make. And although we—me, Rya, and Penny—ended on a good note, these are Ms. Ainsley Anxiety's hours. She's well-rested and ready to go.

I can feel her revving up inside of me.

"Okay. You've figured out that identity stuff, but how are we going to buy this house that Rya's so sure we deserve to live in? And, and, and," she says nervously, talking so fast she's fumbling over her own thoughts, "how are we going to build this company big enough to sustain the family, the house, the business?"

I can feel her pacing back and forth in my head, the questions coming rapid-fire.

"You should've listened to Penny. She was right when she said that our box was small, but it was ours. Who do you think you are to believe that we can do this right now? What proof do you have? What consistency do you have? You don't even have a plan for real."

A heaviness settles in my chest, the weight of everything I've been avoiding pressing down on me. My head feels like it's swelling with all the questions—no, the interrogation—she puts me under. But before I let her have her way with me, I rush to wipe myself clean, flush the toilet, wash my hands, and hurry back to my room to start another writing session.

A muscle in my back tenses as I reach for my journal. Like everything on the floor, my thoughts are all over the place. There's a knot in my stomach, a feeling of unease that I can't shake. I can't find rest or peace of mind. So, I do what I always do when the thoughts in my head take up too much space. I journal. But this time, with the information and questions I have, I don't leave the conversation to myself and the different versions of me. I take it to the manager—I take it to the Higher Up. I take it to God:

Dear Father,

Thank you for loving, guiding, protecting, and leading me. I feel overwhelmed and alone and don't quite know what to do.

You have carried me in ways that I can never explain. I'm forever grateful. And yet, I'm struggling, buckling under the weight of it all. I feel like I'm swimming in the middle of an ocean, and I've run out of steam midway through, and the people around me neither know it nor do they see me. So now what?

Something in me tells me to list all the things that make me feel burdened, and so I do. I feel alone. I'm buying a home that may be out of my league, less because of what I can or cannot afford but more because I can't stop asking the question: Who am I to be doing this? Who do I think I am to believe I should live in anything but what I'm living in right now? I don't know what I'm doing, and I don't have anyone to talk to about how to get from where I am to where I'm going. I feel stuck.

I glance around the room, the chaos reflecting the clutter in my mind. If I make it to the other side of this ocean, I will have to write my way across. With my words, I will have to paddle, row, and swim to the other side of this thing. Returning to who I was isn't an option because I know too much. And the most substantial set of resources I have right now is my faith, my ability to articulate my dreams, goals, and desires, and my ability to write them out.

In my journal, I vent my thoughts and confess all my fears. When I've exhausted all of that "talk," I begin creating through gratitude:

Father God, I thank you. I am a soon-to-be homeowner, and if Ruby can make the impossible possible, I won't just be any homeowner; I'll be the owner of a property that will inspire many and incite envy in many others. Thank you. I am becoming a multimillionaire who can transform the circumstances around my children's lives.

Thank you.

I go on with a list of problems I hope to solve for the people I love with the resources I seek to build. I write:

Thank you for blessing me with the means to do the following:

- Pay off this person's second mortgage because they are on the verge of losing their home: $200k
- Build my mom's home from the ground up (Where she will house my blind brother, care for my dad with dementia, move in my favorite aunt, and have room for me and my children to stay with her when we visit): $500k
- Renovate the family home in Chicago: $200k
- Donate to the causes that matter to me
- Tithe 10 percent of my income
- Pay off my van
- Purchase vehicles for my children
- Pay for my children's college tuition

The more I write, the more comfortable I become with these thoughts, as if they have already happened simply because I've put them on paper—as if by daring to imagine them, I make them real. With each pen stroke, I can almost feel the weight lifting off my shoulders. Each new bullet point brings me closer to the person I dream of becoming. My identity shifts with every word, moving me toward a version of myself that feels authentic and powerful—the version that doesn't just dream but acts. Writing becomes a bridge, connecting who I am with who I'm becoming, each sentence drawing me nearer to the person that I imagine I could be. I'm not just recording possibilities—I'm manifesting them, laying the foundation for the life I want to live and the woman, mother, business owner, and partner I am slowly but surely accepting as the version of me I'm ready to embrace. I close my eyes momentarily, picturing this future, letting it take root in my mind. I am a philanthropist who builds wealth for my family, someone who is virtually debt-free, and a friend who plays a role in breaking the chain of debt binding her friends' lives.

In my room, alone, sitting on a bed surrounded by chaos and clutter, I share my vision with God about who I hope to become. I do this for two reasons. First, in everything I write, I am looking for His approval. Are the thoughts flowing with ease and without a sense of judgment, or am I feeling convicted? And when I say convicted, I'm not talking about the feeling that comes when I'm judging myself, when my insecurities are getting in the way. Instead, I am talking about something so intense that continuing to write feels like a curse. To keep going would feel like entering onto a road that says danger ahead. Second, I write and journal with God because He's the safest person to tell.

Contrary to what others may believe, it's in that sacred space that I feel the least judged. In the process of becoming, I am most vulnerable and sensitive. Brainstorming, sketching, coloring, and filling in all the details about the new me is safest and most secure when only God and I have the vision. With that sense of safety and freedom, I let the words flow without hesitation, and the new invention, me, flows without inhibition onto the paper until we are all exhausted, like the burdens I carried at the beginning of the session. I then move on to the next part of the writing process.

I take a deep breath, ready to face what comes next. I transition from the vision of the woman I will be to the steps that I'll have to take to get from here to there. Now, we're talking about the process:

Dear God,

I have a vision. But I need more discipline and confidence to see it through. This transformation and this purchase are both bigger than anything I've ever done before. Both require more of me than I've ever had to give. Give me the perseverance and grit I need to show up for myself and this vision every day. When things seem unbearable and unlikely to happen, grant me the patience, wisdom, and mental fortitude to succeed internally and externally. To do both, I must embrace the discomfort of growth and the uncertainty of the path ahead. I have to trust that every small step, no matter how insignificant it may seem, is bringing me closer to the person I am meant to become and the life I am meant to live. Remind me that setbacks are not failures but lessons and that doubt is a natural part of the journey, not a reason to give up. Help me to keep my eyes on the vision, even when the road is dark, and the destination feels out of reach. Let me find strength in my faith, and let that strength carry me through each day, no matter how difficult. I know that this journey will challenge me in ways I can't yet imagine, but I also know that I can rise to meet those challenges with Your guidance. Help me to see this vision through, not just for myself but for all those who are counting on me and for the person I am destined to become.

I create another list of milestones and goals I have to accomplish. The pen glides over the page as I write.

Homeownership Milestones:

- Improve credit score
- Come up with a down payment
- Get pre-approved for a mortgage
- Make an offer and negotiate the purchase price
- Finalize mortgage approval
- Prepare for closing
- Transfer utilities

Business Scaling Milestones:

- Streamline processes
- Build a robust and accountable team
- Expand our customer base
- Increase sales
- Secure more sponsorships
- Create a podcast
- Create a game
- Build out Infamous Mothers University (IMU)
- Sell classes
- Automate the business

Personal Growth Milestones:

- Set boundaries for work and personal time
- Prioritize self-care to avoid burnout

- Strength train 3–5 times per week
- Do yoga twice a week
- Treadmill or walk for at least an hour every day

I hesitate, knowing I should put dates next to each one, but the thought tightens my chest. Just writing these things down feels overwhelming, like I'm already in over my head. There's a fear that if I start assigning dates, it'll feel forced, like I'm just ticking off boxes without really committing. And every time I move inauthentically, I fail. And yet, I know that I have to add dates. Otherwise, the contract I'm making between me and God is incomplete. And I will get to it. But for now, this plan, this roadmap, even without dates, is causing a shift in me. I haven't felt a sense of clarity like this in a long time. I'm beginning to see what I need to do to make it to the other side, to go from dreaming to realizing dreams.

I stare at the words I've just written, the ink still fresh and slightly raised on the page, running my fingers and then the fullness of both my hands across the impressions they have made on the paper. The surface is paper cool under my touch, grounding me in the reality of what I've just committed to as if taking in large doses of the new me—absorbing more of the information into my body just by touching the words I've written in cursive across these pages.

But even as I run my fingers over the page, the texture of the paper familiar yet foreign, letting the words sink in, a wave of exhaustion washes over me. As I tire of tonight's session of inventing me, there's still something missing. A hollow ache settles in my chest, and I want to stop writing. It's well into the middle of the night, and I need to get some sleep if I'm going to take care of these kids and do anything on my to-do list, like make it to tomorrow's workout session. But I'm not empty yet. The silence of the night presses in around me, amplifying the loneliness that creeps back in, a cold presence at the edge of my mind. I need some sense of community to help me nurture these dreams of mine.

"Who is my support system?"

The words spill out in messy cursive onto the page, chaotic and urgent. The ink smudges slightly as I press the pen too hard, the question hanging there like a heavy cloud. My hand trembles slightly as I stare at the question, realizing how pivotal it is—how it underpins everything I'm trying to accomplish. It feels like the foundation of a house I'm trying to build, shaky and uncertain. The vision, goals, and milestones are all just ideas without the right people beside me.

"Who do I need to build a relationship with to make all or some of this happen?"

I let the pen rest for a second, the enormity of it all sinking in. My head spins, a dull ache forming at my temples. It's easy to let my hurt, disappointment, and loneliness convince me that I should do all of this alone. The room feels colder, the weight of isolation pressing down on me. It's easy to let anger and resentment convince me that I don't need anyone else and that I can do this without help. My jaw clenches as I fight the urge to prove that I can do it alone. But deep down, I know that's a lie. The truth is this: Every big dream, every significant move, requires a network of people who believe in it and who can offer guidance, encouragement, and a few reality checks.

I think about the people in my life, their faces flashing through my mind like a slideshow. I think about who's in my corner right now. There's Ruby, of course, with her knowledge and belief that the impossible is another challenge to overcome. She's already been a massive part of getting me this far. But who else is willing to fight for this vision alongside me? I begin to mentally sift through the people in my life, the silence in the room amplifying the sound of my thoughts as I assess each relationship, their roles, their strengths, and what they might be able to offer—or, more importantly, what I need to be brave enough to ask for.

Family, friends, mentors—each plays a different part. Mistee, my sister-cousin, comes to mind. She'll hold me up when it all feels too heavy. "Look here, cousin, I stay in my lane. And my lane is support. I'm a good support person," she always reminds me. Her voice echoes in my mind, a soothing balm to my weary spirit. She's as far as I will allow myself to go for now.

But something inside me pushes back, refusing to settle for just that.

Who else? I hear a voice ask, soft but insistent, like a whisper in the dark. *Who are the others that will push me forward when I start to lose momentum? Who are the ones I haven't yet met?* The unknown looms large, a vast, uncharted territory filled with potential and uncertainty. *What connections do I need to seek out? What relationships do I need to cultivate intentionally? Who are the experts, the influencers, the allies, the sponsors who can open doors I don't even know exist yet?* The questions come at me rapid-fire, each one sparking a flicker of light in the back of my mind, illuminating new possibilities. But this time, it's not from a place of anxiety. It's from a place of power, a deep, simmering energy that starts in my core and radiates outward.

The thought of reaching out, of building new relationships, stirs something in me. My heart beats a little faster, not from fear but from excitement, anticipation. It's not just about who I know now but who I need to connect with next. I can almost feel the potential of these future connections, like a current of electricity running just beneath my skin. This is about more than support; it's about creating a community that shares my vision. The realization settles in, like a warm, comforting blanket on a cold night—I can't do this alone, and I don't have to. There's strength in knowing when to ask for help, when to lean on others, and when to admit that collaboration might be the key to turning dreams into reality.

With that in mind, I begin to draft a list of names, qualities, skills, and insights that I need to surround myself with. The pen glides smoothly over the paper, the ink flowing effortlessly as if these thoughts were just waiting to be released. This list isn't just a wish; it's a blueprint for the future I'm building. Each name, each quality, is like a brick being laid in the foundation of something solid, something enduring. This isn't just about finding support; it's about building a team, a community that believes in this vision as much as I do.

And as the list grows, so does my determination. It's like watching a storm gather strength, the winds picking up, the air thick with purpose. The question shifts from "Who is my support system?" to "How do I start building it?"

I end my journaling session with a sense of closure and readiness. The tension in my body eases, replaced by a calm certainty. It feels complete. One last time, I run my fingers over the pages, the paper cool and slightly textured beneath my fingertips, as if to absorb the extra doses of power I've just written. Emptied of all the stuff that I just carried—the chaos, confusion, resentment, fear, and anxiety—I've written myself into a peace of mind and empowerment. I close the journal and let out a long, slow breath, feeling lighter and more focused than I have in a long time.

CHAPTER 10

LOVE + BUSINESS

APRIL 2021

The Quiet One and I are talking on the phone. It's late in the evening, and the sound of his voice feels like home; I could live in it forever. We're discussing the life we plan on building together.

He says, "I don't know why, but I want another baby."

"You want another baby?" I respond, shocked.

"Yeah, I think I do," he says thoughtfully.

"Why? By the time you come home, we'll be closer to fifty. Besides, I don't want more kids. I've worked too hard raising the six I already have. I'm tired. I'm over the baby phase."

There's silence. Then he responds as if removing a dream from his bucket list. "Well, I guess I won't have another baby."

There's more silence.

I interrupt it with another question. "You know what I do want?"

"What's that?" he asks, sounding genuinely curious, not holding the first part of the conversation against me.

"I want a housekeeper," I say excitedly.

The warmth of his voice suddenly cools, like a breeze turning chilly in the middle of summer.

"You trying to tell me you can't clean your house? You need someone else to do it?" he says, disgusted.

"What I'm saying is this: My time is worth $250 per hour. It makes more sense for me to pay someone to clean the house while I work." I try to explain the logic to him.

"So, so, so, what about cooking?" he asks as if he's leading me somewhere.

I answer him. "What about it? I can cook. But I don't have time to cook." Mind you, just a few months back, he told me he could cook and was willing to cook. *So what changed?* I wondered.

"Every child should be able to say that they got a favorite dish that their momma makes for them," he says with conviction.

I don't respond. We sit in what feels like a heated and uncomfortable silence. And while my mouth has nothing else to say, I think, *How did we get here? How did we end up in this place of quiet tension? The conversation started out simple enough, light even, but now there's a heaviness hanging between us.* It's like a shirt that has been buttoned up wrong—each word a button slipped into the wrong hole, leaving the fabric twisted and uneven. I keep hoping that we just missed a buttonhole somewhere along the way and that fixing this misalignment will be easy, a quick adjustment. But as we continue to talk, I wonder if it's really that simple.

How did we get here? How did I get here? This relationship was supposed to be everything I wanted—stable, supportive, and built on mutual respect and shared dreams. And yet, here I am, feeling conflicted. Why?

Lately, I've been mulling over this theory, which I've come to call "Fantasy versus strategy," when it comes to love and business. The idea goes like this: Growing up, my understanding of relationships was shaped by Disney movies, romantic comedies, and the snippets of advice I picked up from my parents. They talked to me about sex, gender roles, and what it meant to be in a relationship, but none of those lessons provided a clear process or set of standards for choosing a partner who was truly right for me.

My dad, for instance, once told me, "Your job as a woman is to shut up, make a man laugh, and feel good." And my mom, while mixing cake batter or experimenting with our new ice cream maker, would say something like, "A man will walk on the lake with you, holding your hand in one hundred degrees below zero weather for ten years. And then when you finally give in and have sex with him, he'll say, 'Bitch, what took you so long?'"

They put me up on game, gave me glimpses of what to expect, but none of it amounted to a strategy. No class or conversation laid out a step-by-step guide for choosing the right partner—just vague notions and contradictory advice. So, I did what I saw: kissed frogs, cussed folks out, settled and traded sex for companionship, all the while hoping that somewhere along the way, I'd stumble into the love story I'd been fantasizing about.

But now, with the benefit of experience, I can't help but wonder—what if I had approached my romantic life with the same strategy and intentionality that I bring to my business? What if I had focused less on the fantasy of what love should be and more on building a grounded, fulfilling, and sustainable partnership? My professional life is built on clarity, goals, and action steps, with no room for uncertainty. I live out my dreams in that realm, but in love, it feels like I've been drifting without a compass, hoping for the best without a real plan.

Maybe, just maybe, if I put as much strategy into my love life as I do into my business, I wouldn't find myself questioning how I ended up here, in a relationship that's supposed to be everything I wanted but now leaves me feeling conflicted. It's time to rethink the way I approach love—not as a fantasy to be fulfilled but as a partnership to be carefully crafted. I need to rethink it not because I want out of my engagement with the Quiet One but because I hope to bring us closer together by presenting us with a playbook that can put us on the same page.

The conversation drags on for a little bit longer, but it's clear we're both just waiting for the fifteen minutes to end so we can retreat into our separate corners of the world and figure some things out. The automation comes on, telling us we have one minute left. "I love you," we say, right before the call ends.

The sound of the Quiet One's voice is still echoing in my ears. It's late, and the house is silent, save for the soft hum of the refrigerator in the kitchen. I sit here, unmoving, letting the weight of our conversation settle over me.

What did I miss? What didn't I consider? What's wrong with me? I drill myself with questions because it's so much easier to fix an issue when I am the problem. *Please, God, let this be on me so I can fix the issue so that I can fix us.*

The Quiet One has finally become the man I thought I wanted—present, loving, committed. He's the dad I always hoped he would be, not just to our son but to our daughter too. I've watched him evolve, calm down, and grow tired of the street life. He's done the work, and now he's ready to settle down, to build a life with me. But is that enough?

Twenty years ago—hell, even three months ago—having a man who loved me and our children felt like enough. But now, with a thriving business, six children, and all of the responsibilities that come with this new life, I realize that love alone might not be enough. The thought makes my chest tighten with a mix of fear and uncertainty.

As I sit with my thoughts, I realize that the reason I was never intentional about love in the ways that I should have been was that I didn't think I was worthy of it. The thought of that used to embarrass me, used to make me feel some kind of way. But I share it so easily now because it was what it was.

Tired of sitting in that chair, I get up to make myself a pot of tea, moving from muscle memory. I gather the pot, then the water, and turn on the stove. Still thinking about my conversation, I move to another chair.

It's a familiar feeling now, this quiet tension that lingers after our talks. It starts small, like a pebble dropped into still water, but the ripples expand until they're impossible to ignore. Tonight, though, I'm determined to do more than just sit with it—I'm going to unpack it, piece by piece, like a business problem that needs solving.

I flip the page in my journal and write at the top: The Business of Love.

I sit back for a moment, tapping the pen against my chin, thinking about what that really means. Love isn't just about the highs, the romance, the feelings that swept me off my feet years ago. It's about the day-to-day, the strategy, the constant work of keeping a relationship aligned with who you are and who you want to be.

I start to write, my thoughts spilling onto the page. But there's hesitation. I want to write a mission statement, just to see what that looks like, but I feel dirty and judged by the voices in my head. "Huh, if you spent more time trying to take care of those kids and less time trying to find a daddy for them, you'll be better off." "Oooo wee, that girl is fast." "Damn, you sho' is boy crazy." It's hard for me to write the mission statement because I don't want to look like my mission in life is to find a man.

Prudence, that version of me that is always about reason, intervenes, stepping in front of the women attacking me in my head. "Think about this. If you don't create a mission statement that guides the way you move in love, that gives you your way, you're gonna have us out butt-asshole naked in this world and being everybody's fool. We need this sense of direction." With a steady hand, I begin writing.

Mission Statement:

"To cultivate a love that inspires mutual growth and authenticity, encourages emotional safety, and promotes unwavering support, where both partners are fully seen, heard, and valued."

"Okay," Prudence says calmly, like she's worried that any sudden moves will make me push a button that will lead to all of us exploding. "Now, that mission statement is meant to guide our day-to-day actions in love and romance. I need you to think five, ten, twenty years in advance about what you want to experience in love. How do you want it to look?"

I feel my stomach get queasy. I tighten my butt. My palms get sweaty. I feel like I want to run. *I don't know, Prudence.* Outside of Prodigal, I've never stayed in a relationship for more than two years. *I can't think that far*, I think to myself as I shake my leg nervously in my seat.

"Yes, you can." I hear her voice in my mind, encouragingly. "Look, what do you want people to experience around love in the next twenty years? What do you want the state of love to be in the world?"

"Um … I want love to be a transformative experience. I want people to be inspired by it. I want fires of love to be (re)ignited all around the world."

"Perfect. Our vision statement is that. We want a love that does that for other people," she says with a sense of satisfaction. "Write it down."

Impressed by how she (I) was just able to do that, I lean forward and then write.

Vision Statement:

"Twenty years from now, I want our love to be so contagious and inspiring that it motivates thousands to say, 'Your love has reignited and transformed me, showing me what's possible.'"

The thought of this makes me smile—a future where the love I build with the Quiet One becomes a beacon, not just for us but for others as well. But then I think, is this something the Quiet One wants? Will he want any of this? I can't dwell on that for now because I am trying to make sense of me. And I am afraid that if I stop to think about him, I may not keep going.

I dive deeper.

I learned from a relationship that I had a long time ago about the importance of being honest about my values. I was dating a guy who pressured me to change my sleep and work schedule so that I could spend more time with him. It had taken me years to get on that schedule. But I changed it to please him. And then our relationship crumbled. He wanted me to change my schedule because he was cheating. It taught me a valuable lesson. Again, at the time, I wouldn't be honest about it. But the truth is I valued having a man and what I thought his validation and support could do for me more than I valued my ambition. In fact, I felt that his support and love were the keys to protecting and easing my journey to my goals. The big takeaway from that was to always be clear about my values and own them. Align your actions with them. And if there is misalignment, I have to either change what I say I value or change my actions.

So, in love, what do I value? I ask myself.

Prudence reminds me that I don't have to get this perfect—just start brainstorming and see what comes out.

I begin writing.

Core Values:

"Adoration, kindness, transparency, authenticity, faith, loyalty, honesty, communication."

These aren't just words. They're the principles that guide how I love, interact, and expect to be treated. They're non-negotiable, just like in business, where certain standards must always be met.

As I write, the recent conversation with the Quiet One replays in my mind—the way his voice shifted from warmth to coolness when I talked about wanting a housekeeper and the tension when we discussed the future. It's clear that while love is the goal, there's a disconnect in the strategy. And that's what I'm here to solve.

My mind shifts to all the times I traded sex for companionship because I never thought I was worthy of being loved. That has been a theme in a lot of my relationships—not feeling worthy, not feeling that what I bring is good enough to, in exchange, experience respect, dignity, and the right kind of support in a relationship. And for years, because I haven't found the strength, I told this boy or that man, "I'll give you my vagina if you give me your time," never really doing the work of demanding much more. So now, I have to face this idea of my value. And I have to actually sit with this idea, own it, and take it seriously.

Value Proposition:

"I bring wisdom, faith, loyalty, and intimacy, offering a deep sense of emotional, mental, and spiritual safety. I create a space where my partner feels valued, heard, and supported, and I seek the same in return. I offer peace and holistic safety. I nurture."

It's about knowing my worth, understanding what I offer, and making sure that my value is recognized and appreciated. If not, just like in business, it might be time to reassess the partnership.

I glance at the clock—midnight. The house is still. I close my eyes for a moment, imagining what continuous improvement might look like in love. How do I keep growing, adapting, and making sure this love doesn't stagnate? The pen moves again.

Continuous Improvement:

"We commit to regular check-ins, honest conversations, and adapting to each other's evolving needs. Just like a business, our love must grow, evolve, and improve to stay relevant and strong."

This sounds good, right? However, one of the things the Quiet One sets his pride on is being a constant man. He stays the same. That's a value of his. And my constant question is this: Where's the room for growth then? And if I value growth, where does that leave us? I never want to think about the idea of us being apart. But if I have to think about that, and the thought is unsettling, what does that look like?

A friend of mine, a gynecological oncologist, once told me that part of her job involves delivering bad news and dealing with hard things. She taught me the importance of imagining the hard thing in all its details and scenarios and then going and doing the hard thing. I close my eyes and think, *What if the day comes when we do have to part ways? What does our exit strategy look like?*

Exit Strategy:
"If our love no longer aligns with our mission, vision, and values, we will part with grace and integrity, understanding that not all partnerships are meant to last forever."

The words are more challenging to write but necessary. I've learned from past experiences that sometimes the healthiest thing I can do is walk away. But that's not the goal here—not if I can help it.

I close the journal, feeling a sense of clarity. This isn't just about love; it's about treating love with the same seriousness and intention as I would a business. It's about understanding that while love is an emotion, it's also a practice, a daily commitment to show up, to communicate, and to grow.

The tea is stone cold now, but I'm filled with warmth. Tomorrow, I'll share some of these thoughts with the Quiet One. I'll invite him into this practice, into this business of love, and see if he's willing to invest in it as deeply as I am.

I take a deep breath, letting the weight of the night settle. The kitchen is quiet but feels different now—less heavy, more purposeful. I stand up, ready to face whatever comes next with clarity and intention, knowing that I've done the work to build a love that is as strong, strategic, and enduring as any business I've ever built.

As I turn off the kitchen light, my thoughts shift. Maybe it's time to take a break from the heaviness of introspection, to step out and clear my head. The idea of a cigar bar crosses my mind—a place where I can unwind and think about something else for a while. Maybe even get a different perspective. I know it doesn't close until two. People who spend long days and nights at the office go there to unwind before they transition home to start over. A friend of mine is one of those people. I can depend on him to be there. He's always there, a regular. Besides, since my conversation with the Quiet One, I haven't been able to settle in for the night. Since I'm still dressed, I might as well go out for a little bit.

The air in the cigar bar is thick with the rich scent of tobacco, mingling with the warm notes of leather and oak that give the place its character. Low, jazz-infused music pulses softly, with a saxophone weaving smooth, winding melodies that fill the space, setting a relaxed but sophisticated mood. The lighting is dim, casting a soft amber glow that dances on the walls and across the faces of the patrons. Men in tailored suits and women in elegant dresses sit in plush, high-backed chairs, nursing drinks and puffing on cigars that send swirling clouds of smoke into the air.

I'm sitting across from a close male friend of mine, a glass of amaretto stone sour—without the foam—in hand. He's relaxed, his posture is easy, and he has a half-smoked cigar loosely between his fingers. There's a confidence about him that's almost contagious, but tonight, it's making me uneasy. He takes a slow drag from his cigar, letting the smoke curl out of his mouth before he speaks.

"A man who makes a minimum of $10,000 per month over three to five years is considered a high-value man," he says, his tone casual, like he's sharing a well-known fact. "But that's not what makes a woman high value."

I raise an eyebrow, taking a sip of my amaretto. The smooth, sweet citrus flavor contrasts with the bitterness rising in my chest. "Oh? And what makes a woman high value then?"

He leans forward slightly as if he's about to let me in on a secret. "The more she earns, the more at risk her value becomes," he continues. "Her earning power can make her more difficult to 'deal with.' A high-value woman is summed up in three simple 'f' words: fit, friendly, and feminine."

I can't help but smirk, a mix of amusement and disbelief bubbling up. "Fit, friendly, and feminine?" I repeat, almost to make sure I heard him right.

"Yeah," he nods as if this is the most obvious thing in the world. "She's attractive to look at, she has an agreeable personality, and she's soft. She smells good, wears dresses and skirts, knows when to speak and when not to, isn't loud or ratchet, and she serves and compliments her man. A high-value man isn't worried about how much she makes because he's a high-value man—he has money. He's interested in her ability to nurture, care for their family, and make him look good in public. A high-value woman is someone who complements, and here's the important piece—doesn't compete against her high-value man."

I feel a knot forming in my stomach as his words sink in. The idea of a woman's value being reduced to her ability to "complement" rather than "compete" with a man feels like a punch to the gut. *Compete?* The word rattles in my mind, stirring up a mix of frustration and confusion. I lean back in my chair, trying to process this. "What do you mean a man wants a woman who will complement him, not compete with him? What woman you know is competing with a man?"

He takes another drag from his cigar, exhaling slowly as he considers my question. "White women go to college to find a husband. Black women go to college to show they don't need one."

The statement hangs in the air between us, heavy and jarring. It's the kind of thing you'd expect from an internet troll, not from a friend you respect. I stare at him, trying to reconcile the man I know with the words coming out of his mouth. The cigar smoke thickens around us like a fog I can't see through. *Is he serious?* I wonder, my mind racing.

"This is the craziest shit I've heard," I finally say, trying to shake off the unease. But even as I say it, I'm reminded of a conversation I had with a girlfriend not too long ago. We were out for drinks, just the two of us, and while discussing dating, she casually dropped a line that echoed this same sentiment: "Black women go to college to get an MS, while white women go to college to get a MRS."

I remember laughing it off at the time, but now, sitting here in this cigar bar, the words are coming back to me with a new level of significance. These two friends of mine don't know each other; they come from completely different walks of life, yet they're saying the same things. A chill runs down my spine as I realize the implications. Are we really that different?

In the dim light of the bar, I find myself questioning the path I've been on. As Black women, we are building businesses, getting educated, and making sure we can take care of ourselves—stand on our own if we must. But what does that mean for our relationships? None of this, it seems, is to prepare us for marriage or partnership—at least, not with a high-earning man. After all we've accomplished, on paper, we look like that man. I'm reminded of a conversation with a Nigerian American friend about his journey to success. At the end of that conversation, I found myself saying out loud, "Damn. Why do I look like a Nigerian man on paper?"

He got quiet then, and with a softness in his voice that I didn't expect, he said, "You tell me."

His words echo in my mind now as my identity shifts, and I step into this new era in my life. I'm presented with models of love every day, models that I have to decide whether fit me or not. What my friend here in the cigar bar is describing is a high-value man, sure, but more importantly, he's describing a man who wants a traditional relationship. And that's not for me.

I look across the table at my friend, who's still puffing away at his cigar, oblivious to the internal storm brewing in me. So what do I want?

My mind drifts back to last year when I was preparing a workshop for our Talk Back Conference. It was called Love + Business. I never finished it or presented it; it was just a casual idea I was playing with. However, I created some interesting and informative models for that workshop. Out of curiosity, I want to know which models fit my relationship with the Quiet One.

I set down my drink, and my decision was made. "I need to check something," I say, more to myself than to him. He nods, taking another sip of his whiskey, seemingly unaware of the shift in my mood.

I head home, the conversation still weighing on me. When I get there, I go straight to my laptop, turn it on, and search through Google Docs until I find the document. As I scroll through it, I smile and then laugh. It's wild that I wrote this back then, but I stand by it. I start rereading the list, getting reacquainted with the models I'd created, remembering the thoughts that went into each one.

Love Models:

Traditional: This model is rooted in fixed gender roles, where the man is the provider, and the woman is the caretaker. It's a model that many of us have seen growing up, and it can work well for some, but it can also be limiting, especially if it doesn't align with our evolving identities.

Wizard and the Healer: In this model, gender roles are reversed, with the woman in the power position while the man focuses on emotional and spiritual support. It's a dynamic that can work well when both partners are aligned in their strengths and values.

Beauty and the Beast (Bad Boy and Good Girl): This model is where the woman's love subdues or saves her partner from a curse or difficult life situation. It's a narrative that many romantic stories are built on, but it can be exhausting and unsustainable if the "bad boy" never actually changes.

Flexi Model: This model is all about adaptability. Partners fill in whatever needs to be done based on who has the capacity at any given time. This couple could shift between different models depending on their circumstances, making it versatile but potentially unstable if not managed well.

Power Couple: Both partners are ambitious, supporting each other's goals and driving each other to greater heights. This model requires a high level of mutual respect and shared ambition, but it can also lead to burnout if not balanced with care for the relationship itself.

Soft Life Model: Here, the focus is on well-being and mental health, with both partners prioritizing a life that's as stress-free as possible. This model can be integrated with any others, adding a layer of mindfulness and self-care to the relationship.

I think back to the dynamic between me and the Quiet One, realizing we were the Bad Boy/Good Girl model. This model can indeed be exhausting and unsustainable if the bad boy never changes. But even if he does, it can be short-sighted. The mission was the conquest, the calming of the bad boy. But as one bad boy said to one good girl, "Now that you have me, what now?"

That model is no longer relevant to us; there have been identity shifts. So, who are we now that we have changed? Or rather, what are we now that the dynamics have shifted?

I can't speak for the Quiet One, but I know what I want. I want a love rooted in a softer life. Raising these children has been hard. Completing that PhD was hard. Building this company has been hard. The love I experience has to make my life easier. It has to bring peace, not more challenges.

The dim light of the kitchen casts long shadows as I sit back down with my journal, thoughts about the Quiet One still swirling in my mind. The air feels thick with unresolved tension, but I know I can't linger here forever. There's only so much I can unpack in one night.

I pick up my pen, staring at the blank page before me. My mind is still buzzing from the conversation with my friend at the cigar bar, the love models I'd created, and the realization that things between the Quiet One and me are no longer as simple as they once were. "Matters of the heart can be so messy, I write," the words flowing like they've been waiting to be released. "And with my identity shifting and his too, there are whole new layers of messiness."

I pause, letting that truth settle over me. The questions that now hang between us aren't easy ones—they're the kind that can reshape a relationship for better or worse. What does support for each of us look like as we make these changes? We'll have to answer these questions together, but even as I write, I feel the uncertainty creeping in.

But there's one question that looms larger than the rest, a question that feels too big and overwhelming to tackle tonight. "Does that support look and feel better as husband and wife or simply as friends?"

I stare at the words on the page, feeling the night's exhaustion settle into my bones. *I can't answer that tonight,* I admit to myself, *especially not with me trying to figure out a similar line of questions for my work life.*

The weight of everything I'm carrying feels like it's pressing down on my chest. I think about how the world seems to punish Black women for striving, for achieving. We're judged for being too masculine when all we're trying to do is make sure everyone is good, including ourselves. We're shamed for doing what needs to be done, whether that's putting a father on child support or raising our babies alone when we don't have that support.

It's enough to drive anyone crazy. The endless balancing act, the constant need to prove our worth, to be soft enough for love yet strong enough to survive— it's a heavy weight that never truly lifts. And after all that, we're told to give up what we've built just to fit into someone else's idea of femininity. How is anyone supposed to thrive under that kind of pressure?

The pen feels heavy in my hand as I close the journal. The thoughts of work and community-building begin to take center stage in my mind, pushing the messiness of the heart to the background for now. But the weight of it all—the love, the expectations, the constant demands—is still there, lingering at the edges of my consciousness.

I'll return to this journal tomorrow, but my focus will shift. I'll dive into the world of work, building something bigger than myself, and creating a community that can grow alongside me. But tonight, I let the pen rest, knowing that the work of the heart and the work of the mind both require their own kind of patience and persistence.

With that thought, I rise from the table, feeling the quiet of the night settle around me like a blanket. The kitchen is still, but it doesn't feel as heavy as before. I take one last look at the journal on the table, a silent promise to return to it when the time is right. For now, though, it's time to rest—and to prepare for the challenges that tomorrow will inevitably bring.

CHAPTER 11

THE ORGASM PROJECT

JUNE 2021

Most of April and May are a blur. Financially, things are looking up. Several sponsorship opportunities secured last year have paid out, allowing us to move forward with our Covet program, continue building Infamous Mothers University, and begin preliminary work on our podcast. Consulting jobs have come through, along with other personal brand work. I take a large chunk of those dollars and pay off all the back bills on my credit report. Within weeks, my score increases. I can check that off my prayer list. My life feels as right as rain—until it all starts to fall apart. And it's that falling apart that has led me to where I am now, in this hotel.

I'm a workaholic. I'm the kind of person who can work through an apocalypse, a tornado, a pandemic, or the deaths of multiple people. It's how I stay grounded and not lose myself when I feel like I'm about to slip. It's how I stay tethered when I am about to snap. Work is how I push through. I think it's in part because it's the one thing I trust. Often, it gives me what I give it. It's reliable, predictable, and gratifying. Although it consumes and never seems to end, it has moments of completion along the continuum. In all of the chaos, it gives me a beginning, a middle, and an end—something to hold on to. It always seems to make sense. And so, I packed my bags—my laptop, a crate full of books and journals, some articles—and I holed away in my favorite hotel until the storm within me passed. I cried. I drank tequila and grenadine with sparkling water. I masturbated.

My fiancé is in federal prison, and I am trying to get as close to him as possible. And so, we have phone sex. I order different adult toys and play with them over the phone. I wear wigs and makeup and lingerie and role-play on video calls just to get closer to him. And I drink and drink, which is a big deal because I don't drink, not even socially. But I want to not feel. I want to be numb as I become other women and take on other personalities as I lose myself. While he enjoys seeing me like this at first, it becomes obvious I am way too inexperienced at this for him. I am out of my league. He has seen and heard it all before, but only better. Back when he was in the world, he stayed in strip clubs and dated a dancer. He forgets I'm not her. He mistakes me for someone who is trying to be a professional. I am not. And he expects to be entertained. I'm not an entertainer. I am a woman spiraling, trying to cling on to my man as he watches, unamused, as I fall from the sky. His cue is missed. He doesn't even know he was supposed to catch me. He doesn't even know how.

For days, I sit in this hotel bed, working, researching, studying, writing, doing the work that will become *Covet: The "Disrespectful" Health and Wellness Journal*. And somewhere between the constant deaths and his not knowing what to do with me, or how to respond, I slide into a deep despair.

One day, I tell him, "I don't feel like killing myself. But I often feel like I'm on a ledge, and I'm afraid of heights. And it feels scary. I feel the urge to jump. But I won't, even though something is calling me to do so. And so I'm going to cling to this bed, like a wall, until it passes, until it all passes."

He listens, and his response is something like, "Only people with something wrong in their head say shit like that. Crazy people." And I hear the fear and the concern in his voice. I hear him see me as broken. And from that moment on, I begin backing away. In all fairness, though, it makes sense that he would respond that way. For almost ten years, I have watched him fight to hold on to his sanity. We talk about the nightmares he faces, the things he sees and hears, and the encounters he's had. He can't save me. So I am going to have to save myself, as I have done so many times before. But how, when I can't stop falling?

Out of desperation and the need to regain control, I step away from the phone sex and turn more to masturbating as a way of reclaiming my power. When I was a little girl, I was by the tenant in the basement of a big house we rented on Chicago's North Side. While I knew it was wrong, it felt good every time he'd lick me on my private parts. As I grew older and started having sex, I'd run away from that feeling, associating it with something dirty and wrong. But at that moment, there was something there I needed. It wasn't the climax I was looking for. It was the ability to lean into the chaos, the unknown feeling that was found in the gap between where I was and where I was going. It was riding, and not running from, that overpowering, intense feeling that comes with having an orgasm. If I could learn to lean into, own, wield the power that came from inside of my body, then maybe I could stop running from my ability to wield and control my power in other ways. Maybe I can stand in my complete power as I navigate this home-buying process. But first, it had to start there, in a place of trauma. I had to take back my control and my first experience with feeling intense power—an experience that had come from inside me, my own body, in the form of an orgasm.

I grab my toy, a pink vibrator—the rabbit.

It looks almost clinical in my hand, more like a piece of advanced machinery than something designed for pleasure. The main shaft, smooth and unyielding, curves with calculated precision, as if engineered for efficiency rather than intimacy. And then there's the smaller piece—the ears. Two delicate prongs, poised and waiting, like an automated system ready to execute a function. It doesn't look like desire. It doesn't feel like warmth. It's technology. Cold. Mechanical. Unapologetic in its purpose.

And yet, I know what it can do. What it has done.

I want to use it—right now. I need this escape. I need this distraction. I need this conquer. But if I'm honest, I'm intimidated, not just by the machinery but by the power. By my power. The power within me that this thing, this pink and plastic mechanism, has the audacity to unlock. This isn't just about pleasure; it's about surrender, about release, about trusting myself enough to feel everything, to let go, to let this moment take me under and bring me back up changed. And that—more than the coldness of the machine, more than the absence of a human touch—is what truly terrifies me.

Fortunately for me, these intrusive thoughts won't let me stay in the present. I'm dealing with my monthly bout of premenstrual dysphoric disorder (PMDD)—an extreme case of premenstrual syndrome (PMS)—something I've been struggling with most of my life, hence the despair, the anxiety, and the horniness, along with the inability to concentrate.

I can't stay in the present. My mind keeps drifting back to the recent past when Prodigal popped back up into our lives.

It was back in late March 2020 when Prodigal arrived at my door to collect his mail. He had a service that allowed him to see online, early in the morning, what items would be hitting the mailbox that afternoon. On this day, he spotted something important. And even though I had told him over the phone that what he was expecting hadn't arrived, he popped up anyway.

I was sitting in my car, talking to the Quiet One on the phone, when I saw Prodigal walking toward my silver van. It felt like seeing a ghost—a reminder of everything I had tried to leave behind. I don't remember if I hung up on the Quiet One or put him on mute; I only recall the sight of Prodigal and the guarded feeling that washed over me. Why was he here now?

We exchanged a few words, and then he asked if he could stay the night in my car to grab the mail first thing in the morning. He looked tired, like a man who had lived through a million wars. No longer the man who once moved quickly and confidently, he now limped—a reminder of the ACL injury he'd gotten while cheating on me years ago. Convinced he was Wolverine or some other mutant with instant healing powers, he had refused occupational therapy and the work needed to restore his leg. Over time, compensating for the ACL injury led to the deterioration of his hip, causing him so much pain that walking became difficult, his foot now protruding sideways instead of facing forward. The fight had left him. Now, he was just a man looking for a place to rest on a long journey.

Thinking about my new relationship with the Quiet One and my very painful history with Prodigal, I was okay with him sleeping in the van. But it was my oldest son—the one who Prodigal had left our home on the worse terms with, the one who had grown taller and more independent in the two years since—who reminded me, "We're not the kind of family that lets a man sleep in his car." He said, "Either he sleeps in the house, or we politely tell him to move on. But there's nothing in between because that's not who we are." He also reminded me that despite all the pain Prodigal had caused, he had stuck it out with our family when no one else had. And that mattered. So, with that, I agreed to let him stay the night on the couch.

Buzzzzzzz.

The sound and the weight of the object pull me back to the present.

The vibration hums against my palm, steady and insistent—a reminder of where I am, of what I was about to do. The memory of Prodigal fades, slipping back into the shadows where it belongs. And I am here again, in this hotel room, alone with this machine, this power, this choice.

The air feels heavier now, charged with something electric. Something inevitable.

I try again.

This time, I let it buzz against my skin—hesitantly, experimentally. The pleasure is instant, undeniable. But the second it starts to feel good, I pull back. My muscles tighten. My breath catches. And before I even realize it, I've turned the toy off. It's too much.

I sit there, staring at it, feeling ridiculous. No, that's not it. I think I feel nervous. Judged? Dirty? Scared? Sneaky? But no one is here but me. Am I judging myself? Is it God? Who told me that I should be afraid of this feeling? That I don't have a right to experience this kind of power, something that lives inside of me. This wetness is mine. And yet, I am afraid to touch it, to slide in it, to live in it, to own it. I tiptoe around it, as if apologizing for addressing this need, moving as if this experience isn't mine to have.

I sit with that thought. Let it settle.

The power from my own body scares and intimidates me. It feels like a tsunami—destructive, out of control, unpredictable, undisciplined, wild, and free. And I don't think I trust it. It scares me.

I think some more.

Maybe it's because the first time I experienced it, my vagina was at the tip of a grown man's tongue. My body responded to him. To his call. I was a child. Too young to consent. And even still, when he summoned it, a surge came through me, warm, insistent, a pull I didn't understand but couldn't deny. It was like being caught in a current, swept up in something both natural and unnatural at the same time.

And I liked it.

That's the part I don't say out loud.

That's the part that sits in the back of my mind, wrapped in silence. I was too young to know what was happening. But not too young to feel it. The pleasure. The sensation. The way my body woke up under his touch, even as my mind screamed, "This is wrong."

Is that why I don't trust it? My own body? My own power? I think I don't trust it because while it lives in me, it has never felt like mine. I think someone else still owns the deed. Or maybe not just one person. Maybe that moment—his breath against my skin, the weight of his presence, the nervousness in my stomach—was just the beginning. A seed planted. A lesson I never agreed to learn. Maybe that experience, that foundational, premature, formative violation, was just the first of many moments that trained me to see my own power as something that does not belong to me. Maybe it's one more experience that has taught me that my power sits and waits for a new master, for someone else to summon it, manipulate it, wield it at their will.

And my only job? To house it. To be a vessel for it. To hold it in silence, untouched, until an external force calls its name.

It makes sense, doesn't it? That I hesitate. That I stop myself the second the feeling grows too strong. That I pull back because this kind of feeling is something I was never meant to hold in my own hands.

I exhale, slow and shaky, trying to recover from this.

It's my choice now, right?

My power now, right?

So why does it still feel like it isn't?

One of those intrusive thoughts comes back again. Little Miss Ainsley Anxiety, with her slick ass comments that no one ever seems to ask for, shows up ... again.

"Yeah, while you're sitting here thinking about the power you have and don't have right now, you almost died. It hasn't been two months since you and your whole house were almost completely wiped out. Choice? Choice? Where was your choice then? Choice is an illusion." I can feel her pacing back and forth in my head. Coughing as she relentlessly puffs her cigarette, eyes heavy and tired.

Shit, where's the lie? I think to myself. *I did almost die. At least I felt like I was about to. And even though I had done everything right, those damn kids of mine put me at the mercy of something I couldn't see: COVID.*

My mind drifts back to the night after Prodigal had shown up. The child I shared with him had developed a fever. It wasn't long before everyone in my home was sick. Symptoms ranged from low-grade fevers to severe headaches. Everyone tested positive for COVID-19, even those who showed no symptoms. But it was my eldest son and I who had it the worst. His headaches were incapacitating, and I lost the ability to walk. The uncertainty of our condition left me angry and scared.

Since the CDC announced safety protocols for COVID-19, I had been strict about following them—so strict that my eighteen-year-old daughter moved out, and my bonus daughter from Prodigal, who had been living with us despite my separation from him, wasn't allowed to come back after breaking protocol. I knew firsthand that COVID-19 was nothing to play with. As an overweight woman in my forties, I was at a higher risk of dying than my children, and I wasn't about to take any chances with reinfection. So, how did we get sick? Prodigal hadn't been around long enough to infect us. Yet, there we were.

After prodding and probing my children with questions, I discovered that one of my sons had been sneaking out to play basketball with his friends after telling me he was practicing his shot alone at the lake. Another child had been sneaking out under the guise of "dumping the garbage," but what she was really doing was meeting up with friends. When this all came out, I was furious. All I could think was, *These kids are going to kill me. I don't want to hear any damn "Momma, I'm sorry" on my deathbed.* I didn't care about their "I didn't know" or any of their excuses. All I could focus on was the fact that these *little motherfuckers have taken away my ability to walk, and they are about to kill me.* As I lay on my bed, soaking the sheets with sweat, drifting in and out of sleep and delirium, that's all I could think.

"Damn."

That's the first thought that pulls me back to the present.

"I really did almost die."

I blink, still caught between worlds, still feeling the fever sweat, the weight of my own body sinking into the mattress. Just moments ago—no, years ago, a lifetime ago—I had been burning up, slipping in and out of consciousness, trapped between this world and whatever comes next. A threshold. That's what it felt like. A line between being here and not. Between life and death.

At the time, Prodigal had been my caretaker, fighting to keep me on the side of the living. I hadn't had the strength or the presence of mind to do it on my own.

And now, here I am. Chasing another edge.

La petite mort. The little death. That's what the French called an orgasm—a brief dying, a surrender so complete it unravels you, then stitches you back together as someone new.

I put my toy in the space between my two thighs and try again. This time, I decide to watch myself. To be my own caretaker. To move between realms, chasing a small death to experience life.

I let the vibrations hum, pressing the toy lightly into the valley between my legs. The pleasure starts slowly and builds, but I freeze before it can take me too far. I stop at the door, in that liminal space between the two worlds, refusing to follow through.

And I watch myself.

I notice how I stop breathing, how my body braces against the intensity instead of relaxing into it. Every time I get close, I panic. Every time I start to lose control, I shut it down. I sit up in bed, legs crossed, the vibrator still in my hand, still warm from my touch. I am avoiding something. And then, the thought hits me: I'm scared to enter.

Like a kid who stands in line for hours to ride the biggest roller coaster in the amusement park, just to turn away when she finally reaches the gate, I back down. More than that, I run as far away from that feeling as possible, back to a place that feels safe, less chaotic, less intense.

I'm not ready to cross over yet. I'm not ready to throw my hands up, scream, and let it take me where it's going to take me. It's too overwhelming.

The irony is, my body has been the threshold men and babies have pushed through to experience beautiful adventures.

And in a similar but altogether different way, it's my body and my labor that will make it possible for my children, my family, and my clients to cross into something greater. A space I will create. A place where they can lose themselves. A place where they can climb to new levels. A place that is warm and safe and transformative.

And yet—while I am the bridge, I can't see myself crossing.

Unable to deal with the pressure of the present, I let the past take me again, dropping me almost exactly where it picked me up. Except this time, I am back with the Quiet One, and we're arguing,

He was furious that Prodigal was even there. And that fury had only deepened the chasm between us.

The night was heavy, thick with the tension that had been building between us for weeks. I lay in bed, the room cloaked in darkness, save for the soft glow of my phone screen. My heart raced, still reeling from the heated conversation we'd just had. His voice had been calm, almost too calm—the way it gets when he's angry but doesn't want to show it. But those big, capital letters on my screen—they shouted at me in a way his voice never did.

"YOU DON'T HAVE TO TELL ME. I STILL LOVE YOU NO MATTER HOW IT TURNS OUT."

I stared at the message, my thumbs at the ready, standing at the starting line of this race—to argue, cry, or scream. I was both unsure of what to say and of what the outcome of our conversation would be. The words felt like a slap, even though I knew they weren't meant to be. I hated it when the Quiet One used all caps. When he wrote in all capital letters, it was as if he were compensating in written form for the volume of a voice he never raised. It made me feel like I was in trouble, like I had done something wrong—even though I knew I hadn't. Or maybe I had, depending on how you looked at it.

I couldn't leave it there. My chest tightened with the weight of everything left unsaid, and I knew I had to respond, to explain myself, even if it was just to try to calm his fears—or maybe my own. I started typing, the words coming out in a rush.

"I might've handled things in a fucked up, messy, wobbly way. But I've NEVER wavered in my commitment to us or my faithfulness to you. Of course, I love you. Even now, I'm still me."

I sent the message and waited, my breath struggling in my chest as the seconds ticked. But the screen remained blank. No response. I could feel the panic rising in my body, the fear that maybe he didn't believe me, that maybe this was the breaking point. My fingers moved quickly over the keys, desperate to fill the silence.

"No matter what, I'm not cheating on you. I've worked very hard to protect our relationship."

Another pause. Still nothing. My asshole tightened, and my stomach dropped. Hysteria was about to take over. Why wasn't he answering? I could feel the doubt creeping in, gnawing at the edges of my resolve. Maybe I hadn't been clear enough. Perhaps I hadn't said the right thing. I started typing again, my fingers moving desperately.

"I didn't put up a fight because I can't win against your pride and trust issues."

Still no response. The silence was deafening, a void stretching out endlessly, swallowing up my words and leaving me feeling hollow. I was exhausted, the emotional toll of the night weighing heavily on me. But I couldn't let it go, couldn't let him think that I didn't care, that I wasn't trying to make this work. *One last message*, I told myself. Just one more, and then I'd let it be.

"But yeah, I love you. Good night."

I sent the message and closed my eyes, trying to steady my breathing, trying to calm Ms. Ainsley Anxiety, convincing her that I had it under control and that all was well. She could go back to her corner. She did, and she sat there, readying herself to pace, to keep me up all night, to think about all the things that had been said, that weren't said, that should've been said. And then, just as I was about to give up hope about having a peaceful night, my phone buzzed. My eyes snapped open, and I saw his name flash on the screen. I held my breath as I opened the message, bracing myself for whatever was to come.

In the quiet of the hotel room, a voice rises inside me, low and insistent. It's not Ainsley Anxiety. This one is way too calm.

"If you want to cross over, you're going to have to stop holding your breath. You're going to have to learn how to breathe."

The words settle into my bones, vibrating against the hum of the city outside. The air conditioner kicks on, sending a cool gust over my bare skin, but my body is still warm, still electric from the last failed attempt. The sheets are damp beneath me, my pulse unsteady, my chest tight—not from exertion, but from restraint.

It brings me back to the now, to the heat of my body and the threshold I keep refusing to cross.

I am ready to enter the world of taboo, ready to push past the edge, because I believe Audre Lorde when she says that the erotic has plenty to teach us.

What lessons wait for me on the other side?

Even though I don't fully understand Lorde's words, I feel them in my core, in the places where language fails but instinct understands: "As women, we have come to distrust that power which rises from our deepest and non-rational knowledge ... The erotic offers a well of replenishing and provocative force to the woman who does not fear its revelation, nor succumb to the belief that sensation is enough."

I let the words settle inside me. My body has something to teach me—if I can stop being afraid and listen.

I wanna learn, I think to myself.

"Well," that not-Ainsley voice comes back. "Move from passively observing to actively studying our body's responses to its power."

Taking her cue, I pick up my toy again. This time, I don't just feel—I analyze. I watch the way my body responds to touch and stimulation the way a yogi studies form and breath, the way an athlete rewatches game footage, studying every movement, every hesitation. Where do I hold tension? Where do I pull away? What makes me shrink? What makes me reach? I need to see me. I need to understand the way I engage and disengage. To map the moments where I let go and the ones where I pull back. I need to record my thoughts, search for patterns. Are there triggers? What am I resisting?

Over and over again, I go back to the drawing board.

First, relaxing. Breathing. Letting the sensation roll over me without judgment. When it starts to overwhelm me, I breathe through it—again, with no judgment. When I get comfortable with relaxing, breathing, and allowing myself to feel without guilt or shame, I push further. I start working on leaning into the power instead of pulling away from it.

I surrender.

Like a body floating in water, I let go of my need to be in control. And part of that surrender means accepting that this is not just research—this is pleasure. This is satisfaction, and I have a right to it.

And it is in that final act of acceptance where the biggest breakthrough is just about to happen but then, once again, progress is interrupted.

Like a flash of lightning across the inside of my skull, I see it.

"I WOULD NEVER LET NOBODY IN THE HOUSE."

The words don't come from my phone. They don't come from the air. They appear in my mind, sharp and sudden, like a verdict being handed down.

"Not even me?" I say to myself, thinking about how he just interrupted my moment.

I blink, the vision of his words so clear it's as if they were carved into the walls.

As if they were waiting for me, just beyond the threshold, ready to snatch me back the second I dared to step forward.

It's almost laughable.

Here I am, finally crossing into myself, into my sacred place, and there he is, dragging me back, telling me what doors should and shouldn't be opened.

I close my eyes, but the memory doesn't fade.

The Quiet One and I had been talking—no, texting—late one night, playing out hypotheticals, stretching the limits of what-if. The conversation had drifted to exes, to whether we'd ever let one move in if they had nowhere else to go. I remember his response. He had been so sure then, so confident in his answer.

"You said that you would let the mothers of your children live with you if they were in a bind. You don't remember that?"

I sent the message and waited, my heart pounding in my chest. But this time, there was no response. The silence stretched between us, a chasm that felt too wide to bridge. I stared at my phone, willing him to say something, anything. But the screen remained dark, and I was left alone with my thoughts, the weight of the night pressing down on me like a heavy blanket.

I set my phone down on the bedside table, the reality of the situation sinking in. I had tried to explain, tried to make him understand, but it felt like we were on different planets, speaking different languages. The night had been a mess, our emotions tangled in ways that neither could unravel. And now, there was nothing left to do but wait to see if we could find our way back to each other in the light of day.

But as I lay there, staring up at the ceiling, I couldn't help but wonder if the damage had already been done.

As much as I wanted to ease the Quiet One's mind, I couldn't. Prodigal was there, right in the middle of what felt like my impending death. Prodigal, the person who had dragged me through hell, was now my caretaker. He was taking care of all of us. He was the one who took everyone to get tested. He was the one giving out medicine and making sure we ate. He was the one monitoring my fever. For three weeks, he took care of me as I fought through my anger and my struggle to walk. By the end of those three weeks, I was better—still fatigued and weak, but the worst was behind me. And the timing couldn't have been better, as it was now the week of my birthday.

That day was about celebrating life—my life. I went to a Thai restaurant and ordered whatever I wanted to experience, tasting a little bit of everything. Pure pleasure.

A thought occurs to me—*own this.*

Own this experience; own this orgasm the way you owned that food.

Take it in without apology.

Taste it fully. Move as if it's your birthright.

Because it is.

This time, I reach for the rose. I turn it on. I do not hesitate. The pleasure comes fast and undeniable. But this time, I don't stop it. This time, I stay with it. The intensity builds, and I let it. I breathe through it, past the fear, shame, and old stories that tell me I should not be here. I let myself shake, let myself lose control, let myself surrender fully to the power that has always been mine.

And as I ride it—as I let it overtake me, consume me, break me open—I finally understand. I can cross the threshold. I deserve to. A sob rips through me, sudden and raw, my body trembling, my breath shaky. Because it was never about the house. It was never about the men. It was about this. About believing I deserved to step inside. Step inside myself. Step inside my power. Step inside the life I built, the pleasure I denied, the space I fought for but never truly let myself claim because I was always waiting at the door, holding it open for everyone else, and never believing I had the right to walk through it myself.

But now, I do.

This was never just about the house. Or sex. It was about power—about unlearning the belief that struggle was all I was meant for. Just as Lorde had said, the erotic had plenty to teach me. I had spent my life shrinking, working, giving, but never feeling worthy of ease. Never trusting my right to claim what I built.

But I do.

And that—more than the orgasm, more than the house, more than the men— was the real breakthrough.

CHAPTER 12

PERSPECTIVE

JUNE 2021

My 2021 started with Nina, a contractor I had worked with a couple of years before, reaching out to inquire about upcoming video projects that she could shoot with me. This back-and-forth with her wasn't just about work. It was about positioning me and my company to scale.

We've been chatting and working together consistently since then, preparing for my trip to Atlanta so that we can record trailers for our Nothing's Wasted course and Infamous Mothers University. But I am most excited about recording season one of our podcast, *Books, Bullets, and Babies*. Could her reaching out be a sign that I should take seriously everything I have imagined and plan to accomplish this year?

The thought of it excites me at first—a chance to scale, to finally see all the pieces fall into place. But then, like clockwork, Ainsley Anxiety slips in through the cracks, seeping into my thoughts before I can even take a full breath. She's a restless, jittery presence, pacing back and forth in my mind, her voice quick and relentless. "You're doing too much," she whispers, then shouts. "Who do you think you are? You'll mess it all up. Just watch."

I try to push her away, but her voice morphs, blending with the voices of people I love and respect, those who've always told me things for "my own good." "Stay in your lane, kid," she says, her tone now low and insistent. "You've got enough on your plate—why add more?"

With every word, I feel a weight in the pit of my stomach, a gnawing unease that spreads until it becomes hard to breathe. That's when Overton Overwhelm arrives, lumbering into the room like a shadow that blots out the sun. He's huge, filling every corner, his presence suffocating. I can barely move under his pressure. My thoughts are scattered, and my focus is shattered. Overwhelm is all-consuming, leaving no room for anything but the sheer enormity of the task ahead.

I close my eyes, trying to find a way out, but Anxiety's voice keeps buzzing in my ears, and Overwhelm's weight presses down on my chest. My mind is a storm of doubts and fears, each one feeding the other, growing stronger and louder until all I can do is sit there, paralyzed by the chaos they've created.

But then, in a moment of clarity, I reach for my journal, my lifeline in the midst of the storm. The familiar feel of the pen in my hand, the crispness of the paper beneath it—these are the things that ground me. I begin to write, each word a small act of defiance against the chaos:

Dear Father,

Thank you for loving and protecting me. Thank you for guiding me and being there for me when I feel most alone. And thank you for your wisdom.

I've been journaling and praying about building a team that could help transform my business and my identity. I've been wracking my brain about how I can make a bigger impact, reaching two million women by 2027. But am I ready? That's the real question. It's one thing to dream, to imagine all the ways your life and your business can grow and how your story can help change women's lives. It's another thing entirely to take risks and push yourself beyond the limits of what feels safe and comfortable. While I am desperate for community and connection, I'm skeptical about people. But when I really think about it, I know people are going to do what they are going to do. I understand that. So I'm less suspicious of them. The person I don't trust is me. I don't trust that I know how to build the right kind of community around my vision. Too much is at stake for me to miscalculate.

And yet, maybe Nina reaching out was just what I needed. Some people believe in this vision as much as I do, and they see the potential in what we're building and want to be a part of it. And if they believe in it and are willing to show up to make my dreams real, then I have to do the same without question, right? And if they are the people who believe in this vision, is that who I consider as part of my team? She's a contractor who works for herself. She stands alone, and yet, is it okay to see this relationship, this partnership, as something more than her business and my business? I imagined team members as people on my payroll who are in the trenches with me daily. But maybe that understanding is too narrow. Maybe I'm missing something major here.

As I reflect on the past year, how much has changed, and how much I've had to adapt, I've been doing a lot on my own. Still, when I really think about it, there've been people around me helping in ways I hadn't fully appreciated. The videographer, for one. She's been with me on and off for years, capturing the highs and lows of this journey. But because she's not on my payroll, I never considered her a part of my team.

The more I think about it, the more I realize how flawed that thinking is. I've been so focused on building a traditional team that I've overlooked the power of who's around me right now. My "team" isn't just the people I pay a salary to. It's everyone who contributes to my vision, everyone who believes in what I'm doing and wants to be a part of it, even if it's just for a project or two.

This realization starts to shift something in me. I begin to imagine new possibilities. What if I stop seeing the videographer as just an outside contractor and start seeing her as a key part of my team? What if I start embracing a more fluid, expansive idea of what my team can be? It's not about who's on the payroll but who's invested in the vision.

I go back to the text thread with the videographer, rereading our conversation. Her enthusiasm and willingness to dive into this work with me make everything feel so much lighter. I feel seen when I talk to her; the vision feels possible. It's exactly the kind of energy I need. And suddenly, I see it for what it is: She is part of my team, whether I've acknowledged it or not. She's been there, contributing to the growth of my business, supporting the vision, and bringing her unique talent to the table. That's what a team is really about, isn't it? People come together, each bringing something different, something valuable. In this moment, I realize how this chapter of my life is part of a much larger narrative—a narrative of resilience, community, and identity. The journey to success isn't just about the destination but the people who walk with us along the way. It's about growth, not by adding more, but by truly seeing and appreciating what's already there.

I put down my pen for a second, letting this mental shift take hold. I started thinking about other people in my life who have been more than contractors. They have been team members helping me build my company through the years. There's Chris, our photographer. Tanisha, our brand ambassador. Ron, our advisor, and Kristin, our graphic designer. In fact, Kristin and I have spent a large part of 2020 and all of 2021 building visual assets for the brand. We've been working on image concepts for the podcast (that I had no idea how to create), logos for classes (that I have no idea how to market and sell), and an icon for our virtual coworking space (that I'm still trying to build out). The work is crisp, beautiful, and top-tier, just like Kristin. A complete professional and even better human. This is my team.

I have Mistee and Damian, who are always there to listen and offer support. I have my accountant, who's helped me navigate the complexities of financial planning and keep my business on track. Every one of these people has been instrumental in my journey, each contributing in their own way.

And as I continue to think about it, the same realization starts to seep into other areas of my life. The friends and mentors who support me aren't just individuals who come and go. They are part of a larger network, a team that supports and uplifts me. It's time to embrace that, to truly see the value in the connections I have, and to recognize that building a team isn't just about hiring people; it's about valuing and appreciating those who are already a part of my life's work.

In the end, this isn't just about scaling my business. It's about scaling my understanding of what a team can be. It's about embracing the support and contributions of those around me and recognizing that this is what will help me reach my goals. This is what will help me build a legacy.

I close my journal, feeling a renewed sense of clarity. The weight of Anxiety and Overwhelm has lifted, replaced by a sense of hope and possibility. The journey ahead is still daunting, but now, it feels manageable, grounded in the support of those who believe in the vision as much as I do. And that's something worth embracing.

I look forward to getting this work done.

CHAPTER 13

BOOKS, BULLETS, AND BABIES

JULY 2021

After a few missed doctors' appointments and one rescheduled operation date due to testing positive for COVID-19 two months prior, Prodigal finally had a confirmed date for his hip replacement surgery. June 29 would be the day he'd go under the knife for the very first time in his forty-two years on this earth. He had so much anxiety. For days, he scanned YouTube, watching different videos of the procedure he understood would be the one he'd be experiencing.

Day after day, I watched him at the dinner table, his eyes glued to the flickering light of surgery videos on his phone. The dim glow cast shadows across his tense face, and his fingers drummed anxiously on the worn wood, creating a soft, rhythmic tap that echoed through the otherwise silent room. "I can't believe they cut into you like this," he muttered, his hand pausing mid-tap, the words barely louder than a whisper. His voice sounded angry and annoyed, but I knew it was really fear breaking through. The Quiet One would've kept his thoughts locked away, but Prodigal needed to voice them, to share the burden. His fears mirrored my own, though neither of us dared to say it out loud. I could almost feel the tension in the air, the unspoken worries swirling between us like a heavy fog.

"I've been watching these videos, and it's just … it's terrifying, you know?" Prodigal said, his voice tinged with panic. "FUCK!" he'd say suddenly, his voice loud and full of frustration. "They're gonna cut into me, open me up. What if something goes wrong?"

"I get it. But you've got this, and you've got the best doctors. You'll come out of this able to walk and be back to your old, scandalous self," I said, laughing but half serious.

"I'm scared that I'm not gonna wake up," he confessed. "There's history in my family—folks put under in hospitals who never woke up. Just the whole idea of going under, knowing that they're about to open up my body ... It scares me. This is just a lot," he hesitated as if trying to find the words. "It's a lot of stress."

"I understand everything you're saying. But let me ask you this. You're counting all the people who didn't get up from surgery. What about all the people who did? Will you consider counting them?" I responded, trying to ease his mind.

"I don't know," he sighed. "It just seems like every time someone changes their life and starts doing the right thing, they die. I ain't lying. But more than that, I just haven't been a good person. I gotta keep it real with myself. Knowing that I haven't been a good person ... I'm afraid I'll go under and not come back up. All the things I've been through, put myself through, and put other people through. I haven't always been a good person to the women I've been with. I've been absent from a large part of my older kids' lives. So yeah, this surgery is making me come to terms with a lot of things. I have a lot of fear and anxiety about it. With the life I've lived, I'm not sure if I'm gonna wake up from underneath."

His words hung in the air, heavy with the burden of his past. I felt a chill run down my spine as his fears resonated with something deep inside me. Here I am, encouraging him to have this surgery. What if he does, and then he dies? Then what? I don't want that on my conscience. But I couldn't dwell on that fear. We had to keep moving forward, one step at a time.

Remember my existential crisis that had me masturbating in a hotel for weeks? I kept saying that one of the biggest reasons for my crisis was that people kept dying. Well, I didn't share that part of what ended my orgasm project was that Prodigal's brother died. From Mother's Day to around Father's Day, seven people had died. And his brother was the seventh one. We don't really know how it happened. Rumor has it a woman killed him. According to that rumor, she was cheating. He was close to finding out. So she put fentanyl in his Hennessy. He called Prodigal about a headache he had. After that, he was dead.

Not long after his death, Prodigal's brother was buried. It was June 18, the day before Father's Day. We had gotten up early to prepare for the service. By prepare, I mean we began the work of making the living brother presentable enough to say his last goodbyes to the one who had passed away.

Up until that point, Prodigal, with all that he was going through, hadn't had his hair cut in months. He had a thick, beautiful mane, the kind of hair that made you wonder if he was Dominican, Cuban, or some other type of Afro-Latino. His features were clearly Black—with his broad nose and chocolate skin—but his hair, full and beautiful like a lot of Black people's hair, had a hint of something else to it. Like the hair on his head, his beard was also full and shiny, rich and lustrous.

Like fresh spring grass, hair grew wildly from his head, down his neck, and from his face. Even though he made it a point to rake a pick through it every day, his struggle still showed. It showed in the unevenness of his antebellum-like 'fro; it showed in the few clean outfits that he rotated several times a week. It showed in his face, hardened by all that he was going through.

That morning, we were going to get him presentable and cleaned up enough so that he could walk to the front of wherever he'd have to go to say "until later" to his brother. It was bad enough that he was hurting—he didn't need to look like his pain.

We discussed where he'd go to buy his outfit. He talked about a store he often walked past when he arrived in Madison twenty-four years ago. At the time, he was eighteen and wasn't yet in a position to afford the clothes he admired from the window: the Stacy Adams shoes and the jeans that seemed to fit just right. That morning, we decided that he'd visit that store on State Street, and for the first time, he'd go in and buy an outfit that was once outside of his price range.

We entered the store hesitantly, the bell above the door jangling in a cheerful contrast to the weight we carried. Immediately, we were hyper-aware of how out of place we were—the only Black folks in the room. The air was filled with the quiet chaos of conversation, customers chatting about the Badgers and sports, as if nothing more serious existed beyond the glass doors. An older white woman caught my eye, her shoulder-length hair swaying as she adjusted a pearl necklace that gleamed under the store's soft lighting. She was dressed in what looked like a tennis skirt, her arm hooked through the large cloth handles of an even larger shopping bag. The way she sipped from her fountain drink, oblivious to us, made it clear this wasn't her first stop of the day—just another leisurely errand on a carefree Saturday. But Prodigal, being Prodigal, wouldn't let our discomfort win. He took a deep breath, straightened his back, and stepped farther into the store, his presence commanding attention even in this unfamiliar, uncomfortable space.

"Excuse me," he said to a tall, well-dressed, slender white man. "Can you help me?"

The man came over to him, but Prodigal invited him closer. Within seconds, the two men were in a huddle, talking quietly, Prodigal speaking and the older white man listening.

"I'm here because my brother passed away, and his funeral is today," Prodigal said evenly. As if forcing himself to speak, he continued, "And I wasn't gonna go at first. But I know I have to go, and now I'm here to get an outfit for today. I think my aim is just to look casual but nice."

The tall, well-dressed, slender white man looked at Prodigal and said, "I'm sorry about your loss. My condolences." Understanding what he needed to do next, he got to work.

The man moved purposefully, with Prodigal following behind. Both had tuned everyone else out. It was all about Prodigal—the man with the uneven afro and the worn-out, somewhat faded clothes. He was following the older white man, who led him to different parts of the store, pulling items from racks and shelves, offering what seemed to be a shopping experience exclusively for Prodigal.

Before long, I noticed the woman with the pearls and the shopping bag hanging from her arm watching Prodigal. I noticed the other shoppers looking. Yet, even in this white space where we were the only Blacks, everyone seemed to have understood the significance of this day and why it needed to be about Prodigal in this moment. They were polite, nodding as if saying, "My condolences."

I don't know how he did it, but he managed to turn a store full of strangers into a space full of supporters and allies. The man with the uneven afro and the worn-out clothes had found a way to get everyone on his side—to notice and see him.

When Prodigal made it to the counter, we discovered that the older white man who had been guiding him throughout his shopping experience was the store owner. This time, he initiated the huddle, inviting Prodigal to lean in. Listening intently, Prodigal looked up, somewhat emotional but composed, and nodded to the man. The man nodded back with a genuine look of understanding on his face.

A woman stood next to the owner on the other side of the counter. She rang up the items as Prodigal stepped away to choose a pair of sunglasses. The total price of a pair of pants, a shirt, and shoes came in at over $500. Prodigal returned with the glasses, but the lady intentionally didn't include those in the total. The items were paid for, and we left with sunglasses, a blue short-sleeved button-up shirt, straight-leg dark blue jeans, and a pair of brown, vintage color, laced Stacy Adams shoes.

It was strange how, even in his grief, he managed to make room for a little bit of pride—to stand a little bit taller from purchasing those three new items. It was time for a haircut.

It was Juneteenth, and a parade blocked off Park Street. I was able to drop

Prodigal off at the barbershop, but instead of turning around and driving back home, I had to keep going straight to get on the expressway because of the parade that was about to take place. Somewhere between his having to wait in a line of chairs filled with other people who had made prior appointments and me finding my way back to him around the parade, at least two hours had passed before I made it back to him.

When Prodigal stepped out of the barbershop, it was like a veil had been lifted. The fresh scent of barber talc clung to the air as he emerged, his hair now cut tight and even, the close taper on the sides and back giving him a crisp, clean look. His goatee and beard had been neatly trimmed, and the rough edges smoothed out so that they framed his jawline with a sharp, defined precision. He paused for a moment, adjusting the new aviator glasses that sat perfectly on his nose, hiding the tired, tear-hardened lines beneath them. He caught his reflection in the shop's window for a second—a man transformed, ready to face the world despite the pain lurking beneath the surface. The transformation was subtle but profound, a silent statement of control during chaos.

We drove home, he showered, put on his new clothes, and we were off to the funeral.

As we pulled up to the funeral home, the gravity of the day pressed down on us with an almost tangible force. The air was thick with the cloying scent of fresh flowers, their sweetness a jarring contrast to the heavy grief that hung like a cloud over the small building. Inside, the muffled sound of quiet sobs filled the space, blending with the low murmur of hushed conversations. A beautiful, brown-skinned woman with a big, full afro approached us. Though there was no evidence that she had been crying, her face bore an astonishing balance of strength, pain, and a calm weariness.

"The service … it was supposed to be streamed, but I don't know how," she whispered, her voice cracking under the strain. Before I knew it, I was ushered to a small table at the back. The outdated computer screen looked heavy and counterintuitive to manage. My hands trembled as I tried to navigate the setup, the keys sticky from the juice left on my fingers from the orange I ate on the car ride over. In the screen's reflection, I caught a glimpse of myself—disheveled, unshowered, and yet somehow tasked with immortalizing this painful moment.

I glanced over at Prodigal, who stood still, staring at his brother's lifeless form. It was bad enough that the man was dead, but his body wasn't in a casket. He lay on a gurney, covered by a quilt, with a sign that read, "DO NOT TOUCH. THIS BODY HAS NOT BEEN EMBALMED. YOUR FINGERS WILL GO THROUGH." Between his brother and us was a stanchion—the kind you see at the movie theater or in line at a bank, with metal posts and a red velvet rope—meant to keep people away or to flow in the right direction. This setup was clearly intended to keep people from accidentally coming too close to the body.

We were so confused and had so many questions. For instance, why had we been told everything was covered and that the only remaining expense was his suit, which we paid for? The room, the service, the day—it all felt surreal, like we were drifting through a nightmare, or worse, some kind of dark comedy that had lost its punchline.

Sitting in the back of the room, I watched Prodigal watch his brother, taking in the bizarre circumstances. There was no falling out, no screaming—just an uncomfortable, awkward look on his face, full of disbelief, as if he were somewhere he didn't want to be but had to be. He didn't linger. As far as I could tell, he refused to look at his brother again, spending most of his time outside the building.

The funeral ended, we left and quickly transitioned to parent mode. Prodigal, wanting to put the events of the day behind him, or at least bury it deep within him, focused on Cho and everything we needed to get him ready for his basketball tournament in Milwaukee. He needed someone to drive him and a few friends there. I was too tired to do so, but Prodigal volunteered. We gathered the children who were under seventeen in our home, loaded them in the van, along with Cho and his friends, and drove close to two hours away to a different city.

The hotel lobby buzzed with teenage boys' excitement, their energy filling the space as they signified with each other, laughed, and recounted the highlights of their last game. I watched from the side, the hum of their voices mixing with the clatter of suitcases being wheeled across the polished floor. My family and I had checked into three rooms: one for me, Layden, and Prodigal; one for Ryland and Brooklyn; and another for Cho and his friends.

As we were settling in, Cho received a text message from his teammates, letting him know which restaurant they were heading to for dinner. Once we had all chosen our beds, unpacked our bags, and flipped through the channels on the television, we gathered in my and Prodigal's room to discuss whether to join the team for dinner. It was a quick decision—we all agreed to go.

When we arrived at the restaurant, it was clear that Cho's coach, a short nineteen-year-old with onyx skin and baby locs, was overwhelmed. He looked frustrated, and it didn't take long to figure out why. He was in over his head, trying to coach a group of young men not much younger than himself, and he didn't have the funds to cover the hotel rooms for the ten-plus players he had inspired to come to Milwaukee on faith.

Seeing his distress, I pulled Prodigal aside and quietly discussed how he felt about us sponsoring the rooms for Cho's teammates and their coach. He didn't hesitate, nodding in agreement. "It's important for Cho and the boys to have this experience," he said, his voice steady with conviction. That was all I needed to hear.

Despite my usual anxiety—the fear of losing sight of my children in a crowd or being caught in a situation I couldn't control—I felt different tonight. Prodigal's calm presence and unwavering support put me at ease, and for the first time, I felt truly involved in one of Cho's big moments.

"Mom, look at this!" Cho's voice cut through my thoughts as he bounded over, holding up the keycard to his room like a trophy. His excitement was contagious, and I couldn't help but smile, some of the tension easing from my shoulders.

"That's awesome, Cho," I replied, hugging him. "Make sure you don't lose it, okay?"

"Don't worry, I've got it under control," he said with a grin, dashing back to his friends, who were already planning their evening.

After we had all settled into the restaurant, I noticed how seamlessly Prodigal supported everything, making sure each player had what they needed, keeping the conversation light and fun, and ensuring that I didn't feel overwhelmed. It was a simple act, but it meant everything to me.

The boys wasted no time diving into the menu, and soon the table was filled with plates of burgers, fries, and pizzas. I watched as Cho laughed with his teammates, his face lighting up in a way that made my heart swell. For once, I wasn't consumed by the usual worries. Prodigal's steady presence allowed me to enjoy the moment, to be present with my son in a way I hadn't been able to before.

As the evening wore on, I found myself relaxing more, joining in the conversation, sharing in the laughter. When the bill came, I covered it without hesitation, knowing this moment was worth every penny.

The next day, they played well but not well enough to win the tournament. Disappointed and frustrated, the boys went back to the hotel, packed their things, and got ready to head back to Madison, with a few of the young men staying behind for a meal and waiting for permission from this teammate or that teammate's parent to drive them back. Noticing that some of his teammates weren't eating, Cho asked me if we could buy their lunch. I agreed, and we did.

This was one of the few times I was present in Cho's—or any of my children's—athletic lives. I hadn't been involved much before, but Prodigal insisted I show up for this tournament. As I looked at Cho, laughing and happy, I was grateful to be there. I knew that this was a memory he would carry with him, and so would I.

The next day, I was scheduled to see the property I hoped to buy. This was my second visit. I took Prodigal and Layden, the child we shared. This visit was meant to include all the children still living in the home with us. But we didn't wake up in time to get everyone dressed and ready. Of course, they could dress themselves. However, I didn't trust that they'd look presentable. So I chose to leave them behind.

Before then, Prodigal and I didn't talk much about the home. The whole thing was new to me. The entire process was so overwhelming, and everything was happening so quickly that I didn't know how to talk to him about it. On the drive over that morning, I don't remember what we discussed or if we talked about anything except small talk.

"I wish the kids were able to come see the place. But we woke up too late to get them ready. You know, they've only seen it online but never in person," I said, trying to fill the silence.

"Aw, yeah?" he asked, playing it cool but also trying to mask his own discomfort about what he was walking into.

"Yeah," I said. "I came without them the first time." What I really wanted to say is that the Quiet One did a video call with me as we viewed the house together for the very first time.

We arrived. Layden jumped out of the car to greet Ruby, and she bent over to his height and welcomed him.

Ruby had no idea what was going on, yet she didn't miss a beat. She knew I had been with Prodigal, was engaged to the Quiet One, and now I was showing up, without warning, with Prodigal by my side. But Ruby, ever the consummate professional, jumped right into real estate agent mode. She greeted Prodigal with the same warm, welcoming smile she had given me and the Quiet One just a month earlier, as if we were all part of the same extended family. As she led us through the house, pointing out details I'd already seen, I watched Prodigal run his hand along the smooth wooden banister, his touch tentative, as if trying to feel out the place, trying to avoid imagining life here. Ruby's calm, fun presence filled the space, easing the awkwardness between us. She didn't pry, didn't judge—just guided us through each room with the practiced ease of someone who had seen it all. She behaved as if this was the most natural thing in the world, even if it felt like a delicate balancing act to us.

In my mind, I was trying to understand who made more sense in this space.

With the Quiet One, I imagined this home as a refuge for him, a space to take him away from it all and for him to recover and heal. But with Prodigal, I saw someone who was comfortable taking care of and managing the property—a person with so much energy, someone who has to always be fixing, tinkering, learning, and figuring out how to maintain the space I hoped could be home.

I see the Quiet One playing and laughing with the kids, but I don't see him picking up a shovel. I see Prodigal managing the snow, caring for the kids, handling transportation for everyone. I see a comparatively easier life with him, in part because he has been on this journey with me in ways that the Quiet One hasn't. Regardless of what we've gone through, he knows my life, my ambitions. He knows my love language is acts of service, and as someone who naturally has to do, do, do, it just makes sense.

But then I think about both fathers and the role this house will play in their redemption and healing of the relationships with their kids. For the Quiet One, it will be the kids he denied before he went to jail. Part of coming home for him means having a safe space to mend those relationships.

"Man," the Quiet One had said, thinking over his absence from the lives of kids he once denied, "I know I was bogus for that. And only time is going to fix it. But you know that's what I'm on when I get home, bringing together all of my kids. That's all I think about in here."

And then there's Prodigal. Between the two of us, there are twenty-one children. Because our relationship was riddled with so much drama and toxicity, my children have only met two of them outside of the son he and I share together. Throughout our seven years as a couple, I always talked about buying a house big enough to blend the families adequately. I wonder if he imagines that happening here.

Ruby didn't skip a beat. She laughed with him, and they talked about the landscape together, as if he was a potential buyer or my partner or support for me. Somehow, she managed to find a sweet spot that melded together all of those possibilities without making it awkward or making me feel judged as the woman caught in some weird triangle that even I didn't understand.

As we left that day, I couldn't help but ask him, "So, what do you think?"

Prodigal looked around, his eyes lingering on the house as if trying to memorize every detail before responding. "It's nice. I think this is good for you and the kids. You worked for it. Y'all deserve this." I knew him well. I could hear him trying to be a good sport. For seven years, he'd watched me dream and talk about one day moving into a home just like this. We'd been broken up for two years, and now I was on the cusp of making that dream real. I knew that deep down, he was probably sick about the possibility of someone else fulfilling that dream with me, standing in the place he felt he should be in. At the same time, I heard that he was genuinely happy.

The weekend was over, and I had to get back to work. If I wanted to generate enough dollars to buy that home, maintain it, and care for my family, I was going to have to scale my business. And I had to do it in a way that didn't feel desperate or forced. It had to be thoughtful and considerate of all the segments of people I do business with and attract. It also had to add real value to people's lives.

I was already working on Covet, a health and wellness journal that I was creating for IMpreneurs (infamous mothers who are entrepreneurs). I wanted to create something that allowed women to think about their wealth alongside their health, and I wanted this thing—whatever it would be—to cost next to nothing or nothing at all, at the same time offering high value. I can't stand it when entrepreneurs lure me in with a "free" gift that is flimsy and weak. Not only is it insulting, but it feels desperate and dishonest. It makes me feel like they just threw anything at me to get my attention so they could bombard and pressure me to buy their service, program, or item.

That's not what I wanted my relationship with my future customers, clients, or members to feel like. I wanted to create an experience for them, offer solutions for things they'd been praying about, and start conversations that made them think. I wanted to inspire them. After all of that, if they chose to invest in themselves by purchasing a course, workshop, or item from the Infamous Mothers brand, it would be because they trusted our work and understood that they were more than a transaction to us. They were part of a larger movement, a mission to make the world better by helping them grow their own power.

I decided that it was time to create that podcast I had been thinking about and tinkering with since I created the Infamous Mothers brand.

For days, the words *books, bullets, and babies* echoed in my mind, a mantra I couldn't escape. *Books, bullets, and babies. Books, bullets, and babies.* I repeated them over and over again, each time trying to tease out their relevance to my current life. I sat at the kitchen table, my notebook open, fingers wrapped around a mug of tea that grew cold as I wrestled with the thoughts swirling in my head.

I flipped through old journals, jotting down ideas, comparing them to the present, trying to connect the dots between who I was then and who I am now. The repetition of those three words became a rhythm, a heartbeat of sorts, guiding me to uncover what lay beneath the surface of my daily responsibilities. The more I wrote, the more the words started to make sense, revealing the juggling act I was still performing, even if the players had changed.

And then, one day, after all the reflecting and writing and decoding, it came to me—a very basic idea became apparent. *Books, Bullets, and Babies* is about juggling competing and sometimes contradictory responsibilities. If I were going to host a podcast by that name, it would have to be about doing just that. Although I was no longer managing those three things, I was still juggling things that didn't make sense together.

Having completed my PhD in 2019, I was now a full-time entrepreneur, mothering six kids as a single mom. That's not how one would describe the typical business owner. We often imagine them to look like Mark Zuckerberg, Steve Jobs, or Elon Musk. And yet, there my Black ass was, trying to grow a brand and build not only a company but a movement. People often don't associate women, especially mothers, with business because of the risk involved. Business is very risky. Mothers are nurturers, protectors, and the way our society understands it, we should be risk-averse.

The way that I understood it was that I was taking more of a risk by not charting my own path as a business owner, as I needed to earn a living that accommodated my responsibilities. A professor's salary for someone with one or two or three kids was nice, especially with another income to add to it. For me, however, I realized that it would be more than a stretch trying to send folks to college, buy a home, pay for food, purchase clothes, etc., for so many people on $60,000 to $80,000 per year.

It was more of a risk for me to stay in a traditional career, locked into a salary that wouldn't grow with my needs. I also understood that as a mom, I was supposed to be all about the home and self-sacrifice. I was supposed to be about service, not profit. I had come from a family of women who dedicated their lives to nonprofit work. I watched them make a difference in the community. They helped people keep their homes or fought for voters' rights. I watched them do all of the things that people admired and applauded. And I watched them come home at the end of the day fulfilled, excited, and proud of the work they had done. I was proud. So proud, in fact, that I wanted to start a nonprofit called Capable Women, inspired by the Bible's Proverbs 31 woman.

Two things deterred me. First, it was the control nonprofit boards had that I couldn't quite submit to. For years, I had been following an organization that I really admired. It was created in response to women in police custody birthing children while being handcuffed to beds. I had never heard of this phenomenon, and I wanted to keep an eye on it, as I knew it was relevant to my work. One day, I came across an article that featured the organization's founder. It explained that her board had ousted her from the very organization that she had founded. I imagined myself being fired from a place I built from the ground up, a place that would exist only because of my vision, a place that would be a culmination of my life's work, just to be taken away for whatever reason. No, ma'am. I couldn't let that be my story.

The second reason I didn't want to start a nonprofit was because, quite frankly, I wanted to earn a profit. Without exploiting others, I wanted to make as much money as I could because I had lived so long in poverty. And it was because I had lived so long in poverty that I needed to create a business model that benefited people beyond me. I wanted to be on the other side of philanthropy, writing the checks to causes that I cared about. I had witnessed how organizations that I loved competed for grant dollars, turning people who should've been allies into enemies. I also noticed that people writing the checks often didn't look like me, and I wondered what difference I could help make if I could put dollars behind the causes that directly affected me and people who looked like me with similar experiences. No, I wouldn't be starting a nonprofit. I would be starting a company, juggling all the things that people associate with men—managing money, taking risks, being in the public. And I would also be raising my kids, juggling all the things people associated with being a mother: children, the private sphere, self-sacrifice, faith, and the home. I was doing all of this while also trying to manage my health and love. These had become my new *Books, Bullets, and Babies*.

The idea of this crazy juggling act was something beyond the idea of dreaming and doing the impossible. This was a whole new level of inconceivable. It was the kind of crazy you see when a person rides a unicycle while juggling fire. The two don't go together, but more than that, they shouldn't be together. They're a dangerous combination, and not in a "dangerous as good" kind of way. At least, that is how some people would see it. But I was a writer. For years, before I became comfortable with writing prose, I was a poet. And poetry often puts together things that shouldn't be together to create something completely different.

Early on, I learned the value of metaphors. A metaphor is defined as "a direct and vivid comparison between two things usually considered distinct or unrelated. Metaphors discover the connections between unique things and emphasize their similarities poetically without being taken literally." Metaphors are about bringing together two unrelated things to emphasize their similarities. Except, unlike metaphors, I needed this marriage of unlikely concepts and identities to be taken literally.

For example, I intentionally brought together two terms that were unrelated within the context of our society—*infamous mothers* and *millionaires*—when I started working on the question for season one: Can the women we call infamous mothers become millionaires? And yet, like metaphors, I also understood that doing so would create something new in the mind. Yes, people who failed to see the poetry and needed to focus only on the realities they understood to be fact wouldn't get it. They wouldn't see the beauty or the emotion pairing these two together. In fact, some would be downright offended because the very idea messed with their understanding of who could be what in this world. But the more imaginative would ask questions. They would wonder, why not? They would interrogate their own biases, they would examine the meaning of it, and if they were really adventurous, they would wonder how to move beyond poetry, creating a society where it's normal for these two terms to come together as a way to point out someone real.

I both loved and was intrigued by the concept. What would be our process? How would we do this thing, from start to finish? I reached out to Nina to add this to our list of projects. She agreed and became the videographer and producer for *Books, Bullets, and Babies*. I explained to her my concept for the show and shared with her the question I was trying to explore. She didn't cringe or turn me down as I began to explain my idea. Instead, her only real feedback was that we'd have to come to Atlanta.

Because of COVID-19, the places we'd normally record something like this weren't available, so we'd have to go to Georgia. But what was that going to look like? How was that going to happen?

We had planned for me to be in Atlanta in June of 2021. But between dealing with overcoming COVID-19 in April of that year and struggling with the seven deaths between Mother's Day and Father's Day—the losses that dragged me to the existential crisis—June seemed to have had plans of its own.

Why go through the trouble of buying a home? Why produce this podcast? Why write these books? We're all going to die. I know, depressing, right? In my defense, I was going through it. And if all of this wasn't enough, Prodigal would be having surgery, getting his hip replaced on June 29. Between anxiety about the possibility of long-haul COVID-19, a bunch of unexpected deaths, Prodigal having to bury his brother, both of our battles with depression, and a surgery, my June was booked. I would not be traveling to Atlanta that month.

Instead, the producer and I would plan out as many of the details as possible in June so that July would be a more than reasonable time to pack my family up in our van and drive to Atlanta—all of us seeing it for the first time.

In the past, I didn't understand the importance of planning the details of photo and video shoots. I thought it was enough to look nice, show up, and smile. I thought it was enough to be able to talk about a given subject. It never occurred to me that building content for a brand wasn't like picture day in elementary school.

It required so much more. It required organization and foresight. It required an understanding of how these smaller pieces would fit into or serve a larger initiative or message. It required me to create sceneries and ambiance. Wardrobe mattered. Props mattered. Hair and makeup mattered. I had learned those lessons the hard way.

Once, a major newspaper interviewed me and insisted on using their own photographer versus using the images Chris, our photographer, had taken. The outcome? I looked like a mammy on somebody's plantation. The light was too harsh against my skin; in fact, the entire image represented me as harsh, asexual, and old. I would've accepted that reflection as my truth had I not experienced something different with Chris, a photographer who knew how to capture the beauty of darker skin, or Nina, the videographer who somehow made my skin bronze and beautiful through her video shoots. I had no idea how she did it, but I always felt seen through her work.

With both of them, I walked away seeing myself in ways the world hadn't reflected back to me. And so, with those experiences and that knowledge, I learned the importance of planning. The *Books, Bullets, and Babies* podcast was no different.

There was so much work to be done before showing up. Planning episodes, choosing guests, booking studio time, pulling together wardrobe, getting hair braided, and creating makeup looks. We had to create show segments, plan for show notes, design a logo, choose books, and gather props. June was about doing all of that. I didn't want to wing it in Atlanta. I had winged it too many times before. Freezing in front of a camera because I didn't have an answer to some key question for an ad I was creating for my own company. Wearing an outfit and offering a look that communicated something in direct opposition to the message I was trying to convey.

No, I was not going to waste time and money on not showing up prepared. I needed to come up with a better plan and a clearer vision. June's work in Madison was going to ensure that July's work in Atlanta was not going to be about winging it. It would be about the beautiful execution of a well-thought-out and organized plan. And so, that's what we did. Sometimes I would plan and dream with our videographer on my two-hour-long walks. Other times, I would imagine and think alone. I would take notes on my phone and then circle right back to my videographer. I needed her to see everything that I saw from every angle that I saw it.

And she would deliver. Every step of the way, she understood, changing sets from the one she imagined to the one that I imagined. She was in my head. She saw my vision, so much so that she was able to help me refine and tweak it until it was better than even I had imagined it. Before I knew it, July had come, and we were ready—at least, we were ready enough to get on the road.

On Sunday, July 11, 2021, just past noon, Prodigal and I loaded up my van with our children, luggage, and snacks and headed to Atlanta with Google Maps leading the way. We were supposed to leave Friday or Saturday, but somewhere between managing teenagers and their attitudes, packing, and the lack of sleep that comes with doing last-minute work, wild, full of excitement and anxiety, we got on the road later than expected.

The van rumbled along the highway, the steady drone of tires on asphalt creating a monotonous backdrop to our tense silence. The sun beat down through the windows, casting sharp, almost harsh shadows across the dashboard. Inside the van, the air was hot and filled with the scent of road trip essentials—salty chips, sweet soda, and the faint, lingering tang of sweat from too many bodies in too small a space. Prodigal reached for the radio, his hand hovering for a moment as if unsure, before finally settling on a station playing old R&B. The familiar melodies of Marvin Gaye and Al Green drifted through the van, their soothing harmonies a welcome balm to our frayed nerves. I caught a glimpse of the kids in the rearview mirror, each lost in their own world, headphones on, staring out at the endless fields that blurred into a green and gold tapestry outside. Occasionally, the landscape was interrupted by a lone barn or a cluster of trees, but mostly, it was just miles and miles of the same. I kept my eyes fixed on the road ahead, but my mind was miles away, wandering through the days to come, the challenges that lay waiting in the heat of Atlanta. "You think this is gonna work out?" Prodigal's voice broke through my thoughts, low and filled with uncertainty.

I glanced at him, his face half-lit by the golden sunlight, and nodded, offering a small, reassuring smile. "We've come this far. We'll make it work." But as the miles stretched on, so did the gnawing doubt at the back of my mind, a quiet, persistent whisper that refused to be ignored.

CHAPTER 14

MORE BOOKS, BULLETS, AND BABIES

JULY 2021

Before leaving for Atlanta, I had taken my taxes to the bank, written a letter of intent, and put in an offer for the house. Things were getting real, and now, more than ever, my family was depending on my business to succeed. Everything was riding on my ability to make it work. And this road trip would be crucial in determining whether we would sink or swim. But the Atlanta trip came with its own set of books, bullets, and babies: family drama, balancing my work with a botched attempt at a family vacation, building the foundation of Infamous Mothers 3.0 while also making good on promises I made to my sponsors, and trying to stay in contact with and be responsive to my real estate agent about the house. Everything was time-specific and critical. One wrong move, one missed step, and the whole tower would come crashing down like a game of Jenga. I wasn't about to let that happen, and yet we hadn't even made it to Atlanta, and things were already so uncertain.

My family and I were accustomed to taking road trips. We'd traveled from Madison to Chicago countless times. The kids and I traveled to Chicago every weekend for the first three years we lived in Madison. We've traveled dozens of times from Madison to the Twin Cities for conferences and to visit friends and family. These trips were between two and a half to four hours, respectively. But driving the family to Atlanta? That was a twelve-hour and nineteen-minute drive, according to the GPS. Except for the two times in my life that I'd driven to Texas—one about fifteen years prior and the other two years prior—I had never driven that long with five children ranging from six to seventeen years old.

There was that time my entire family had gone to Shreveport, Louisiana, for my aunt Pudding's funeral. But this would be different. I would be the elder, the person in charge of this journey—not my aunts or my older cousins. And I would be solely responsible for all the driving. If we left at five o'clock in the morning, we'd be there by a little after five o'clock that afternoon, meaning most of the drive would happen during the day when the sun was out. But we're not a five-in-the-morning kind of family. We left sometime in the late afternoon or early evening, meaning we'd arrive early in the morning. This meant we wouldn't be driving straight there on dark, unfamiliar roads, and we'd have to get a hotel somewhere along the way.

As if that wasn't enough to throw off our ETA, there was Prodigal's recent surgery to consider. It had barely been seven days since they'd replaced his hip, and the instructions from the doctor were clear: He had to stop every hour to stretch his legs; otherwise, he risked getting blood clots. With those two factors alone, a twelve-hour trip quickly morphed into a twenty-four-hour one.

Our eight-passenger, 2017 silver Toyota Sienna was packed to the brim, the scent of worn leather mixing with the faint odor of spilled juice and leftover fast food. What space the humans didn't take up, the luggage did. Suitcases were crammed into the trunk, their zippers straining against the fabric. Backpacks and gym bags stuffed with technology and clothes were wedged between seats, the smell of unwashed clothes mingling with the sweetness of half-eaten snacks. Shoeboxes balanced awkwardly on the headrests in the third row, teetering with every turn, while a cooler of snacks with half-melted cheese sticks, cold soda cans, and fruit slices sat between the seats, within easy reach of small hands. The floors were littered with random items like t-shirts, candy wrappers, and socks that had been hastily thrown in during our last-minute packing frenzy. It was a tight fit, and with tight fits and a car full of anxious, excited, and later tired kids, that meant hours of nonstop arguing, bathroom breaks, and complaining. The sound of bickering voices echoed off the windows, the space too small to escape from each other.

Not to mention, I was worried about Prodigal. I hadn't traveled that far with someone fresh out of surgery before, and he had never had surgery, so neither of us knew what to expect or how to manage his care. The questions swirled in my mind, relentless and nagging. Did we have to stop precisely every sixty minutes, or did we have some leeway? How would we know if he had a blood clot? Would there be pain? Sudden death? Would his skin turn blue first? The thought of it all sent a shiver down my spine. What had I gotten myself into, traveling to another part of the country with this unpredictable brew of people I call my family?

Our energy was everywhere; an ADHD/ADD family cramped into one space was a recipe for chaos and frustration. The kids' voices overlapped, their energy bouncing off the van's walls, making it hard to think straight. But music always centered us. My children, Prodigal, and I are all riders. We love being in the car, the hum of the road beneath us, and we love music—the rhythm and beat soothing the chaos in our minds. So, to bring order and some comfort to all of us, I kept our favorite songs on rotation, the familiar melodies filling the car and helping to calm the storm. And when the favorites ran out, I took requests, their excited voices shouting out song titles as I scrolled through playlists.

We drove from Madison through Illinois, the landscape flattening out as we passed endless fields, the giant windmills turning lazily in the distance, their blades cutting through the air with a faint whoosh. Cows dotted the fields, their heads bowed as they grazed, oblivious to the cars speeding by. When we got tired, we pulled off the highway and stopped at a hotel in southern Illinois, the air outside cool and refreshing after the stuffiness of the van. The beds were lumpy, and the room smelled faintly of bleach and stale cigarettes, but we were grateful for the chance to stretch out, to let our tired bodies rest. The next morning, we piled back into the van, bleary-eyed but determined, and started our playlist again, the familiar songs filling the space as we hit the road, the miles ticking away beneath us.

It was midday when we ended up in Paducah, Kentucky, where we stopped for snacks and gas. We swapped out our music with YouTube clips of pastors speaking about courage and purpose—whatever else we needed to hear to keep us focused, inspired, and positive as we traveled. Those words sustained us through the thunderstorms that came out of nowhere, the sky darkening to an ominous gray before unleashing sheets of blinding rain. The rhythmic thud of the windshield wipers barely kept up, and the roar of the rain against the roof was deafening. At one point, I would've seen this weather as a challenge, a test of my driving skills and nerves. But now, in my early forties, it made me understand why my aunts and uncles, who used to love driving, at different points in their lives, announced that they'd no longer be making those trips from Chicago to Madison. It was just too much for them. This trip made me feel my age. My nerves couldn't handle all the unpredictability—the weather, the stop-and-go traffic, and the sheer exhaustion that crept into my bones. By the time we reached Nashville,

I was frazzled—a shaken, hot mess.

Somewhere in Tennessee, hunger and fatigue got the best of us, and we decided to stop for brunch at a small roadside restaurant that served breakfast all day. The outside of the place looked weathered, with chipped paint and a faded sign that barely hinted at the name. As we pushed open the creaky door, the clatter of dishes and the low murmur of conversation stilled, replaced by a suffocating silence. The air inside was thick with the smell of fried food and something stale, like old grease that hadn't been changed in too long. The cook, a gaunt man with a stained apron and a few missing teeth, paused mid-sentence, his gaze narrowing as he looked us up and down. His eyes were hard, unwelcoming.

My son, Cho, who was seventeen at the time, was the first to venture inside. He barely made it a few steps before he turned around and walked out, his face tight with discomfort.

"Man, dude looked at me and was like, 'Y'all lookin' to eat here?' But the whole time, he had a loogie he was working up from his throat. Naw, man, I'm good," Cho reported back, his voice laced with disgust.

With that, all of us were good. We stood outside, the sun beating down on us, processing what had just happened. The tension was thick, a silent agreement among us that we weren't welcome there. As we debated our next move, two cars rolled up with Wisconsin plates. The doors opened, and two guys got out of one of the cars. They glanced around, taking in the scene, and before long, they were walking back out of the restaurant, looking just as uneasy as we felt. When I asked what made them leave so quickly, the one with gold and diamond grillz in his mouth said he didn't feel safe. There was something in his eyes that mirrored our own unease.

Prodigal asked him where he was from in Wisconsin. The man with the grillz told him he was from Milwaukee, which is right next to Madison. They bonded for a bit, their voices low and serious, sharing a moment of camaraderie in a place where neither of us felt entirely safe. Before long, we were back in our cars and pulling out of the lot, the unease still clinging to us like a bad smell. But before we parted ways, the people from Milwaukee told us where it was safe for us to eat, and that's where we went, grateful for the tip.

As I drove through the South, the sight of Confederate flags fluttering in the wind made my stomach churn, a visceral reminder of where we were. They weren't just symbols of history here; they were markers, staking a claim that felt hostile and intimidating. Northern racism, I mused, was so much more polite— smiles from neighbors who later sent the police for "wellness checks." But this was different. It was in your face, bold, and deep-rooted. Fear gnawed at me, a constant undercurrent, but so did determination. We had to make it to Atlanta. No stopping for food, no unnecessary breaks—just keep going until we reach our destination. My family agreed, their silence a testament to the tension we all felt. This wasn't just a road trip anymore; it felt like a test of our resilience, of how much we could endure.

After a few short hours, we made it to Atlanta. The air was thick with the humidity that comes before a summer storm, and within minutes of our arrival, I had gotten a text from our videographer with a YouTube link to Jermaine Dupri's song, "Welcome to Atlanta." It wasn't quite rush hour when we arrived, but the expressway was busy. The roads were a chaotic mess of cars speeding through the lines, sliding diagonally from one lane to another with little regard for order. We had survived the rainstorms; we had survived a potentially racist encounter; we had survived that long-ass travel in a packed car, but surely it would be the driving in Atlanta that was going to kill us. The roads twisted and turned, the GPS guiding us blindly as we made unexpected turns on a winding expressway. And yet, somehow, we survived that too, my knuckles white on the steering wheel, heart pounding in my chest.

We drove past signs that read "Tyler Perry Studios," and each time, my heart swelled with pride. Perry had purchased and turned an old U.S. Army military base into a film production campus. The thought of it filled me with a sense of possibility. I was proud because he was Black, but I was just as proud because he was a business owner who had come from very little, and I was inspired. The sight of those signs felt like a small victory, a reminder that success was possible, that we were all part of something bigger.

That was the thing about being in Atlanta—without effort, almost everyone I had done business with was Black. When we showed up to our Airbnb, the owners were Black. When we had our first meal, the restaurant owner was Black. When I showed up in the studio to shoot the first episode of the podcast, I met the owner—he was Black. And when we went to the peer space to shoot our ads for Infamous Mothers University and the Infamous Mothers campus, the owner of that space was also Black. None of this was intentional. That was the norm here, and it was both refreshing and empowering.

For the first time as a business owner, I didn't feel out of place. In Dane County, Wisconsin, where I live, I've heard there are over 5,000 nonprofits. I don't know how many Black-owned businesses are in Madison, but outside of hair salons, barbershops, a few restaurants, and CocoVaa Chocolatier (which, by the way, has the best chocolate in the world), successful Black brick-and-mortar locations are rare. Most of the Black women I know in Madison are offering free services to those living in poverty or to other disenfranchised groups. But I sell books, classes, workshops. I'm in the empowerment business, and I charge—sometimes a lot. In a city of nonprofits, being a for-profit business doesn't always sit well with me.

And yet, there is so much honor and dignity in being a business owner. We spend a lot of time talking about the wage gap, but research shows that successful entrepreneurship can be a major key to closing both the wealth and wage gaps for Black people, especially women. It's a pillar of wealth, right up there with homeownership and inheritance. Seeing thriving Black businesses in Atlanta affirmed that I might just be on the right path. In that way, Atlanta was truly inspiring.

The kids were yet to have their own experiences. Cho had his heart set on visiting a mall to explore what he described as one of the largest shoe stores in the country. Brooklyn, who was eleven, couldn't stop talking about going to a theme park and riding the go-karts, her excitement bubbling over like soda fizzing out of a freshly opened can. Layden's birthday was just around the corner—the day after we arrived, he was turning seven on July 13. The anticipation in the air was palpable. Everyone, especially the children, was buzzing with the expectation of a grand celebration. After all, we were in Atlanta! The city was alive with possibilities, and their wide-eyed excitement made me wish I could give them everything they were asking for. But the weight of balancing work with their vacation was like a stone in my chest, heavy and unyielding. I quickly regretted the promises I had made to them.

The thought of Prodigal driving them around didn't sit well with me—at least, not in our minds. We had taken a risk bringing him South, just seven days post-surgery. Now, we were considering putting him in charge of chauffeuring around a bunch of energetic kids in a city completely unfamiliar to us. His hip was still healing, and his body was a foreign landscape he was just beginning to navigate. The thought of him behind the wheel, stiff and aching, made my stomach churn.

I couldn't drive them around because I was buried in unexpectedly long hours of work. We had already arrived days later than planned. We were supposed to arrive on July 10, but the reality was we didn't hit the road until July 11, finally making it to Atlanta on Monday, July 12. My anxiety about not wanting to mess things up was like a tight band around my chest, making it hard to breathe. When I finally showed up at the studio, my perfectionism kicked into overdrive, and I became fixated on getting every detail just right. The props had to be perfect, the lighting had to hit just so, and the sound had to be flawless. Out of the twelve episodes we were shooting, three or four had no guests. Those solo episodes

A POT TO P*SS IN

meant the spotlight was solely on me, and we reshot the scenes multiple times to get everything just right. The pressure was suffocating because we had sponsors counting on us, and I wanted to make them proud. More than that, I wanted our listeners to find real value in what we were offering.

Each day, the hours in the studio stretched longer, and our videographer's patience, though steadfast, was wearing thin. As if that wasn't enough, every morning, I found myself paralyzed by the fear of messing up, which only made me show up hours late. I would obsess over the show notes, replaying the previous day's mistakes in my head like a broken record. Although I had meticulously picked out all my clothes in advance, I second-guessed every choice, wondering if I had made the right decisions. So much was riding on me getting this right— my reputation, future funding, downloads, followers, future business, and the Infamous Mothers community. I needed to nail this for the brand, for the movement we were hoping to build, and for scaling our company. In my mind, the success of this podcast was directly linked to whether I would be able to consistently pay the mortgage on the house I was hoping to get. I had placed so much unnecessary pressure on myself that I couldn't bring my head up long enough to even begin making good on the promises I had made to my kids. By the second or third day, everything came to a head, and our family erupted like a long-simmering volcano.

It was late afternoon, inching toward early evening, when Prodigal came to pick me up from the studio. Until that point, I had been driving myself from the East Point suburb where we were staying to the Atlanta location where we had been recording our episodes. The summer heat hung thick in the air, and the city seemed to hum with energy as we drove through the streets. On this particular day, Prodigal expressed the need for him and the kids to be more mobile, and move around as they needed so they could do simple things like go to the grocery store. I could sense the frustration in his voice, the need for some semblance of independence gnawing at him. I understood their point, and so I was okay with being dropped off.

That day, the videographer and I were both frustrated and overwhelmed with my constant fussing and whatever else was going on in our respective worlds, so we ended the day early. Prodigal and the kids picked me up, and the air conditioning in the van felt like a cool relief from the hot studio lights. We ran a few errands, the mundane tasks providing a temporary reprieve from the intensity of the week. But beneath the surface, the tension lingered, waiting for the next opportunity to rise.

To decompress, I sat in the car and listened to music. Neighbors walked by and noticed that I wasn't from there. One set of neighbors, a couple with a dog, talked about the history of the area, the owners of the Airbnb, places to eat and shop, etc. As the nice couple with the dog was about to walk away, Prodigal stepped out onto the porch, his face tense. "Sagashus," he called, his voice low but urgent, "you need to come in here and get the kids."

I sighed, feeling the weight of the day settle even heavier on my shoulders. "What's going on now?" I asked, already bracing myself for whatever awaited inside.

Prodigal shook his head, frustrated. "I told the younger kids, the smaller boys, they didn't have to clean up, and now Brooklyn's having a fit. She's talking back, and it's getting out of hand."

I could already hear Brooklyn's raised voice from inside the house, her tone sharp with frustration. As soon as I stepped through the door, I caught the tail end of her argument with Cho.

"Why are you acting like Prodigal? You're not even supposed to be in charge!" she snapped, glaring at him.

Cho bristled, his voice tight with anger. "Say that again, Brooklyn. I dare you."

"Since you want to act like this, you are acting like him!" Brooklyn shot back, her defiance rising with each word.

"Stop it, Brooklyn! You need to calm down!" Cho shouted, gritting his teeth as he held her back.

"No, you let me go! You're not in charge of me!" Brooklyn fought back, her eyes blazing with fury.

Their shouts filled the room, the tension thick and suffocating. Brooklyn grabbed a chair and hurled it across the space, narrowly missing Cho as he dodged to the side. Moving faster than I could react, Cho lunged, pinning her to the floor in a desperate attempt to stop her from causing more damage.

"That's enough! Both of you, stop it right now!" I rushed forward, my voice commanding, trying to bring an end to the chaos.

"Let me go!" Brooklyn struggled under Cho's grip, her voice filled with defiance.

"Not until you stop throwing things!" Cho countered, not budging an inch.

I stepped between them, my heart felt like it was being dragged to the ground from the gravity of it all. Prodigal stood helplessly off to the side, clearly in no condition to intervene. The room was a mess of emotions, and I knew something had to give.

"Cho, let her up," I said, my voice firm but weary. "Brooklyn, we don't solve problems by throwing things. You need to calm down."

Cho reluctantly released her, and she scrambled to her feet, still fuming. The room fell into an uneasy silence, the aftermath of their outburst hanging in the air. Brooklyn's eyes still burned with anger, but there was also a flicker of regret. Prodigal watched from the sidelines, frustration and helplessness etched on his face, knowing he couldn't step in like he wanted to.

I watched them retreat to their corners. Exhausted, I wondered how I was going to get through all of the work when they were fighting like this. I couldn't fight on two fronts: fight to get us a better life and fight to keep my home from falling apart. They knew the mission. We talked about this. They knew what it was. I expected them to do their parts. But maybe I was putting too much on them, expecting too much from them. They're kids. And they still needed a momma who would guide them. I got that. And, as rough as it sounded, they knew the assignment: chill and let me finish the mission. As my aunt always said, Little Tommy Tucker sang for his supper. This is what they're going to have to do for theirs: act right.

The tension in the Airbnb was thick, the air heavy with unspoken words and unresolved conflicts. When Aunt Business finally arrived, she didn't waste time with pleasantries. She took one look around, her eyes quickly assessing the situation. Without too many words, Brooklyn, Aunt Business, and I gathered in the car, and I dropped them off at a bed and breakfast inside the city.

With Brooklyn gone, the house felt different—emptier but also less charged. The kids retreated to their corners, and I finally had a moment to breathe. Prodigal was still flipping through channels, his presence a steady charge of uncertainty, but the immediate crisis had passed. Now, it was just a matter of getting through the rest of the trip and figuring out what the hell I was going to do next.

I glanced over at Prodigal. His face was drawn, the pain and exhaustion clear despite his attempts to mask it. It reminded me of a moment not too long ago when we were in the hospital after his surgery.

I'm sitting in the small, dimly lit hospital room with Prodigal, the sterile scent of antiseptic lingering in the air. The fluorescent lights buzz softly above us, casting a pale glow on his face. He's just had surgery, and though the pain has dulled him, his spirit is still as lively as ever. The stiffness in his movements and the occasional wince tell me he's in discomfort, but it doesn't stop him from trying to make me laugh.

He shifts in bed, adjusting the thin hospital gown as he looks at me with a mischievous grin. "So, do you think you'll ever have more kids?"

I laugh softly, shaking my head. "No, I'm done with that chapter. Besides, I'm forty-three—those days are long behind me."

But even as I say it, my mind drifts elsewhere. In truth, deeper thoughts are swirling beneath my easy response. First, I'm thinking about the Quiet One and how, not too long ago, he mentioned wanting another baby. What is it with men nearing fifty and suddenly deciding they want more kids despite already having a bunch? Then there's the guilt gnawing at me. The Quiet One's been reaching out, calling, trying to check the pulse of our relationship, but I've been dodging. "Let's talk after we get a house," I keep saying, using it as a convenient placeholder for all the conversations I'm not ready to have. Maybe I'm just buying time. And then there's Dorothy Roberts, whose words from *Killing the Black Body* haunt me—about how so many young girls have children, not because they want to, but because they don't have a reason not to. That resonates with me. For years, I didn't have a reason to stop either. But now, I do—my dreams, hopes, and ambitions—the weight of raising children without the support of a fully present partner. I simply don't have the bandwidth to start over, to commit to another eighteen years of mothering.

Lost in these thoughts, I almost forget where I am. But Prodigal, as always, is in an entirely different headspace, ready to lighten the mood. Without missing a beat, his face lights up with that familiar spark of creativity. "Oh, so you're really done, huh? Well, let me tell you how your eggs feel about that." His voice shifts, adopting the persona of an elderly woman, shaky and high-pitched. "Lemme introduce you to Ms. Shirlie."

I raise an eyebrow, chuckling softly, already knowing I'm in for a show. Before I can say anything, he launches into an impromptu skit, his voice cracking and trembling like an old woman who's seen too much.

"Ms. Shirlie, here," he begins, his voice quivering with exaggerated frailty. "I'm just one of them old unfertilized eggs, been sitting up here for years now. Ain't much left of me, to be honest. I seen Layden shoot out—oh, I said bye, but Lord, we didn't realize he took half of what we had in here. That's why he so intragetic!"

I burst out laughing, caught off guard by the ridiculousness of it all. Prodigal's delivery is spot on, each word dripping with the sass and wisdom of a woman who's clearly been through it all.

"But I tried," he continues, his voice wobbling with faux determination. "She gonna hide me, but I try to tell ya right now, I don't look all that well. Got some situations going on with my face, and these legs? They don't walk too well no more. Neck too weak to suck off your teet, so I'm just hoping I get a good pair of feet if I ever gotta walk. But let me tell ya, we sat in here too long. You're forty-three now, trying to have a baby? You shoulda just weighed that shit."

I'm laughing so hard now that tears are forming in the corners of my eyes. Prodigal grins, enjoying the effect he's having. He doesn't even pause as he shifts

A POT TO P*SS IN

into the next character.

"Now, let's hear from Ms. Betty," he says, his voice dropping lower and louder, like a woman who's both tone-deaf and entirely unaware of how loud she is. "Betty, how you feel about being fertilized?"

He takes a deep breath, readying himself for Ms. Betty's debut. "Uh, uh, I'm okay with it. I mean, uh, uh, we been sitting here so long. Oh, Lord Jesus, she talkin' 'bout having another baby. Oh, Lord. You know Layden took so much out of us. Oh, Lord Jesus, I guess we'll pray on this later, but it don't matter. She already unleashed the berms!"

The voice is so loud, so unexpectedly deep, that I'm doubled over in my chair, my sides aching from the force of my laughter. I frantically grab my phone, fumbling with it to start recording.

"Hold on, hold on!" I gasp, tears streaming down my face as I finally hit record. "Okay, go!"

Without missing a beat, Prodigal continues in Ms. Betty's shrill voice. "Ain't no telling which one of us really had to go. You remember what happened last time? I'm not feeling up to it these days. I'm gonna come out all fucked up! Oh, Lord, I just sat up here and thought about it. I don't know why she waited so long. Do she know? She forty-three!"

He switches back to Ms. Shirlie, the old lady voice full of exaggerated resignation. "Yeah, she knows. She forty-three."

Ms. Betty picks up again, even louder. "She know goddamn well she too old to be trying to pull this shit off! Then her diet up and down, up and down. It's down right now. She doin' good."

Prodigal suddenly launches into a horribly off-key rendition of "Take Me to the Mountain," his tone-deaf Ms. Betty singing at the top of her lungs. The combination of his ridiculous lyrics and the awful singing voice sends me into another fit of laughter, my body shaking uncontrollably as I record every moment.

By the time he finishes, we're both breathless. Him from the effort of making me laugh so hard and me from laughing so much that my stomach aches. I can barely speak, wiping the tears from my eyes as I shut off the camera.

"Okay," I say, still catching my breath, "You know we're gonna go to hell for that little politically incorrect skit of yours, right? And for laughing, I'm going right with you."

Prodigal smiles, the pain momentarily forgotten in the wake of our shared laughter. "Glad I could help. And ain't nobody going nowhere," he adds, with a glint in his eye, "because if we got pregnant right now, no matter how that baby comes out, you know we're going to love him or her like we love the others."

I laugh again, softer this time, and shake my head. "Don't worry. I'm done."

Could humor and shared memories really be enough to make me consider giving him another chance? I wasn't sure. But as I watched Prodigal on the couch of the Airbnb, flipping through channels like nothing had happened, I couldn't help but remember how we met in a writing class at UW–Madison. He was a student, and I was a graduate student shadowing a class, but I wasn't enrolled. I was somewhere between a student and an assistant. The teacher, a clean-cut and witty professor who wore plastic-rimmed glasses, had given an in-class assignment. The task was to write a story without picking up your pen. I watched everyone tap out at some point, laughing about how the assignment was more challenging than it seemed, everyone except for Prodigal. He just kept writing and writing.

When the time was up, and the students read back their work, everyone had funny and silly things they had written to keep going as long as they could. But Prodigal had taken all of the lessons from that day, everything that the teacher had said, and created a story from it. I remember looking at him and thinking, *He's either a damn good liar, or he's brilliant*. During our seven years together, I learned he was a terrible liar. But his brilliance and creativity were something that never got old. And I just felt like there was something left to explore. I know the dangers of getting caught up on potential. And yet, I still wondered.

If I'm honest, I saw myself in him. Like me, he had a lot of children, and like me, he had been discounted because of that. And yet, even with all he had going on, his hidden vices and all the chaos he brought to my life, I still felt the urge to bet on him. As much as I wanted to be completely through with him, I wasn't, not yet at least. But something about him made me believe that we had a chance in the right environment, under the right circumstances, at the right time. I wondered if this new home brought all of those things together.

After nine days in Atlanta, we finally wrapped up recording and began preparing to get on the road, saving the tenth day for just relaxing and experiencing the city together. The sun was warm on our skin as we wandered through the bustling streets, the air thick with the scent of food from nearby vendors. We stumbled upon a Black vendor who had set up his Italian ice cart on the corner of a gas station. The cart was a bright splash of color against the concrete, and the sweet, icy treats provided a welcome relief from the heat. Across the street, a Black-owned car wash buzzed with activity, sprays of water catching the sunlight as they cleaned cars. None of this was intentional; it just was. This was Atlanta.

We ate at a restaurant called The Real Milk and Honey, the savory aroma of soul food filling the air as we walked in. The restaurant was alive with chatter and the clinking of silverware against plates, every bite a reminder of the rich culinary heritage of the South. The ambiance felt like a warm embrace, a space where we could just enjoy the day without any of the pressures that had weighed on us.

As we headed back to Madison, the uncertainty of the house deal loomed large. But even more pressing was the choice I had to make between Prodigal and the Quiet One, a decision I knew I couldn't avoid much longer. With so much at stake, the road ahead felt more uncertain than ever.

After that exhausting day, we drove home from an experience that was all at once chaotic, exhilarating, and intense. I was finally able to relax and just enjoy the quiet in my head while taking in the freedom of the highway. My phone buzzed insistently on the console beside me. It was Ruby, my real estate agent, calling with an update about the house. I knew I needed to take it, but the quiet was everything in that moment.

I hesitated, torn between the importance of the call and the pressing need to stay present and unwind. I glanced at the screen one more time, my heart racing. Every decision felt like a critical move in a game with impossibly high stakes. Finally, I picked up, trying to keep my voice steady as I balanced my attention between Ruby's updates and the peace I was desperately holding on to.

"Hey, Ruby! What's the word?" I said in my "what's the tea" voice, like I was talking to one of my girlfriends because, to an extent, I was.

Her voice was calm, professional, with just a hint of urgency, maybe even some concern. "We've got to figure out our next move, Sagashus. They're pushing us to see how serious we are. We need to show them we mean business with a bump clause."

"Okay, what's a bump clause?" I asked, trying not to allow myself to get nervous or worried before I needed to.

She went on to explain that a bump clause allows the seller to keep their house on the market until I meet certain criteria. In this case, I needed to come up with an additional $3,000 (for a total of $5,000).

"After everything we've spent on this trip, producing content, printing the game, and just living in general, I only have the $2,000 that I thought they had agreed to. But, okay, I will figure it out."

As for the pre-approval letter, that's altogether different. I was going to need proof of more income, which shouldn't be a problem because of the contracts that were soon to pay off. But then there was all the paperwork, and it was a lot of paperwork: taxes, profit and loss statements, etc. The bank wasn't going to give any kind of approval (pre or otherwise) if they didn't think I could handle the loan. And the only way I could show that was by showing numbers. I had been building relationships to help me navigate the system. But it was crunch time, and they were looking for numbers to support the story I was telling.

After hanging up with Ruby, I took a deep breath, leaning my head back against the seat. The conversation weighed on me. In the rearview mirror, I saw Layden's sleepy eyes in the backseat, a reminder of the quiet moments I was struggling to find amidst the noise. I needed a moment to collect myself. I was going to have to make something shake. But for now, I needed to just enjoy the ride home.

The house was still a looming question mark, just like the unresolved tensions within my family. Both felt like ticking clocks, counting down to decisions I wasn't ready to make.

CHAPTER 15

MARY AND ELIZABETH

AUGUST 2021

As I sat in the car, waiting for the meeting with the bank, my mind drifted to one of my favorite Bible stories—Mary and her cousin Elizabeth. Elizabeth was too old to be pregnant, yet there she was, six months along, when Mary got the news of her own miracle. A virgin, pregnant by the Holy Spirit. The angel Gabriel had pointed to Elizabeth, proof that God made the impossible possible.

I let out a slow breath, imagining Mary's journey to visit her cousin, the baby inside Elizabeth leaping at the sound of Mary's voice. "Blessed are you among women," Elizabeth had said. I needed that kind of blessing right now. If only someone's blessing could confirm that my miracle was coming, I'd take it and run with it.

So much was up in the air. Like a high-stakes tennis match, the offer to purchase the house had been a back-and-forth between my team and the sellers' team. They were selling the house for $775,000. We put in an offer for $750,000. In a market where people were selling their homes for almost 30 percent higher than expected, with a low inventory of houses for sale, it was definitely a seller's market.

Ruby was nervous about us offering to buy their home at $25,000 below the asking price. But I wanted to go even lower. She then told me a story about a couple selling their home, and a buyer made an offer that was egregiously low to them. Offended by what they saw as disrespect and a lack of appreciation for the value of their property, the couple closed down that deal altogether.

"Wait, they can do that?" I asked.

She assured me that they could, and they did. I didn't want that to be my story. So, to play it safe, I settled for the $750,000 offer. In addition to that, we made other bold requests. For example, we offered an earnest payment of $2,000, which, again, seemed to concern Ruby. She explained that that was an awfully low number, but it was all I had to give. At the time, there was about $3,000 in my bank account. Although I was expecting more dollars to come in, that wouldn't be until the end of the month or sometime in September.

Finally, we asked that they accept proof of financing from the bank within ninety days, putting us right at the deadline for the October 15 closing date that we were also offering. We knew that it was cutting things close, but I was working to generate two sources of funding simultaneously: one source for scaling my business and the other for the soon-to-be scaling costs of providing for my family as we secured a new home.

Everything was happening so quickly, and I was pushing harder than I ever had — moving from overworked to overwhelmed. My normal was six days a week, eight to ten hours a day. Now I was at seven days, ten to sixteen hours, without pause. I wasn't working my ass off just to survive — I was working my ass off to reach a goal. I was trying to buy a house, and I didn't know how long I could keep this up. The workload wasn't sustainable, but I was in too deep to stop. I was committed, and I wasn't backing down. This fight would be to the death — and at one point, it almost was.

But I'm getting ahead of myself. (By several chapters.)

We put that offer in on July 15. By July 21, they sent back to us a counteroffer. Again, surprisingly, they accepted our offer of buying the house for $750,000, $25,000 under their asking price. But they asked for $5,000 in earnest money, that's $3,000 over the initial proposed amount of $2,000. The problem was this: I would have to deliver the earnest money within six days of the accepted offer. Even if I had wiped out my bank account and was willing to starve my family and myself until other money came in, we still wouldn't have had enough.

On top of that, they added a bump clause, meaning that even if they entered into a contract with me, they could still keep their property on the market. If a buyer came along and made a better offer, the buyer could bump me if I didn't make a better offer within a specific time. These nice people were really playing hardball. And understandably so. They had a buyer at one point, and things fell apart at the last minute. They had learned from that experience and were protecting themselves by keeping their options open. That was good for them but made things more challenging for me.

As if that wasn't stressful enough, they also wanted us to provide proof of financing within forty-five days after the accepted offer, not ninety. Again, impossible! June, July, and August have always been slow seasons for the Infamous Mothers brand. There were no speaking engagements, book sales, sponsorships, classes, or anything else during that time. If we accepted their offer, which we weren't going to, there was no way that I was going to be able to provide my bank with the kind of proof that they needed to make this deal work so that they could, in turn, finance the mortgage based on that proof, by early September. We needed more time.

Ruby wasn't backing down, though. She created another counteroffer. We accepted their request for $5,000 in earnest money this time, but we asked if we could pay in two installments. The first $2,000 payment would be delivered within three days after the accepted offer, and the second $3,000 payment would be delivered by September 21. We didn't dispute their bump clause. But we did dispute their request around financing. We found a middle ground between our initial request for ninety days and their counter of forty-five days, asking to provide proof within sixty days of an accepted offer. That would still be challenging, but I was confident it was doable. It seemed like a happy compromise because it would be enough time to let sellers know if an October 15 closing date was actually feasible.

Then came the twist. They rejected our counteroffer, except not really. On July 28, they sent us yet another offer that accepted all of our terms in the previous offer, with a few new terms of their own. They wanted to keep operating their Airbnb until the day of closing. As a businessperson, that made sense to me. So on July 30, we accepted their offer and signed the document. On that same day, I delivered $2,000 in earnest money to an address provided to me by Ruby's husband, Chris, who was her partner in a company they called Conrad Development. As the real estate agent, Ruby was the face of the business, but as we got deeper into the process, Chris became more present.

We entered August with a major win under our belt, but the clock was ticking. The signed offer meant deadlines were now breathing down our necks—there was no room for error. With every step forward, I knew I needed my accountant's guidance more than ever. (His name was Ryan, by the way.) Even if we worked diligently to produce everything according to the schedule, some stranger interested in buying the house could show up and complicate everything. August was all about playing a delicate balance between offense and defense. In a sense, we had the ball and were committed to doing everything in our power to make sure that we didn't drop it, including satisfying the bank.

On a Friday evening in late July, Kelli from the bank sent me an email that started off friendly.

"Hi Sagashus, I hope you and your family enjoyed Six Flags today! I'm sure you're exhausted!!!"

On our way back from Atlanta, we stopped in Louisville, Kentucky, to visit my uncle Degree. It would be in Kentucky that my kids would experience some of the getaway and fun they were hoping to while in Atlanta. I glanced over the seemingly nice email and made up my mind that I would dedicate more time to it once we made it back to Madison. July had come and gone. It would be early August when I'd revisit the details of her message. And it was overwhelming. They wanted everything, it seemed: 2019 and 2020 tax returns and 1099s (if applicable), 2021 year-to-date profit and loss statement, three most recent months of business bank statements (all pages), two most recent months of personal bank statements (all pages), two most recent months or most recent quarterly statements for investment or retirement accounts, copy of driver's license photo identification, letter from my accountant stating that "using up to $50,000 for the down payment and closing costs for your home would not negatively impact your business," proof of any sponsorship dollars for the business, letter of explanation regarding 2019 income, and accepted offer paperwork.

The sheer volume of documents required was daunting, a reflection of the high standards needed to establish financial credibility.

Fortunately, August was also during Ryan's slow season. While Ryan had other clients he was working with, it was nothing like tax season. It also helped that we had a good relationship. Some years ago, when Ruby and I were excited about the possibility of buying a home the first time, she introduced me to Ryan. Always a straight shooter, humble but very honest, he gave me the sobering reality check about how things might not go as planned with the book sales and launching of the brand. And he was right. We didn't do nearly as well as we expected; in fact, it was a total flop.

Over the years, I had grown to appreciate his honesty, and this time around was no different. Always conservative with numbers, erring on the side of saving and not counting chickens before they hatched, I really valued whatever input Ryan would have about the possibility of purchasing this home. Hell, he knew my finances better than I knew them. He also understood ownership better than me. What he'd have to say would be critical.

The pressure weighed heavily on me as I sat at my dinner table, which also doubled as my desk. The wooden surface cool under my palms was hidden by papers scattered across it like fallen leaves in disarray and deadlines looming like dark clouds. The air in the room was almost suffocating, and empty water bottles toppled over everywhere on top of the papers. If we were going to make this purchase—if it was even possible—we needed approval from my accountant. The clock's ticking on the wall seemed to grow louder, each second amplifying my sense of urgency. Ryan, in many ways, would be the deciding factor. If he weren't the one to green-light the overall purchase, he would certainly determine whether we could close by October 15. I knew I had to act quickly.

Fortunately, Ryan and I had been discussing the possibility of this house ever since I discovered it. My fingers felt slightly damp as I picked up the phone, wiping them on my jeans before dialing his number. Each button pressed echoed in my AirPods, blending with the room's quiet as a mix of nerves and determination settled in. The phone rang a couple of times before Ryan answered.

"Well, hello, Sagashus. How are you?" he greeted me, his tone warm and familiar.

"I'm good, Ryan. How about you?" I replied, trying to keep my voice steady.

"I'm doing a lot better now that tax season has wound down," he said with a slight chuckle. "So, what can I do for you?"

"I wanted to get your opinion on something," I began, feeling the strain of the decision pressing down on me. "You already know I'm looking to buy this house, right?" My voice sounded steadier than I felt, the room around me almost too quiet as I laid out the details. Ryan listened patiently, not interrupting, letting me explain everything. When I finally finished, there was a brief pause, and I could almost hear him carefully weighing everything I had said.

"You know, you're in the business of inspiring people," he said. His voice poured gently through the speaker, warm and familiar. "And where you live plays a role in that for a lot of people. They need to see something concrete, not just hear your words. They need to see proof that you are living a certain kind of life. So I guess this makes sense."

As his words sunk in, relief washed over me, but I knew Ryan well enough to expect that he would have questions I needed to be prepared to answer.

"Aren't your kids leaving soon? Do you really need that much house?" he asked, his voice thoughtful. The concern in his tone was evident, cutting through any niceties and bullshit that I might have hoped for. But still, he was thoughtful.

I took a deep breath before responding, the air feeling cooler as it filled my lungs. "I understand where you're coming from, Ryan. But this house is more than just a place for me to live. I want it to be an intergenerational home. You know, I stayed way too long in toxic and dangerous relationships because I had nowhere to go. There was no space for a woman with as many children as I had in my family. Physically, it was impossible. I don't want that for any of my children. Even though they're leaving, I want them to always have a place to come back to and for their children to sleep comfortably in the family home."

There was a pause on the other end of the line as Ryan processed what I said. I could almost hear the gears turning in his mind.

"Okay, I get that," he finally replied. His tone softened slightly, though still measured. "But if you get into a bind, you know, slow seasons or whatever, how will you cover the cost of such a large house? I don't want you to be house poor, where all your money is going to maintaining your home, but you can't live."

I had anticipated this question. "The house isn't just a residence," I explained. "It's also an income property. The previous owners ran an Airbnb from the property, and I'm hoping to do the same. It's already set up for it, and with the right marketing, it could bring in enough income to cover the mortgage and more."

Ryan was silent for a moment, and I could hear him tapping on his calculator, the soft clicks of the keys faint but distinct. He was crunching the numbers as he always did. I felt a bead of sweat trickle down my back as I held my breath, waiting for his verdict.

"Well," he said finally, a hint of caution in his voice. The sound of his chair creaking as he shifted was almost audible through the line. "I still have some reservations, but you've done your homework. And honestly, I've seen how your business has grown over the years, especially in the past eighteen months. If anyone can pull this off, it's you."

"Thanks, Ryan," I said, feeling a mix of gratitude and determination. My fingers relaxed around the phone, and I was able to breathe. "I really appreciate your support. This means a lot."

"Just make sure you stay on top of things," he added, his voice firm but kind. "And if you need anything, you know where to find me."

I hung up the phone. The end of the call felt complete in a way that was bigger than the conversation itself. My mind raced with possibilities, but there was a calmness now, a sense of resolve. This wasn't just about buying a house—it was about creating a future, a place where my family could always find refuge. And with Ryan's cautious blessing, I knew I could make it happen.

Those factors, combined with what he knew about my personality, made him feel positive about this next step. Knowing the ebb and flow of my business, the slow seasons, and the money-making seasons, with little to nothing in my account at the time, he wrote the comfort letter, confirming that using $50,000 from my account would not jeopardize the business. Ryan's words kept me thinking long after he was off the phone. *Can I really do this? What if I'm out of my league? But then again, if I don't do it, where else will I go?* I found myself nodding along to his words, even though doubts kept surfacing, one after another.

Ryan was putting his word, his professional opinion, and his reputation on the line. I knew that, and I am forever grateful to him for doing so, especially since he is a man who doesn't count chickens before they've hatched. My job was to get the money into the account by the time the bank checked, but for now, I was safe with Ryan's word. One item on the list was checked off.

What we needed from Ryan was more time-consuming and messier. Yet, I imagine it was easier because they were more objective and didn't require his opinion. The math was just the math. It was my taxes and profit and loss statement.

I have to be honest. For several years, my taxes have been a mess. The first years I started Infamous Mothers, I was a broke student. More often than I am proud to admit, I ended up in ChexSystems for overdrawing accounts and not being able to replace the money in time. I laugh now, but then, I was so embarrassed about the times I tried to open a new account while being in ChexSystems, just to be denied because of my outstanding debt. For this reason, there was a period when I only had a business account.

That's how Ryan and I got to know one another over the years. My accounts were so messy, and he was so meticulous about getting them right that I had to parse out every business expense, separate it from every personal expense, and explain it to him each year. He'd often say, "You know, Sagashus, if you'd just opened up a personal account, we wouldn't have to have these awkward conversations about whether or not purchases from A Woman's Touch are personal or business."

A Woman's Touch is "a woman-owned and operated sexuality boutique" that I absolutely love here in Madison. Ironically, the purchases from there were business-related, especially during COVID-19. I was teaching a class on intimacy and social distancing. And those toys and books were part of either the curriculum or research. But I understood his point. As much as I respected and appreciated Ryan, who was a good man and a great person, he was also a very conservative Christian and a white man. Explaining my sex toys to him was pretty awkward. We could avoid those conversations if I had a personal account. And yet, as we had done in past years, through strong communication, a lot of laughs, and his hard work, we got those taxes done. Another item checked off the list.

We had waded through the mess of 2020, and with more income and stability, I surprised him with the beauty of 2021's work. For the first time in a long time, I had kept most (if not all) of my business expenses confined to my business account and my personal expenses confined to my personal account. For the first time in a while, I didn't owe a bank. I wasn't in ChexSystems, and I was able to get a personal account. This saved Ryan a lot of time, making it easier for him to work within the constraints that we had.

And with all the numbers crunched, I could see that 2021's earnings were even better than 2020's. The realization sent a thrill through me, like the first taste of victory, the kind that makes your heart race and your breath catch just a little. Not only had we checked off another item on our list, but this achievement felt like a tangible step closer to pulling off something that had once seemed impossible. The thought that we might become homeowners soon filled the air with a kind of electric anticipation that makes the hair on your arms stand up.

But this was life. And like any major event that happens in life, I knew better than to get too comfortable. The room around me felt charged, as if the very walls were tense from all the unknowns. I reminded myself to keep my head in the game and to stay focused. My eyes darted back and forth over the papers spread out on the table, as if watching the ball, ready for the moment I might need to switch from offense to defense without a second's notice. Or worse, realizing too late that I had missed the shot, and now it was time to rebound. The unpredictability of it all kept my muscles taut, ready for whatever came next.

And then, just as expected, life threw its curveball. We had been waiting anxiously to hear back from one of our sponsors. They had promised that a decision would be made and announced in August. As I waited to hear back from them, every sunset and sunrise felt like a year had passed. Although they couldn't offer any guarantees, their tone had been optimistic, giving me a false sense of security that we'd receive the funds needed to cover our startup costs. With those dollars, we could build out and launch Infamous Mothers 3.0, including 3rd Space Coworking and the courses that made up Infamous Mothers University.

The funding would also help us put the final touches on the *Books, Bullets, and Babies* podcast, the editing and polishing steps we'd been itching to complete, while also covering the content and technology for our *Wanted* newsletter. I was already miles ahead of myself whenever I thought about hiring new people to help us scale. The deadline was August 24, and I found myself glancing at the calendar repeatedly, my stomach tightening with each passing day.

When August 25 came and went in silence, I couldn't take it anymore. I reached out, my fingers trembling slightly as I typed out the email, asking for an update.

The reply came quickly, the words on the screen sharp and cold. They hadn't met. Our proposal would be delayed for another two months. The news hit me like a punch to the gut, and the breath knocked out of me as the room seemed to close in around me.

This meant that we wouldn't know until after the closing date whether we'd receive the funds. Our crown jewel of sponsorships was now up in the air, dangling precariously without a definitive answer. The future of scaling the brand, which had felt so sure just days ago, now felt as fragile as a house of cards. The uncertainty was suffocating, like a dense fog that I couldn't see my way out of. With it, my ability to generate the income needed to sustain the costs of buying this home became just as uncertain.

In one sudden move, we went from offense to a very desperate and aggressive defense. My mind raced, searching for a play, but there was nothing. No strategy, no backup plan—just a heavy silence filled with the weight of what-ifs and missed opportunities. It was like standing on the edge of a cliff, the ground crumbling beneath my feet, and knowing that there was nothing I could do to stop the fall.

As if this wasn't enough to worry about, I called a meeting with my older three kids because it had become clear to me that Prodigal and I deserved another try. Four months had gone by since he came back into our lives. We had survived COVID-19, the deaths of our loved ones, his surgery, a trip to Atlanta, and his presence just felt right. We still had to work through things, but in my gut, I knew we had to explore this new possibility. One Saturday night, he and I discussed it, and by Sunday morning, I had called an emergency meeting for my three oldest children to join me at the Original House of Pancakes.

I figured that if we met in a public place over good food, we'd be able to get through a tough conversation without things getting too out of hand because, after all, we would be in a restaurant surrounded by people. We weren't going to make a scene, right? I was wrong.

We arrived at the Pancake House separately. Cho rode with me, while Dianna, my oldest, drove herself. Yemi, who, like Dianna, was living outside my home now, showed up too, though I don't recall exactly how she got there. The place was packed, so getting a booth was out of the question. We were seated in a tight corner, with one side of the table pressed up against the wall with bench seating and the other side equipped with regular chairs. We were so close to the party next to us that it didn't feel like an arm's length away; it felt more like an elbow's length. There was no privacy, and that was my mistake.

The booth's seat dug into my back, the tightness amplifying the suffocating tension in the air. The scent of butter and syrup mingled with the bitterness that hung between us. Each clink of a fork against a plate made me flinch, the sound a reminder of the weight of what I had to say. I don't even remember exactly how I broke the news—I just know I did.

Before I could fully process it, Cho rolled his eyes, his tone a mix of anger, annoyance, and frustration. "I knew this was going to happen. No, no, no. I don't want him there." He wasn't loud, but his words were firm and consistent.

Yemi, my second child, spoke up more forcefully. "Mom, are you seeing someone? I thought you were seeing a therapist because, seriously, have you spoken to your therapist about this? Something is wrong with you if you're making this choice."

I tried to stay composed, letting them vent their thoughts. I explained that Prodigal was different today than he was before. I tried to explain that I had stayed longer than I should have in a toxic relationship with him in the past—not because I didn't know it was toxic, not because I had been tricked or manipulated, but because I felt that as a single mom with six kids, in the environment we lived in, the community wasn't going to let me peacefully raise my kids alone.

If I wanted the "wellness checks" calls from CPS to stop, and if I didn't want to be treated like an eyesore or seen as a stain, or if I wanted my children not to be treated like charity cases, I was going to need to stay partnered. And so I did. For the first time in my life, I stayed with a man for more than two years—seven years to be exact—because I felt that had I done otherwise, I would have lost my kids. As sincere as I was, as much as I felt that that was my truth, they weren't buying that.

"So you're saying that you stayed with him because of us? You're blaming us?" I don't know who said that, but whoever did, I felt like he or she spoke for all three of them. I fought to stay objective and to hear them out. But the anger and hurt were so potent, it overwhelmed me. I fought back the tears. I was determined not to be one of those women who starts crying and making it about them when they have clearly hurt someone else. So, I refused to let a tear drop.

They had the right to feel whatever they were feeling. Life with Prodigal traumatized all of us. And just when life was getting good for us, he came again. On the outside looking in, it was the ultimate Fuck Boy move. It was the kind of manipulation that you see from sadistic and cruel sociopaths. The torture that we saw Ramsay do to Theon in *Game of Thrones*.

The kind of torture where the tormentor captures someone and makes a sport of making them think they've been set free, just to capture and carve away parts of them. We saw this kind of torture from Shakespeare's Aaron the Moor. The kind of torture that comes with finally getting over the loss of a loved one, just for their corpses to be pulled from their graves with a note carved into their bodies saying, "Let not your sorrow die though I am dead." Yes, I understood what this looked like and how they must've felt. But Prodigal wasn't Ramsay or Aaron. He was a person who was tired and had been through things, facing his mortality at worst and compromised mobility at best. He learned that he wasn't invincible and that his shit did stink, and since he never tricked me in the first place, I believed that the changes I saw were real.

"I need you to trust me," I said, my voice trembling slightly despite my effort to stay composed. "Just give me a year. If he turns out to be anything like before, I swear, I'll walk away. But right now … right now, I need to believe in second chances. Can you understand that?"

Cho responded, "I will support a year of you and him being together if Prodigal doesn't live with us."

I couldn't even pretend like that was a possibility. I didn't want him to live outside of us. I wanted him in this new space with us if we were to be a couple. I needed that support.

Dianna, possibly my child with the most adverse feelings toward him, was quiet. With thoughtful consideration, she said, "I know what it's like to have the support of a partner," she was referring to life with her now live-in boyfriend, Andy. "Maybe if I didn't know that feeling, I would be saying the same thing. But I do know that feeling, and I want that for you, Mommy."

I knew that wasn't easy for her. In fact, I expected her to be the most vocal about her opposition to us being together. In her senior year of high school, Prodigal and she had a fallout that they never returned from. For over three years, they hadn't said more than a few sentences to one another, and now this. She was firm and consistent in her dislike for Prodigal, but she still believed in the idea that Black women deserved to be loved and supported, and if this was the person who could offer her mother that, she wouldn't get in the way. She'd give me that pass.

In exchange, she needed me to understand that my choice to forgive him was not hers and that she was committed to keeping the distance between them as a result of the bridge that he had burned some years ago.

Somewhere during the conversation, a thought occurred to Yemi. "Wait. It doesn't matter what we were going to say. You were going to be with him anyway, weren't you?"

Cho looked at my face, wanting to know the answer. I looked down and, after a short time, back up again.

I knew this would be hard, but seeing their faces now, I wanted to hide. But I couldn't, so I just sat there and took it because I had to and because I was already in it.

I reminded them that I raised them differently from how I had grown up.

They grew up in campus housing on a college campus. My circumstances were different. I explained, "Everyone around me struggled with addiction: alcohol, drugs, sex, gambling. Over time, I watched my uncles get clean, cousins. Everyone around me got clean except the men who were directly connected to me. For a change, my prayers are being answered. I want to experience this. Give me a year. Please, that's what I'm asking."

"You are going to do this no matter what we say," Yemi responded, annoyed.

Cho's face was a combination of hurt, betrayal, and disappointment. I don't remember how we left the table. But I'm pretty confident that Yemi said more about therapy for me.

Yemi was right. My mind was already made up going into that conversation.

Here's why. Yes, I believed in Prodigal's transformation. His change was consistent, and I trusted what I saw. I believed that this version of him deserved another chance—a chance to do right by our son, a chance to be to me the man he promised he and my older children he would be, and a chance to experience a promised land that he and I had spoken about for so many years. Yes, he had been a problem in our lives, yet, he had also been a solution to many problems. The old version couldn't return, but the new version was much better. But those are not the only reasons my mind was made up.

When I was a little girl, I heard an argument between a mother and her adult son. The son and her boyfriend didn't get along. And so, the mom put the man out. One day, when the mom came home from work, a woman was in her tub. She screamed to her son, "What is this strange woman doing in my house, in my tub?"

He responded, "You're just mad that I have a woman, and you're alone." That taught me something about grown children and their parents' love lives. They want to weigh in and have a say-so, but that say-so is not always a two-way street.

My grown children would make choices over the years that I didn't like. And because they are headstrong, I imagined they would make those choices regardless of what I had to say. I didn't want to resent them over the years for being the people I had raised them to be while denying myself that same freedom. They were grown and living their lives, and I had to live mine. I hoped that we'd love each other enough to meet in the middle—when possible—but also to be respectful and to remain united no matter what. This choice of mine was going to put that hope to the test.

While August started out so promising, it was getting heavier as the days went by. Out of the blue, a friend I hadn't connected with in almost a year reached out to me via text. Her message read, "Hey, my dear friend! Hope all is well. I am having a small get-together/birthday celebration this Saturday. Are you in town?

I hope so!! Let me know!" She included the day and time, along with her address.

I responded, "It's Virgo season. Yes! I've been thinking about you. And I will be there." I immediately followed up with, "Thank you for the invite."

She fired right back, "Gurrlll, it's my time!!! Wouldn't be a party without you."

To be clear, I don't party, and neither does she. For us, a party is more about a meeting of minds over good food, where the conversation flows as freely as the dishes being passed around. Sophie and I have always had an interesting friendship. We're both super busy with our large families' entrepreneurial ventures, and we were both homeschoolers at one point. Our lives are so full that we rarely find time to hang out, but when we do connect, it's always rich and meaningful. I can still recall the warmth of her kindness—how she has taken from whatever storehouse she built for her family and brought food that nourished mine. The scent of her homemade Sloppy Joes would fill my kitchen, or the sweetness of a random sheet cake from the bakery would linger in the air long after it was gone. She has sat in the car with me for hours, the interior filled with the scent of worn leather and the faint aroma of fast food, helping me work through some crisis at home or bad news I had received. And when those weren't the cases, she spent countless hours singing my praises, her voice bright and confident, reminding me that "I am somebody." With her perfect smile, revealing those gleaming white teeth, she'd say in a very official voice, "You are the Docta." No, we don't do parties, but this event was something I had to show up for.

When the day arrived, she sent another message. "Hey! I'm grabbing some extra food. Just wanted to make sure I have enough. Are the kids coming, too?! They're totally welcome!"

I was happy to announce, "No, ma'am. Just me." It was my night out alone during COVID-19 when I rarely ever went out, and I was going to enjoy it. I followed up with, "Happy belated birthday, Beautiful!!!"

She wrote back, "Ahhhhh, I feel that in my soul! Well, come on through, friend! Thank youuuuu!"

That evening I got dressed and left Prodigal with the kids. I got into the van, entered her address into the GPS, and drove where it led me. We hadn't seen each other since before COVID-19, and I had only been to her apartment once or twice. I didn't remember exactly where she lived, but I knew this was the wrong direction. I kept driving anyway. It led me to an unfamiliar neighborhood and to a building with an odd but really cool design. I parked the van and got out.

I walked up a set of stairs that cascaded alongside the most beautiful landscape I had ever seen. Lush greenery surrounded me, the smell of fresh earth and blooming flowers filling my senses. Some older white people sat on a deck, a couple, I believe, their laughter mingling with the sounds of the evening. *What was this?* I wondered, scanning the area for any clue that I was in the right place.

As I looked beyond the couple, my eyes landed on Sophie. She was sitting next to a woman who looked like she could be her twin, their similar features illuminated by the soft glow of the setting sun. Around them were other people, chatting and laughing, their voices blending into a comforting chatter. As I climbed toward the group, a realization hit me like a wave: *Wait a minute, this is Sophie's house!* Excitement bubbled up inside me, quickening my pace as the thought took hold. Sophie went and bought a motherfuckin' house and didn't tell anyone. I bet this is hers!

When I got close to her, I gestured for her to come to me. She gestured that I come her way, but because I wanted to be tactful, I wanted her to be away from everyone when I asked her to confirm my thoughts. She got up, politely excusing herself from her guests. As soon as she came over to me, the anticipation spilled over.

"Is this your house?" I asked, barely containing my excitement.

"It is," she said proudly, her smile widening as she recognized the significance of her achievement for both of us.

I couldn't hold back my joy as I walked into the house, the excitement bubbling up and spilling over in quiet, gleeful screams. This was the Elizabeth to my Mary; the miracle I could see in her life was confirmation of the miracle that would soon be a part of my life. The air in the kitchen was warm and inviting, filled with the aroma of something delicious simmering on the stove, and as she recounted the details of how she had quietly owned this home for about a year, I listened intently. Her story was filled with twists and turns, each detail more inspiring than the last. What was for her was for her, and not even a better offer from another buyer could keep her from it. This was the inspiration I needed to enter September, a month where everything felt like it was hanging in the balance— money, my relationship with my children, and the conversation I needed to have with the Quiet One.

And yet, witnessing Sophie's triumph felt like my own Elizabeth experience. The certainty in Sophie's voice, paired with the tangible reality of her new home, reinforced my belief that I was on the right path. It reminded me that I wasn't just hoping for a miracle; I was in the process of building one. I made up my mind to keep moving forward, trusting that what was meant for me would come and that no obstacle would keep it from reaching me.

CHAPTER 16

NAKED

AUGUST 2021

It's ten o'clock in the morning, the day after Sophie's birthday event, and I'm still reeling. I stayed up late replaying everything in my head—the conversations, the food, the beauty of her new home, and that last-minute miracle that made it clear to everyone: that house was meant for her.

But now, I'm left wondering, *Is the house Ruby found meant to be mine?*

I want to believe it is.

But the only way to know for sure is to retreat to my mountaintop, my sanctuary—to connect with my Father.

Some people have prayer closets, sanctuaries filled with scripture and silence. My sacred space is my shower. It's where I strip away not just my clothes but the layers of fear, doubt, and the lies I've been told about my worth. When I really need to talk to God, I brush my teeth, wash my face, and step into that space— completely naked.

Unlike most days, when I'm in and out of the shower without a second thought, these moments are different. They're ceremonial. I handle myself with a special kind of care, paying attention to every curve, every inch of skin. The white lather against my deep brown skin feels like an anointing. These are the moments I am tender with myself. I cleanse with intent.

I am a sinner—a fornicator, a glutton, a gossip. I cuss, covet, and blaspheme. I will never be "pure" or "clean" again. And I accept that, without apology. Life is

174   DR. SAGASHUS LEVINGSTON

tough, and my soul is just as worn and lived-in as my baggy eyes and my saggy breasts. I've made peace with that.

This cleansing isn't about hiding who I am or what I've done. I know I can't *literally* wash away my sins.

On the contrary, it's about uncovering and discovering. It's about being seen clearly. The warmth of the water makes me feel safe, unashamed, and comfortable in my own skin. I pray naked, exposed, knowing that in His presence, I am accepted—flaws and all, FUPA and all.

This is my mountain.

And I stand here, as an offering, in exchange for prayers being heard and answered. In this vulnerable space, I confront my deepest fears and desires, laying them bare before God. It is here that I dare to ask for what society tells me I shouldn't: wealth, power, success.

On this mountain, I lay it all out:

"Dear Father, break the chain of addiction from the lives of those I care about." I call out each name of those struggling with alcoholism, drugs, and cigarettes.

"Dear Father, thank you for loving me and for blessing me. Thank you for protecting me."

"Dear Father, help this child or that child manage their fears and insecurities. Walk alongside them, keep them safe in this world."

"Dear Father, bridge the gap between me and the people I love. Show me how to speak with love and compassion."

But of all the "Dear Fathers," the one that has raised the most eyebrows among my loved ones is this:

"Dear Father, bless me with a strategy that will turn my company into a multimillion-dollar brand and a movement that will transform lives."

I know—you're not supposed to pray for wealth and riches. But I've lived with poverty all my life, and it's a hard thing to endure. If I can't ask the ultimate Being that I call Father for a life of comfort, ease, and satisfaction, who can I turn to?

Praying for wealth has always felt rebellious—a defiance of the norms that tell us to accept less. But I'm not content with less—not for myself and not for my children.

Every day, my kids ask me to pay this bill or buy that thing. Surely, the God I serve—my ultimate parent—can do more for me as His daughter than I can for my own daughters and sons.

Aunt Business loves to tell the story of how my cousins and I would come to her as kids, asking for money to buy candy at the store. They'd all ask for 25 cents, and she'd give it to them. But I'd ask for $1.25. She'd adjust herself in her bed, raise an eyebrow, and ask, "What do you need all that money for?"

And I'd tell her, "So I can buy a honey bun, a 7UP, and a Kit Kat."

Because I could account for every cent, she'd fulfill my request, giving me five times what my cousins asked for.

If my aunt could do this, so could the God I call Father.

Over the years, I've made requests that were both sincere and bold. I believe God has answered my so-called big prayers—the kind of prayers only He could answer—because He knew that one day, I'd be telling you about them, and He'd get all the glory.

And I'm good with that.

Because I know for sure, where I have run out, He's always run in.

And I have to give credit where credit is due.

Amen?

Amen.

But as soon as I step out of the shower, I'm back in the valley. The cold air sends shivers down my spine, pulling me out of my sanctuary and into a place full of chaos, danger, and unforgiveness. Here, I'm not just physically exposed but emotionally raw. The valley is where shame and insecurity reign, where I'm no longer in the comforting presence of God but in a harsh reality where I feel discounted, like an item on the clearance rack.

I towel off, wrap it around myself, and stand in front of the mirror again. I stare at my reflection, at the history written across my skin—stretch marks, scars, soft places. Evidence of a life lived, of battles fought, of sacrifices made.

I press my hands against the cool ceramic sink, taking a deep breath.

Where did this begin?

I know the answer before I even finish the question.

When we came into this world, none of us knew about worth or value. We cried when we needed something, reached out when we wanted comfort, and didn't question whether we deserved it. We didn't know that the world assigns value to bodies. We didn't know that one day, we'd be walking through life with an invisible scorecard, always being measured, always being marked up or down.

And by the time I became aware of this reality, I still had it wrong because I thought my worth was rooted in who I was, not in what I looked like. I thought you built value through your character, work, and love. But slowly, I started to see the truth—the unspoken scorecard that grades us all.

Every body is evaluated. Some are marked up, praised, and welcomed. Others are marked down, discounted, and dismissed. It's not personal—it's the system. A game with very real consequences.

And my body—like most—has its fair share of deductions and additions. Five points added for this, three points taken away for that. Twenty points gained for this, twenty-five taken away for that. And I get lost in the math, not always knowing my value in any given room I show up in, not aware of the final grade.

But here's another truth: I'm not just being graded. I'm doing the grading, too.

I see a tall and thick woman walk into a room with long, straight, or wavy hair, and I assign her points: *Stallion. Put together. Probably has money. +10 points.*

I see another woman with less curves, natural hair, and a child on her hip, and I do the same: *Tired. Struggling. Probably got a story. -5 points.* And maybe the score isn't the one I would assign to either. Maybe it's me just having a vague sense of what the market values.

It's automatic.

And I hate it.

Because I know, deep down, that the system is broken. That I'm not just a player in this game—I'm a pawn. That, like so many others, I'm participating in my own devaluation, letting these invisible scorecards determine what I ask for, what I accept, and what I believe I deserve.

And now, standing in front of this mirror, preparing to enter the world of real estate, wealth, and negotiations, I can feel that scorecard hovering over me. I can feel the weight of every deduction, every mark against me, and I wonder: *How do I build an empire when I'm still walking around like I'm on clearance?*

I know what my body says before I even open my mouth.

They see: Black. Woman. Fat. Single mother.

They hear: Risky. Expensive. Questionable return on investment.

I have worked. I have built things from nothing. I have turned $1,500 a month and food stamps into a vision, into a business, into a life. But in their eyes, my body is still tied to struggle—not wealth.

And so, I compensate.

I lean in too much. Smile too much. Work too damn hard to put them at ease. I cushion my asks, soften my demands, wrap my worth in disclaimers. I position myself carefully—palatable, non-threatening, easy to digest.

Because deep down, I have been trained to believe that I should be grateful to be here at all.

A POT TO P*SS IN   177

I have learned to make up for what the world does not see in me. I offer more. I give more. I work harder. I do not ask for full price. I slash my own worth before they get the chance to do it for me.

And it is this silent negotiation—this unspoken markdown—that makes building an empire feel impossible.

Because the truth is, no one else needs to mark me down. I'd become an expert at doing it myself..

I had spent my whole life believing that banks weren't for people like me. That financial institutions were like Ivy Leagues—reserved for those who had already proven themselves worthy. And in many ways, that belief had been reinforced over and over again. But then, I found Project Money.

I don't even remember how I first learned about Summit Credit Union's Project Money. Maybe it was through a flyer, a random email, or one of those deep-dive Google searches that seem to happen when you're desperate for a way out.

All I know is that the concept grabbed me.

Project Money was a financial coaching program where real people—like me—got a chance to transform their finances with the help of a coach. They shared their stories, learned new strategies, competed for cash prizes.

But what stood out the most? It made banking feel human. For the first time, I thought, *Maybe this could be for me, too.*

I never got the nerve to apply for Project Money—that felt too big, too public. But it led me to Summit Credit Union, where I started to believe that maybe I could belong.

That's how I met Adam.

Adam was the first banker who didn't treat me like I was in the wrong place. Instead of just reviewing my financial history and making a decision based on numbers alone, he asked me a question: "Why do you believe you can be successful here?"

I wasn't sure how to answer.

The old version of me might have defaulted to shame, rattling off a list of reasons I probably wouldn't be successful. But something told me to reach for a different story. So, I told him about Weight Watchers.

I told him how I had learned to track my food, manage my portions, and stay disciplined with numbers. How I had transformed my health by following a system, by working within a structure, by committing to the process. And somehow, that connection made sense to him. So, he let me in. He opened the door.

But getting in the door was one thing. Learning how to manage it was another. That's when I learned about Red Shoes. Unlike Project Money, Red Shoes was private. No cameras. No competition. Just a guided program designed to help people take control of their finances.

And so, I took a chance. I applied to the program and paid a fee so reasonable that even a single mom of six, completing a PhD on a very limited income could afford it. I was accepted. And after a coach or two, I met Aidan, my Red Shoes coach.

And much like Weight Watchers had taught me to track my food, she was teaching me to track my money through Red Shoes.

Sitting across from Aidan at Summit Credit Union was like getting butt naked in front of a stranger—saggy boobs, stretch marks, unshaved nether parts, rolls, back fat, and all. The vulnerability was terrifying.

In the beginning, every meeting was like standing under a harsh spotlight, exposing all my financial wounds—the ones I had kept hidden, even from myself. But Aidan wasn't just someone helping me manage money. She was both a witness to my reckoning and my financial bestie.

She didn't just throw numbers at me; she helped me understand them. She sat with me, meeting after meeting, as I learned how to stop treating my money the way I had treated my body—detached, careless, without a sense of purpose.

Every session with Aidan became a mirror, not just to my bank account but to my life. She helped me recognize the patterns that had kept me stuck—the ways I undercut myself, the ways I handed over my power without realizing it.

She didn't ask me to dig into the roots of my financial habits, but after each session, I would go home and journal, trying to unravel them myself. I'd sit with questions like: *Why did you spend $3,000 on homeschool supplies when you knew that money was needed elsewhere?*

And I'd answer myself, brutally honest: *Fear. I spent it because I was afraid. If I looked like I knew what I was doing, maybe I could silence the voices of the critics.*

It was uncomfortable. Sometimes painful. But necessary. And then, something shifted.

One day, I found myself actually enjoying a budgeting session. Instead of feeling like I was drowning in scarcity, I felt something else—control.

Even though I had more month than money left, as Dave Ramsey would say, I wasn't being dragged by the numbers. I was driving them.

And for the first time, I wanted to understand this process.

That night, I bought every finance book I could afford because I wasn't just surviving my finances but was engaging with them.

This work with Aidan and Red Shoes wasn't just about numbers but about reclaiming my power.

I wasn't just handing over money—or my body—without thought or care anymore.

I had questions.

I had boundaries.

I had new ways to say no.

Every dollar I had was on a clear assignment.

My money was working for me instead of running over me.

And that sense of ownership started to ripple into every area of my life. I wasn't just taking control of my finances. I was taking control of me.

Adam opened the door. Aidan walked with me through it.

She gave me the tools, the strategy, the knowledge. She didn't just tell me to see myself—she showed me how.

Unlike the older man, whose strategy wasn't protective and wasn't for my safety, Aidan's approach didn't leave me feeling exposed. It didn't make me feel like I was "put out there" without armor. Instead, she gave me a way forward.

As I go through this process of trying to secure a home, I think back to that season of my life—the time when body, money, and story balanced each other like the Holy Trinity. I need to hold on to that. Because no matter how many deductions my body is hit with, I still have a say. I still hold power.

I have the ability to address what I can—to turn negatives into positives, to shift the narrative where possible. I have the strength to let go of what I cannot change, to refuse to let those unchangeable "deductions" define me. And, most importantly, I have the power to control my story—at least the one I put out into the world.

When I come to the table—whether it's a bank, a boardroom, or a closing meeting for a home—I can't afford to discount myself. No matter how much those in power may want to mark me down, I have to walk in with my full price tag. Because the truth is, the only person who can truly put me on clearance is me.

Stories shape us. They define how we see ourselves, how the world sees us, and—more importantly—what we believe we deserve. But what happens when we decide to rewrite them?

James Baldwin once said, "I had no secrets. You couldn't blackmail me. You didn't tell me, I told you."

That's what it means to be naked. To own the stories we've been given, to expose the ones that have been used against us, and to write new ones on our own terms.

For years, my story—my body's story—was told by others. Like the elder in my family who would smirk and say, "Sagashus doesn't have many vices. She doesn't drink. She doesn't smoke. She doesn't party. She just loves having a lot of sex." She said it like it was a joke, something for other people to laugh about.

But one day, I stopped letting the story be hers. I asked, "How do you know I like having sex?"

She had no answer.

Because the truth was, I didn't. I had sex because I felt like I had to. Because I had been taught that my body wasn't something I could own. That it was a thing to be traded—for love, for attention, for safety. That it was something other people had the right to claim.

But I reclaimed that story. And when I did, I started to reclaim my power.

And my bank account? It was no different. For years, I lived inside the story that I wasn't supposed to have wealth. That money was something I could access only in scraps. Overdraft notices, declined debit cards, bad credit—I let them narrate my worth.

But those weren't failures. They were proof of something deeper: I had been fighting for something I didn't even believe I was allowed to have.

Yet, I kept pushing. I kept choosing a different story.

I remember the girl who walked into a bank, terrified, convinced she didn't belong there. The woman who sat across from Aidan, slowly learning how to assign every dollar a purpose, how to take ownership of her financial life the way she had learned to take ownership of her body.

That work I did with Aidan was years ago. And since then, I've ebbed and flowed, fallen and climbed. But that work let me know what I was capable of. It gave me a foundation, a reference point—an experience to always return to.

And right now, more than ever, I need to tap into that.

So I do the thing that always brings me back to center.

I step into the shower.

The water rushes over me, hot and steady. It washes away the tension in my body, but more importantly, it reminds me—I have been here before. On the edge of something bigger than myself. Facing uncertainty. Pushing past fear.

And so, I start praying:

Dear God,

As the water beats down upon me, I am reminded that this body—this sacred vessel of my experiences and dreams—is powerful. It has carried me through the darkest times, and I trust that it will carry me through the challenges that lie ahead. This body is not just flesh and bone; it is a statement of Your grace, a testament to the resilience You have placed within me, and a reflection of my ability to thrive in a world that often tries to undermine my worth.

Lord, I acknowledge that this same body moves through financial struggles, navigates a world of numbers and transactions, and faces the realities of life with courage. It is this body that owns its story, that pushes through workouts and sits in quiet reflection. It is this body that confronts the uncertainties of life and transforms them into narratives of empowerment, guided by Your wisdom and strength.

I pray that You continue to fill me with the power to honor this body, to see it as more than just a vessel but as a tool for Your work in the world. Help me to embrace my journey with confidence, to navigate every challenge with the assurance that I am equipped and capable. Let my body, my mind, and my spirit be a testament to Your unending love and grace.

Amen.

I step out of the shower, feeling renewed. The water has done its work, cleansing not just my skin but my spirit. I wrap myself in a towel, feeling the soft fabric against my clean skin and realizing that the connection between my body, my finances, and my story is not just theoretical—it's lived. It's real.

I walk back to the couch, where my journal lies open, the ink still fresh on the pages. I glance down at the last words I wrote, feeling their truth settle into my bones.

Power isn't just something I wield; it's something I embody.

It's in the way I move, the way I speak, the way I engage with the world around me.

It's in how I care for myself—physically, financially, emotionally.

And so, I will continue to embrace this journey, owning every part of my story, my body, and my finances. I will continue to push boundaries, to challenge the narratives that others try to impose on me, and to write my own story with confidence and clarity.

Because, in the end, it's not just about surviving.

It's about thriving.

It's about living fully and unapologetically in my skin, in my purpose, and in my power.

CHAPTER 17

NET WORTH

SEPTEMBER 2021

Damn. I haven't spoken to my bestie in a hot minute, I think as I scroll through my contacts. The names and numbers blur together, a reminder of how much this housing process has consumed me. The magnitude of the decisions I've had to make presses down on me, and I can feel the tension building in my shoulders. I take a deep breath, trying to shake off the heaviness. *Let me call this man and see what he's on.*

The phone feels cool against my ear as I listen to the ringing. My heart races a little, not from nerves but from the simple anticipation of reconnecting with my best friend since the third grade. I've been so wrapped up in this whirlwind of responsibility that I haven't been connecting with the people I love most. Part of it is because I can't afford distractions. But if I'm honest with myself, there's a fear in the pit of my stomach of having to go back and tell everyone that things fell through if I don't get the house. But not talking to my A1, Day 1? That's crazy.

The phone rings twice before Damian picks up on the third. In the background, I can hear the soft hum of activity—pots clinking, the distant sound of music playing, and the chatter of his kids. Despite the noise, his voice is like a balm to my frayed nerves, grounding me in a way that only a lifetime of friendship can.

"What up, Say? Long time. You good?" His voice is calm, steady, with just a hint of warmth that reminds me I'm never too far from his thoughts, even with everything he has going on.

"What up, jerk face? Yeah, I'm good. You?" I reply, trying to sound casual, but there's a rush in my chest that I'm trying to keep at bay. As much as I've been holding back, trying to keep things under control, I feel the dam within me about to break. I'm about to tell it all.

"Yeah, I'm good, jerk face." He chuckles, and I can almost see the grin on his face, that easy smile that's always been a part of who he is. I can hear Bri in the background, humming along to the music as she stirs something on the stove. Their baby, Kai, is babbling in that adorable way toddlers do, filling the kitchen with the kind of life and energy that makes me smile despite everything.

Damian, the master of long pauses and the king of smacking his food, does both as we sit on the phone catching up. Even with the distractions around him, I know he's fully present, listening intently as I tell him about everything that's going on—the house, the business, the pressure that feels like it's suffocating me. He listens, like he always does, and I can almost hear him nodding along, taking it all in because he's the Yoda of that shit, the Yoda of good listening.

When I'm done, he lets it all hang in the air for a moment, giving my words the space they need to breathe. There's a comfort in the silence, a reassurance that he's really heard me.

Then, with that calm confidence that's been his signature since we were kids, he says, "Aye, man. Look, I got you on the $3,000. If you still need it at the end of the month, I got you."

Relief washes over me, like a warm wave that starts in my chest and spreads outward. It's more than just the safety net of his dollars—it's the reassurance that I'm not in this alone. Knowing I have one more person in my corner, believing in me, helping me get to the finish line, lifts some of the weight off my shoulders. I can feel my body physically relaxing into the couch, the tension in my muscles easing just a little.

"Thanks, Damian. You don't know how much this means to me," I say, my voice softer now, filled with a gratitude that goes beyond words.

"That's what we do. We come through for each other. I know you'd do the same for me if the tables were turned," he replies, his tone steady and sincere. "We gotta look out for each other, especially when the stakes are this high."

I nod, even though he can't see me. "You're right. It's just … sometimes it feels like so much, you know?"

He lets out a thoughtful breath. "Yeah, I get it. But you've always been a fighter, Say. You've got this. And you've got people who believe in you. Don't forget that."

We talk a little longer, the conversation easing from the heavy stuff into lighter memories—laughing at old jokes, reminiscing about the times we've had. The sounds of his family in the background—Bri calling the kids to dinner, Kai's laughter—are a soothing reminder of the life Damian's built, one filled with love and stability. It makes me feel grounded, too, knowing that even as he's stirring a pot on the stove or handling daddy duties, he's still there for me, just like always.

As we say our goodbyes and hang up, I feel a little lighter. Damian's words stick with me, grounding me in a way that I didn't realize I needed.

I sit for a moment, the silence in the room settling around me like a blanket. My thoughts drift to something I read a while back—how one reason Black people struggle to build wealth is because many of us don't have a circle of family and friends who can lend a minimum of $3,000. And for those of us who have $3,000 to lend, we're often the ones taking care of others around us. Those dollars aren't circulating back; they're just flowing out, like water from a faucet.

I think about that, and while I'm proud that some members of my circle have it, I realize I've been hesitant to lean on them. Part of me wanted to prove that I could do it independently and didn't need to rely on anyone's resources. Part of me doesn't want to be among the ones pulling from and not pouring into those around me. But the truth is, we are not meant to do this alone. We're stronger together, and sometimes, leaning on your network isn't a sign of weakness; it's a sign of strength.

September 2021 was a month that tested my resolve in every conceivable way—financially, emotionally, and personally. The days were still warm, with just a hint of the autumn chill that would soon follow. As I navigated these overwhelming challenges, it became increasingly clear that my true wealth wasn't just in the dollars I would have to grow or the house I was looking to buy or the business I was scaling, but in the people who stood by me, reminding me that our network is indeed our net worth. Whether it was the late-night conversations with my Australian friend, whose voice crackled over the phone lines, offering comfort from across the globe, or the unexpected financial support from Damian, my closest friend since childhood, I realized that the people in my life were one of my greatest assets.

Even as I navigated the financial maze, the tension at home was a constant undercurrent, a reminder that my challenges were not just monetary but deeply personal. The atmosphere in the house felt thick, like the heaviness of unspoken words hung in every room, making it hard to breathe.

One early afternoon, as the sun filtered through the windows, casting long shadows on the floor, Prodigal came to me, his face etched with concern. The sunlight highlighted the worry in his eyes, making the lines on his forehead more pronounced as he spoke. He was concerned about his daughter, Nari, my bonus child, who had come home from college and was staying in a hotel instead of with us. He wasn't sure why she was there or if anything was wrong. Given his past experiences and anxieties, the unknown—especially when it came to his kids—made him nervous. His hands, which usually rested calmly at his sides, were now fidgeting, betraying his unease.

Instead of letting him spiral into worst-case scenarios, I suggested we visit her so she could explain what was going on and why she'd been staying at this hotel. Reluctantly, he agreed, his sigh heavy with a mixture of relief and lingering worry.

As we drove down East Washington, the bright afternoon sun glinted off the buildings, making everything seem sharper, more vivid. The hum of the car's engine filled the silence between us, a silence heavy with unspoken concerns. Prodigal's anxiety was palpable; I could see it in the way he gripped the steering wheel. The air in the car felt thick, weighed down by the tension that neither of us could shake.

When we arrived at the hotel, the lobby was a surprising contrast to the worry that had filled our journey. It was full of color, bright and beautiful, as if the space had been recently redesigned to be more welcoming. The walls were adorned with cheerful artwork, a refreshing change from the sterility of most hotel lobbies. The vibrant atmosphere made me feel slightly more at ease, though I could tell Prodigal was still on edge.

We walked down the brightly lit corridor, the carpet soft under our feet, muffling our steps as we approached her room. When Nari opened the door, a scent of citrus wafted out, mixing with the faint smell of vanilla candles burning somewhere in the room. Inside, the room was a reflection of her—a mix of practicality and comfort. She returned to her desk, where books lay scattered across the surface. Sitting down, she wrote in her notepad, the soft scratch of her pen the only sound breaking the quiet.

The room reminded me so much of my own hotel getaways when I'm deep into a new book, crafting a sponsorship proposal, or tackling something significant. You never really know what lessons stick with your kids, but seeing her handle things with such a familiar calm and focused energy made me feel both proud and honored. It was like catching a glimpse of myself in her—steady, intentional, turning a small, temporary space into a sanctuary for getting things done.

It gave me a sense of comfort, reassuring me that she's been listening and watching all along. Prodigal, on the other hand, was confused, his brow furrowing as he tried to understand why she felt the need to be here.

"Why are you here?" he asked, his voice tinged with concern and a hint of frustration, his confusion still evident.

"I just needed to be in my own space. I had some things I was working on, and I couldn't really think where I was. So I decided to get a room," she replied, her tone calm but with a slight edge, as if she had anticipated the question and was ready for it.

"Has some boy been staying here with you?" he asked, still not satisfied with her answer, his voice betraying his lingering fears.

"No, Dad," she responded, her voice lightening, annoyed but more playfully, a small smile tugging at the corners of her mouth.

He relaxed a bit, the tension in his shoulders easing as he looked around the room again. His gaze landed on the candy scattered around and a collection of chocolate on her desk, and he seized the opportunity to tease her.

"I see you made sure you got yourself a stash. You need a bump? That's why you're a sugarhead, just like the rest of them," he joked, referring to her siblings. His laughter was a welcome sound, breaking the tension that had filled the room.

We all laughed, the sound echoing softly off the walls, and for a moment, it felt like everything was okay. We chatted for another fifteen minutes or so, the conversation flowing more easily, and then we all left. As we walked back to the car, the afternoon sun cast long, golden shadows across the parking lot. Somewhere between the hotel and the drive, we broached the subject of her moving back into the apartment with us.

She had lived with us off and on during my first seven years with Prodigal, and even after our breakup, she stayed with us for a bit. But then COVID-19 happened, and because of other obligations she had to family outside of our home, she couldn't quarantine, and I didn't want to risk infection. We parted ways, only seeing each other a few times since then. We never discussed the way we separated, me telling her she couldn't come back in and putting her clothes outside. Deep down, I knew this was a sore issue for her. To be honest, it was sore for me, too. The memory of that day still stung. A dull ache that resurfaced whenever I thought about it. And yet, I hoped it wouldn't get in the way of her deciding whether she should move back in. The car was filled with the hum of the engine and the faint sound of the radio as we drove, the city lights blurring past us. She listened to our offer, her face thoughtful as she gazed out the window, and said she'd think about it.

About a week later, Nari reached out to her dad and took us up on our offer. Until then, Prodigal had been sleeping in the one bedroom downstairs while the other kids and I slept upstairs. But with Nari moving back in, things needed to change.

The house, occasionally filled with the comforting smells of home-cooked meals and the loud chaos of daily life, now seemed to hold its breath, waiting. The familiar scent of lavender from the diffuser in the wall's outlet mixed with the mustiness of the old carpet, which had seen better days. The carpet had once been a soft gray, but years of wear and tear had left it matted with dirt in some places and crusted with stains in others. The sound of footsteps, once muffled by the thick pile, now echoed faintly through the house, a reminder of the tension simmering beneath the surface.

Nari moved into the downstairs bedroom with her suitcases, full-length mirror, books, and all. The small and cozy room quickly filled with her presence—the scent of her floral perfume lingering in the air, the quiet rustle of pages as she organized her books on the makeshift shelves. Prodigal, ever the vigilant father, gave up his room without complaint and moved back onto the couch in the living room. The couch, covered in a worn, faded blanket, had become his new resting place. It was far from ideal, but he accepted it with the quiet resolve that had become second nature to him.

As we tried to settle into this new arrangement, the undercurrent of tension was never far away. Prodigal was always on edge, his senses heightened as he kept a close eye on everything, especially his daughter. The living room, once a space of relaxation, now felt like a watchtower, where Prodigal sat, alert to every sound and movement. The tension finally snapped.

Across several nights, Cho made a few trips past Prodigal and into Nari's room, carrying a television. The sound of their footsteps on the dirty carpet didn't go unnoticed. By the third trip, Prodigal's patience wore thin. The day had started quietly, the soft sounds of morning routines filling the house. But as Cho made his way once more toward Nari's room, Prodigal's unease turned to confrontation. The tension that had been building finally boiled over.

He approached them the next day, his voice tight with frustration. "Y'all just gon' do this right in my face?" he asked, his words heavy with the weight of his suspicions.

Cho and Nari didn't quite understand what he was implying. They exchanged seemingly confused glances, their expressions becoming frustrated as they realized what he was suggesting. I watched the whole thing in slow motion, not sure what to think. We had raised them both as brother and sister, but did they really see themselves that way? Or was Prodigal just tripping? I couldn't figure it out, and because of that, I didn't know how to respond in that moment. Meanwhile, Nari's eyes flashed with a mix of embarrassment, hurt, and anger, while Cho's fists clenched at his sides, and his posture was defensive.

The argument that followed was inevitable. Voices were raised, sharp and bitter, filling the house with a tension that seemed to press down on all of us. The air grew thick with the smell of anxiety and frustration, a far cry from the comforting scents of home-cooked meals that sometimes filled the space and the laughter every day. Dianna just so happened to pull up, and quickly, all the kids joined together, becoming one strong voice of anger against Prodigal. The air felt charged, as if a storm were brewing inside our home.

Dianna and Cho, older and more sure of themselves now, were not going to walk on eggshells. Dianna's voice, though steady, carried the weight of years of unresolved hurt, her words cutting through the air like a knife. Cho's anger was raw, a mix of teenage rebellion and a deep-seated need to protect the family from further pain.

With all the yelling going on, I couldn't understand a word being said. And yet, I could feel every emotion in the room: anger, sadness, fear, disappointment, resentment, and hurt. The argument spilled out onto the patio and then to the playground in the middle of our apartment building's U-shaped courtyard. The sky, filled with clouds, mirrored the atmosphere within our family. As the yelling continued, a call came in from Ruby. I walked to the side of the apartment, the sound of my shoes crunching on the gravel, trying to shut out the noise as I spoke on the phone with her and the bank about the closing date that was fast approaching.

As insults were hurled back and forth behind me, Ruby's voice was steady, calm, and focused on the task at hand. She outlined my options if I couldn't come up with the proof of funds needed: a land contract, in which the current owners would provide financing, or a rent-to-own agreement. Neither option appealed to me, but the reality of our situation weighed heavily on my mind.

Also, I wasn't renewing my lease. With the amount I had earned the year before, I would be paying over $4,000 per month to stay in that apartment. That's three times the amount I was paying at the time and not far from the mortgage I'd be paying on the new property. It didn't make sense to renew that lease. And with all the noise and hurt playing in the background, I knew we needed to own our space. I didn't want to enter into any relationship other than one that meant I'd own my home within a few weeks. As the voices clashed outside, I found myself grappling not only with the immediate chaos but with the larger question of how

A POT TO P*SS IN   189

to secure a stable future for all of us in this new home.

Amid all the yelling, Prodigal gathered his wallet, shoes, and shirt and got in the car with me. Hyper-focused on my call about the house, I tuned him out as I watched the kids gather in my rearview mirror. The sight of them huddled together, their faces a mix of anger and confusion, tugged at something deep within me. In doing so, my mind returned to something a woman named Felicia told me years ago. She said that when God has something for you, Hell sends out its biggest hounds to come after you.

In these months, I had survived COVID-19. I had survived the deaths of people I cared about. I fought my way out of depression and anxiety, overcame an existential crisis, and refused to let the odds of my credit score at the start of the process and my financial predicament at this point in the process break or discourage me. But the implosion of my family, I wasn't prepared for. The world's weight seemed to press down on my chest, making it hard to breathe. Everything I had done for the past twenty-one years was to place me and my children in the best possible position.

And while they couldn't see it, part of my reason for giving Prodigal another chance was for my children. Let's not get it twisted—I was choosing him for me. But I was also choosing him for the son we had together and for my teenagers. Although I spend a lot of time working from home online, I also travel. I didn't want them to be home alone, living with the constant insecurity that comes with being left to their own devices before they are mature enough and have enough life experiences to navigate all that comes with that. The thought of them moving through this world without the guidance of a present adult made my chest tighten with a protective instinct. Don't get me wrong. While I worked and went to school, my older kids spent most of their early years at home with each other, depending on their older sister, Dianna, who was still a child herself, to guide them. But it wasn't ideal then, and it's even less ideal now. Even though my adult children couldn't see it now, I was choosing him for them too. Prodigal loved all six of my children, and he'd be there for them in a heartbeat whenever any of them called, no matter if it was the dead of night or the quiet of a Sunday morning when the world seemed still.

None of my children had grown up in a two-parent household. No matter how much we loved, laughed, and stood by each other, we all still noticed the absence of dads from my kids' lives. It was apparent in all the different last names that didn't match my own. It was apparent in my struggle with discipline. We noticed it in the shortage of income. It was apparent when kids were being bullied and assaulted. And it was evident when no one showed up to games because the only parent in the home had to work. All of that could never quite be warmed away, no matter how many blankets of love I wrapped around them. While I never regretted not being in relationships with their fathers as I raised most of my children, I saw how that choice had left its mark. Although I explained to them that just because my relationships with their dads didn't work out, that didn't mean that both of their parents didn't love them. Their understanding still didn't change the fact that many of them craved that day-to-day connection.

My youngest had an opportunity to tell a different story. The thought of him growing up in a home where he could experience the presence of his father brought a warmth to my heart that I hadn't realized I needed. More than that, two of my children who had troubled relationships with their dads saw Prodigal as a father figure. They'd never admit it out loud, especially not in front of their siblings, but they'd expressed it to me in those late-night heart-to-hearts when the world was dark and quiet, and the air was thick with unspoken truths.

I had to step out on faith, accepting that things might have to fall apart before they could come together. It was like the way a storm tears through the trees, bending them until they almost break, before the sunlight filters through the clouds, casting everything in a new, hopeful light.

Within a few days, Cho had left. The door closing behind him felt like a final, definitive click, a sound that reverberated through the house long after he was gone. He needed space from everything, especially from me and Prodigal, so he went to Michigan to live with his dad. The drive there was long, the highway stretching out endlessly under a sky that seemed too vast, too empty. I didn't want him to leave, but I also understood. He had just turned eighteen that month, the candles on his birthday cake still fresh in my memory. He was a young man, and now, he needed a soft place to land during this time of uncertainty for him. A momma's boy, he was trying to figure out what it meant to assert himself as an adult and to handle conflict as a man against another man. I knew he was also trying to figure out how to trust, or if he should trust, this person who had hurt him so badly, even though they cared for each other so deeply.

Prodigal had been through a lot with Cho over the years. I could still picture them at the lake, Cho's small hand tightly gripping the fishing rod as Prodigal patiently showed him how to cast his line. The air was crisp, carrying the scent of water and earth, while Cho's eyes sparkled with excitement. It was also Prodigal who stood up for Cho when he felt his son had been overlooked at school. His voice was firm yet calm, tinged with the pain of recounting the day he found Cho sitting alone on a bench after school. Prodigal had approached the afterschool teacher and asked if he could point out Cho. The teacher responded, "I do not know him."

Frustrated, Prodigal replied, "He's the one child's name you should know, as he's sitting right there, all alone, in the middle of all these kids running around and having fun. Cho is a lively kid, and the fact that he's just sitting there should alarm everyone." As Cho grew older and became a teenager, it was Prodigal who drove him to and from where he needed to go, especially when I was too buried in schoolwork to step away and, later, so consumed by my business that I couldn't tear myself away from the keyboard.

Prodigal and Cho, the two comedians of the household, often roasted one another in the evenings, the rest of us laughing and admiring Cho's quick wit and Prodigal's vivid imagination. The living room, usually filled with the warm glow of lamplight, would echo with their banter, the sound wrapping around us like a cozy blanket on a chilly night. Their relationship was complex and damaged, like so many of the other relationships that Cho had with the men in his life. I watched him as a child, looking to male figure after male figure to learn what it meant to be a man, just to be disappointed by flaws that left him hurt, traumatized, and confused. The sadness in his eyes, the slump of his shoulders, told me everything I needed to know about the weight he carried.

I understood my son's anger and his need for distance. The room he left behind felt emptier than before, the air heavy with the things left unsaid. Yes, it was because of what happened the other day. But it was also about the things that were triggered as a result of that thing—the scars that ran deeper than either of us wanted to admit.

Prior to the blowup, we had already been packing a little here and there. The rustle of cardboard, the smell of packing tape, and the sight of our belongings slowly disappearing into boxes had become the backdrop of our days. We didn't know where we were going, but we knew we were leaving. Days were going by, each one marked by the slow, deliberate movement of our lives being folded up and packed away, and I still didn't have the answer to the money situation. But I kept packing, the repetitive motion grounding me in a way nothing else could. Hours went by, still no answers, so I kept writing. The scent of ink filled the air as my pen moved across the paper, trying to make sense of the chaos. *Covet* was still incomplete, and if I could just pin down one thing that was up in the air, maybe that would be the answer.

I started taking longer walks. The crisp, cool air of early autumn filled my lungs, the sound of leaves crunching underfoot offering a brief respite from the storm inside my head. I was still walking as part of the mental health hygiene I began in June. But now, I was becoming obsessed, surpassing my daily goal of 12,000 steps; I was coming in at 15,000, 20,000, and sometimes 25,000 steps. My body ached from the walking, the muscles in my legs burning with each step, but the pain seemed to ground me. It made me feel accomplished at a time when everything seemed to be standing still or, worse, falling apart. The rhythmic sound of my footsteps on the pavement became a kind of mantra, a steady beat that kept me moving forward when everything else felt like it was crumbling.

If I could just get one sponsor, I'd be back in this race.

My first encounter with the idea of a sponsor came from my experience attending a Catholic elementary school. A lot of my friends were going to Catholic high schools, and they were joining a program called LINK Unlimited. Several people I knew who went on to attend St. Ignatius or Loyola were part of that program. They'd often talk about their sponsor's role in their lives: the trips, the dinners, the outings. Sponsors usually offered these experiences in addition to paying for a student's tuition. Although I would've been a perfect candidate for LINK, I chose to go to a private boarding school, which made me ineligible for that opportunity. But fortunately for me, a nun from my elementary school named Sr. Helen still encouraged my mom to find a sponsor for me. And she did. That experience taught me that people would invest in you—whether it was for a tax write-off, because they believed in your abilities and wanted to see you succeed, because they were rich and felt guilty, or because they realized that money was only one resource that goes into the pot, and they wanted to contribute to the pot. There are a thousand and one reasons why people do not mind sponsoring a person's cause or work or experience. And there are people actively seeking an opportunity to do so.

From experience, I knew the importance of securing reliable sponsorships, which had become integral to my business's revenue model. But sponsorships could be unpredictable. Sponsors would agree to provide funding in exchange for marketing to my audience, often involving large sums of money. Most of the time, they delivered as promised, but there were also times when things didn't go as planned. Without explanation, two of my biggest sponsors had postponed their commitments indefinitely. Closing was next month. How would I scale my business and buy this house without those two heavy hitters? I was desperate to make things right. I needed a new sponsor, fast.

I prayed for guidance, and my gut pointed me toward one person. I hesitated, afraid they might turn me down. They had supported my work in the past, and I worried they might think I was asking for too much, too often. But desperation pushed me forward. I prayed for confidence and the right words to say.

When I finally gathered the courage to make the call, she didn't answer. I left the phone in one part of my apartment and walked away, needing some distance from the anxiety of waiting. About a half-hour later, I returned to find she had called back and even left a text message. Summoning my strength once more, I called her back. This time, she answered.

"Ah, my dear Sagashus. How are you?" she said, her voice warm and welcoming in an accent I have yet to locate.

"I'm well," I replied, trying to steady my voice. "How are you?"

"Very good. I'm very good. As we speak, I am preparing to welcome my family from out of town. They will be vacationing with us. I am excited. But you didn't call to hear about my family. What about you and your travels? How may I help you?"

There was no turning back now. With all types of butterflies in my stomach—the monarchs, the mourning cloaks, and every other you can think of—I went into my spiel, explaining my situation. I told her about the house, the financial challenges I was facing, the business, and how close I was to achieving something truly remarkable—but only if I could secure this piece of funding. I laid it all out, hoping she could hear the sincerity and desperation in my voice.

When I finished, there was a brief silence on the other end of the line. My heart pounded in my chest as I waited for her response.

"You've always been a visionary, Sagashus," she finally said. "And I believe in what you're doing. I'm going to do what I can to help you."

My heart skipped a beat. "Thank you so much," I whispered, barely able to contain my emotions.

"But," she continued, "there are a few conditions."

I nodded, even though she couldn't see me. "Of course. Whatever you need."

She explained that she could grant most of the $180,000 I had requested, but it would come in two parts. I would receive $50,000 immediately, and the rest would follow in a month. She also outlined a few other terms that aligned with my values and my work—terms that I was more than happy to agree to.

With those details sorted, she offered to send an official letter of commitment that I could take to the bank, satisfying their requirements for proof of funds.

As we wrapped up the conversation, I felt relief wash over me. This was the breakthrough I had been praying for. I thanked her profusely, and when I hung up the phone, I let out a breath I didn't even realize I had been holding. Then, I did the only thing that felt right in that moment—I got down on my knees and thanked God.

It wasn't lost on me that this was the third person I had contacted, and she had accepted my offer. I hoped this was a sign, that this third attempt at owning a home would finally end with the outcome I had been working and praying for.

For now, we had a win worth celebrating. If nothing else came in, we had money for the down payment and the earnest payment, which I paid on September 21. On September 28, the bank provided our pre-approval letter. But it came with conditions. First, I had to come up with the remaining $50,000 by October 11. Second, two unexpected things showed up on my credit when the bank pulled my report that none of us saw in the initial pull. I was exhausted, at the end of everything I had. And I didn't know if I could muster up anything else. I had thirteen days left, and with the curveballs on my credit, I didn't know how or if I was going to pull it off.

Through all of this, one thing became clear: my network was one of my greatest assets. Every dollar raised, every conflict resolved, every step forward was a testament to the power of the people in my life. This journey wasn't just about buying a house; it was about realizing that my net worth was woven from the strength, support, and love of those around me.

CHAPTER 18

CLOSE

OCTOBER 2021

In graduate school, I wanted the word *lotus* to be included in my dissertation's title. I was fascinated by the idea that this flower grew from the mud of a river or pond. Rooted in the muck, it rises out of the water to bloom as an elegant and clean flower. I used to think of myself as a lotus, and briefly, I entertained the notion that it could be my story now. In many ways, it is. But the truth is this: I may emerge from this with more elegance and grace, but I'll be far from clean. And I damn sure won't be pure. There will be trauma, marks, stains, wounds—reminders of the battles fought. October made sure of that.

But first, let's revisit September 28, a Tuesday evening. Our entire team had been moving forward as if the deal would go through. The owners of the house were moving that way, too. Because this was the wave we were all riding, we made plans weeks in advance, agreeing to meet at the property on this day. We needed more rooms for our large family, so we planned to build out the unfinished basement—a space with endless possibilities. The owners had been so meticulous and thoughtful with the original design that all the bases seemed to be covered. That basement would be our contribution to the house, our way of rooting our family's presence in the foundation of the home. The redesign of the commercial wing would come later.

As I walked into the basement, the cool, damp air enveloped me, contrasting sharply with the warmth of the main floor. The concrete walls were rough to the touch, their coldness a reminder of the work ahead. I imagined the space transformed, walls painted in soft hues, the echo of our voices replaced with the hum of daily life. It felt as if the future was within reach, just waiting for us to carve it out of this raw, unfinished stone. Ruby and I exchanged a glance, a shared acknowledgment of the challenge and the potential that lay ahead.

I explained our vision to Ruby, and she put together an entire team to help make that happen for us: an interior designer, contractor, flooring experts, etc. And on that Tuesday, everyone showed up at the home we expected to purchase.

Prodigal and Layden accompanied me. But before we made it there, we had to stop at my credit union. They needed proof that I had enough money in my account to cover the down payment. I got the printout they needed, and we continued on our way. With that bit of information, the bank was able to begin writing our approval letter.

As we drove, I found myself lost in thought. The trees lining the road, their leaves just beginning to turn with the season, seemed to whisper of change—of endings and beginnings intertwined. The weight of the moment pressed down on me, not just the significance of the house but the culmination of every step that had led us here. How many times had I walked this road, metaphorically speaking? How often had I faced obstacles, only to push through, bruised but not broken?

Contractors and future partners rolled in and out of the home like clockwork. Ruby had timed the visits with such care that an hour or so was allotted to each contractor without overlap. Once again, we toured the house. It was our final walk-through before the changing of the guard. As the contractors moved, Ruby and I were still aware that five o'clock was approaching—the time we had agreed, in writing, to have the approval letter presented. The interior designer asked the owners if she could borrow the home's blueprint to make design choices based on the shape of the space. This was serious business, as my son Ryland often said about the house, and I felt the heaviness of it all.

Time was still ticking. The owners and I made small talk, all aware of the clock and just as anxious. The house, bathed in the golden light of late afternoon, seemed almost to hold its breath with us. When we couldn't take it anymore, we called Kelli, who informed us they had just sent the approval letter. But there was a catch—we had been approved, but with conditions: provide proof of another $50,000 coming and resolve the two judgments on my credit.

I knew about the $50,000. That stress was familiar. But those judgments? I had fixed my credit months ago. Nothing should've been on it. I monitored it daily and had pulled all three reports. How could this happen just when I was about to bloom?

Later, I would learn that these items weren't on my credit report. They were judgments that, if left unresolved, would put us at risk of a lien being placed on the property. The bank wouldn't take any chances; they needed this cleaned up. If I didn't pay my mortgage and went into foreclosure, the entities associated with these judgments would have priority when it came to placing a lien on the property. It made sense why that would be a problem. But the real problem was how I was going to fix it.

At this point, I had a better chance of coming up with a letter promising me another $50,000 than resolving the almost $8,000 in judgments against me. The latter required cash in hand now. The former required proof of income from reputable sponsors. The clock was ticking, and I didn't have time to panic.

I began tackling the highest judgment, which seemed most accessible: the University of Wisconsin Hospital & Clinics Authority. According to the information that the title company shared, I owed them $5,594.05 from October 1, 2014. Earlier that year, I paid off a series of hospital debts. Going back over my records and notes, I called the number I had reached out to before and gave my information to the representative. She looked me up just to tell me what I already knew.

"Sorry, Ms. Levingston. We don't have any accounts with your name on it."

My heart sank. The sterile, impersonal voice on the other end of the line contrasted sharply with the warmth of the home I had just been walking through. Frustrated, but determined to resolve the issue, I reached out to a good friend of mine who worked at the hospital. As I understood, her job was to help patients with any billing questions, including payment plans and hardship options. She was on her way out of the country but gave me a number to call. Again, the response was the same.

"Sorry, Ms. Levingston. We don't have any accounts with your name on it."

Desperation tightened its grip on my chest. For the first time in my life, I was desperate to reach a bill collector to resolve an issue. I needed this fixed, and I needed it now. Finally, if I remember correctly, Ruby's husband, Chris, had suggested that I contact the state collection agency. I did, and my account was there. Finally! I didn't have the almost $6,000 that I supposedly owed, but at least I was in the right place.

I told my story to the representative, hoping for a solution. To my surprise, she explained that I did not owe close to $6,000. Thanks to them levying my account over the years, most of that debt had been paid. But I did owe something. I don't even remember the amount. All I know is that I still didn't have it. The representative agreed to settle the account at a rate that was still a stretch for me, but I had it. I paid for it right then and there. Everything was all good until it was time for me to get the proof that I needed.

"Due to COVID-19, we are not keeping regular business hours. The person who handles the Satisfaction of Judgment won't be in until next Thursday."

Another wave of anxiety was threatening to pull me under. That was cutting it a little too close, but I had to trust the process. She assured me that once the document was notarized, I could pick it up from the office. Fine, whatever you all say, as long as I can close this chapter and present the proof. Things went as planned, and I was able to meet one of the three terms.

While handling that, I enlisted Prodigal to help me chase down the other judgment. Trying to find these debt collectors was like chasing ghosts. We couldn't figure out who they were. The debt had bounced around from collection agency to collection agency, making it nearly impossible to trace. One had gone out of business, being bought out by another. But somehow, the company that bought out the previous company managed to keep some of the accounts while doing away with others. I was given a number to contact, leading to sketchy customer service. Representatives claimed they did, in fact, have my account, but they couldn't tell me what or who I owed. It was a nightmare.

As I hung up the phone, I stared at the screen, my reflection faintly visible against the backdrop of a blank page. The frustration that had been simmering within me now threatened to boil over. Everyone was exhausted by the process— tired and at the end of their ropes. It was September 29, and we still couldn't figure out who to pay so I could zero out this mystery debt.

Sitting there, phone in hand, I couldn't help but reflect on the journey that had brought me to this point. Life had thrown so many challenges my way, each one seemingly more insurmountable than the last. Yet, here I was, still fighting, still pushing forward. The weight of it all pressed down on me, but beneath it was a bedrock of resilience. I had learned, through every trial, that I could endure more than I ever thought possible. But the cost of that endurance was high— each victory left scars that I carried with me. I realized then that this house, this moment, was not just about securing a home for my family. It was about proving, once again, that I could overcome the odds. But I wondered, at what point would the fight become too much? When would the mud I was rising from finally swallow me whole?

Fortunately, as hush-hush as I had been about the entire process, about a month prior, I had decided to tell my mom that I was buying a house. She's a well-known housing counselor in Chicago, and she helps people all over the country. Not telling her would've hurt her deeply, both as my mother and as a professional in the housing industry. Sharing that news with her was the best decision because I knew she was the only one who could've gotten me on the right side of this judgment. Over the years, I've watched her advocate for people in foreclosure.

On any given day, she'd be on the phone with a client and some other institution, like a bank, for hours. It was always impressive how, when I knew others would've ended the call, the clients, my mom, would outlast everyone, asking the questions, staying on hold, asking more questions, and complimenting everyone involved to keep the conversation sweet and energized. She was relentless, never giving up until her clients' needs were met.

I had faded. I had no more fight in me and needed my momma to do what she did best. I needed her to fight. I needed her to get me to the other side of this.

She made the phone calls, going down all the paths I had taken until she ended up with the exact same woman who told me that they had my account but didn't know what I owed or who I owed. This seemed to excite my mom, and off she went.

"Ma'am, let me repeat back to you what you've just said and tell me if it makes sense to you."

My mom, the agent, and I were in three different states, and I was both cringing and sliding down in my seat. I always say, "The sky's the limit when it comes to what may come out of my mom's mouth." And between the three of us, there was nothing but space.

In a voice that seemed to be saying, "So let me get this right," she began, "You just said, yes, we have your debt. Yes, you owe us. But we cannot tell you who you owe, nor can we tell you what you owe."

The lady confirmed back to my mom that what she had just repeated was correct.

"Ma'am," my mom said, now sounding like a lawyer who has gathered all the evidence she needs to make her argument, "This sounds like fraud."

The tension in the room dissolved as the representative burst out in laughter, her serious demeanor cracking open with unexpected joy. The representative, who had been somewhat nasty and dry toward me and more serious toward my mom, was now laughing as if we had just shared a great joke. It was an unexpected moment of lightness in a dark situation.

Before I knew it, my mom, who had never identified herself as my mom but rather as a HUD-certified counselor, continued talking to the woman, and before I knew it, she had a plan. She would email their law department, explain my situation, and expedite the process.

That Friday, I was in a personal session with my yoga instructor when my phone went off. I missed the call, and when my session ended, I listened to the voicemail. It was from a woman named Chrystal. She told me she was calling about the debt I was inquiring about and gave me a number to call her back. I did, and we talked. Although she knew my circumstances, she wanted to hear the details directly from me. I explained everything to her, including that I had only a few days to pay this debt. The pressure was on, and I needed her to understand that.

After listening intently, she finally said, "Ms. Levingston, this debt is from 2000. It's over twenty-one years old. As far as Illinois is concerned, because that's where it comes from, you are beyond the statute of limitations. We can't collect money from you and consider the judgment satisfied."

Tears welled up in my eyes. The tension, the fear, the anxiety—all released in that moment. What else could I do but cry?

"Thank you, Chrystal." And thank God.

I looped her into an email chain with the bank, the title company, and my real estate agent, and she wrote everything she had told me. But this time, she stated it even better.

On October 1, she sent an email to the title company that stated this:

Thank you for your email and for the additional information. Our records indicate that the original judgment was obtained in Cook County, Illinois, on 9/28/2000 and that it expired on 9/28/2007 (pursuant to Illinois law). Please see attached. Somehow, we do not have a record of the current judgment that was obtained in Dane County, Wisconsin on 2/9/2015. This is why we show the account to be closed in our system. The judgment is still valid. However, due to the situation, I will proceed with preparing the Satisfaction of Judgment/Satisfaction of Lien. It will be Monday before it will be executed/notarized and then it will be submitted electronically to Dane County Circuit Court for filing. As soon as I receive a file-stamped copy, I will send a copy by email.

Sincerely,

Chrystal

That email was more than just a resolution; it was a lifeline, pulling me out of the mud I'd been stuck in for so long. If you are reading this, Chrystal, thank you. You did everything you said you would, and I am forever grateful.

Although finding this creditor was stressful to uncover, we actually closed our business with them much sooner than we did with the UW. Chrystal sent that letter on the same day she called me. Two down, one to go: $50,000.

But as one hurdle was removed, another obstacle rose before me. I still had no idea how to overcome it.

Throughout the process, I had been in contact with a Black store owner in Chicago. We'd known each other our entire lives. She had housed our coffee table book in her boutique since 2017. While I was working on the new project, she and I talked about new possibilities. Coming from generations of property owners, she had recently moved into a new property herself, and her stories provided a much-needed balm to my stress.

This time, she listened to me as I explained how I had run out of solutions.

"I'll write the letter on your behalf. I'll sponsor your work," she said as normally as anyone would say, "pass the grits" or "hand me my shoes."

Her words were like a bridge over the swamp, offering a way forward when I felt stuck. That was on Saturday, October 8, three days before my time would run out. By the end of the day, I had the letter in hand. All conditions were met. Finally, I could rest.

As I held that letter, I couldn't help but reflect on the kindness of strangers and friends alike who had stepped in when I needed them most. It was a reminder that even in the darkest moments, there are lights—small, steady, and bright—guiding us forward. This journey had been long and arduous, marked by setbacks and heartaches. But it was also marked by resilience, by the people who refused to let me fall, and by my own refusal to give up. The lotus may bloom from the mud, but it does not do so alone. It is nourished by the unseen forces, by the elements that surround it, and by the will to thrive.

Somewhere during all of this, Cho had come back from Michigan. While he was away, using CADD, the general contractor had taken my vision for the basement and turned it into a blueprint. I shared the vision with Cho prior to his return, as he played a big part in my decision to get the downstairs started so soon.

The first time he and the other kids had visited the house, everyone was so excited. They had seen it virtually a million times. Ryland had made a habit of projecting the "virtual tour" onto our television screen, guiding everyone through the home like a seasoned real estate agent. My more laid-back kid, he's easygoing, always observing and then imitating each of us for laughs and fun. This was one of those rare times I could say that I had really seen him concentrate and take charge. Ryland is my kid who quietly does his chores without being asked. He's an in-and-out kind of person who does things quietly behind the scenes. When it came to making sense of this new place, he was at the forefront, working with technology in ways that I didn't even know he was capable of.

And yet, even after all of the tours and the pictures, none of it had done the house justice. He and his siblings were finally able to visit the real thing. As he moved from room to room, the only thing Ryland kept saying was, "Wow, this is serious."

Cho, on the other hand, had something very different to say. To put it nicely, he was frustrated that his temporary room would be one of the old acupuncture-turned-Airbnb spaces on the commercial wing of the property. Unlike the other rooms with walk-in closets and bathrooms, those rooms had only sinks—no bathrooms or closets. It was a far cry from the rooms that Ryland and Brooklyn would live in. As the oldest son who had gone through the most, he clung to my promise of a better life. He had believed in the vision I painted of a future where everything would be worth it. And now, in his promised land, I was essentially offering him a hospital room. As entitled as he sounded, I understood his disappointment. I was there when he was being bullied for not having a decent haircut and for wearing worn-out clothes. I knew that with all the things he had gone through—being talked down to by other family members and having to walk miles to practice when other kids rode by him—it was the promise of a better life that gave him what he needed to push through. And once we got here, to the place I had been giving them so much hope about, he found himself getting the short end of the stick again. I didn't want to understand, but I did. Seeing his disappointment, I made one more promise. I told him that I'd begin on the basement immediately. With the blueprint from the contractor, I had proof that I was keeping my word.

One Saturday night, Prodigal and I sat up in bed watching television. He wasn't feeling good, so I invited him upstairs to watch a movie with me, giving him respite from the couch. As we enjoyed the movie, Cho came in and asked if we could talk about the blueprint. I showed him the different rooms. I got to his, showing where we planned to install his bathroom and closet. He was proud. And that made me proud. I went on to explain the space. When I got to the flex room, a space that could occasionally double as a television room for Prodigal so that I could have a break from the noise that came with him watching his shows at night, Cho flipped.

"It's bad enough that you are getting back with him, but now, you want to put me next to him? What sense does that make?"

The tension in the room thickened like mud. He went into a panic. I was shocked. There I was, going above and beyond trying to please this kid, and it wasn't enough. Prodigal was shocked, too. Neither one of us grew up in families where people finished basements for us and designed rooms to our specifications. We didn't understand his reaction.

"Cho, how are you going to get mad at your mom about how she is spending money building things out in her own house?" Prodigal said calmly, in defense of me.

But that only added fuel to the fire. In all the chaos, one of the kids called Dianna (or maybe she called them.) I don't know. However it went, before I knew it, Dianna was on the phone, and then she was at the house. Everyone was yelling.

"I hope a bus runs over you."

"You're a piece of shit."

"Good luck living in that big house by yourself because none of your kids will be there."

"You'll die before I will."

In all my years of raising my kids, we had never been this way as a family. The chaos felt like I was drowning in quicksand or a bottomless, muddy earth with no clear path out. Desperate for a resolution, I called someone I hoped could mediate. I called one of Cho's relatives on his dad's side, who often brags about her two master's degrees and her position as a therapist. I knew she and Cho had a good relationship, and I knew she and I cared about each other enough to maintain a bond long after my relationship with his dad had ended. I explained to her what was going on. While Cho's dad was on the phone with him, I kept talking to her. One of the kids announced that Yemi was coming over, and she was bringing all of her rage with her. I told the woman on the phone, who was also Yemi's relative, as Yemi and Cho share the same dad. She replied that, as a licensed therapist, she knew how to handle Yemi. I countered with a gentle caution.

"Yemi is my most compassionate child. But she's also very good at directing her anger in places she believes it should be aimed. For years, she's been angry and resentful with your side of the family because she believes that as successful as you all are, you left us to struggle. I don't see her taking advice from you. I see her telling you to stay out of this. Cho, on the other hand, you have a better chance with. But Yemi, she's going to speak her mind."

The woman assured me that she had things under control. Not even five minutes later, Yemi walked in and unleashed her fury on Prodigal, on the word of her siblings. When the family tried to calm her down, Yemi responded just as I knew she would.

"With all due respect, stay out of this. You haven't been in our lives. This is between me, my siblings, and my mom."

Embarrassed that my understanding of my child was more accurate than her skills as a therapist, she immediately turned on me.

"I should've called DCFS on you a long time ago," said the family member/therapist. (And to help her save face, I'll keep her name anonymous.)

Her words hit me like a slap, the kind that leaves a mark. I was speechless. Of all the things she could've said, she chose to say the thing she knew would hurt me the most when it wasn't even me that had insulted her. I tried to protect her from going down that path in the first place. The wounded family member/therapist continued to take out her hurt feelings on me, explaining how I was selfish for calling her in the first place, knowing that she had hypertension, etc. My eyes started to fill with tears. And I told her that, with all due respect, I would be getting off the phone.

As soon as I ended that call, I got a notification from the Quiet One. In all the chaos, Ryland and Brooklyn had told him about me and Prodigal. And he didn't hold back.

"Bitch, I knew you wasn't shit." And he continued with all the things he felt he needed to say to make it clear that he would protect his children at any cost. This man, who has always been so mild-mannered and patient toward me, was unleashing all his fury.

As I sat there, absorbing the verbal blows from every direction, I felt a deep weariness settle over me. It was a bone-deep exhaustion that came from years of fighting battles on multiple fronts. I had always been the strong one, the one who held everything together. But in that moment, I felt myself cracking under the weight. I realized that strength is not just about enduring; it's about knowing when to let go. The house, the move, and the promises I had made were all important, but at what cost? I wondered if, in my pursuit of stability and a better future, I had lost sight of the present, of the relationships that mattered most. The lotus flower that I had once identified with seemed so far away, its beauty marred by the very mud that had given it life.

By that Monday, Cho was back in Michigan. Meeting all the bank's requirements in advance, I had taken three steps forward. But with the state of my family, I had taken ten steps back.

It was closing week. Over the following days, Prodigal, my three youngest kids, and Nari kept packing. I rented a U-Haul, bought some more boxes, and we worked as a unit to get the job done, working literally around the clock. Prodigal packed and loaded during the night, me and the kids during the day, while Nari loaded the truck during the evening. At some point, I wired the down payment from my credit union to wherever it had to go and went back to packing. I was excited that we had made it through the struggle of gathering the paperwork, filling out the documents, being pre-approved, and then actually being approved with conditions, and then completing those conditions. But I was also very sad that my older children weren't there with me.

On Wednesday, I got a call from Cho's football coach with big news—scouts would be at the upcoming homecoming game, and they wanted to see him play. Despite the turmoil at home and his recent move to Michigan to create some distance between us, his talent on the field hadn't gone unnoticed. The coach understood the situation but recognized his consistent performance and potential. He didn't want him to miss the chance to shine in front of the scouts.

Although my son had been homeschooled, he continued to play sports with a local high school, keeping his athletic dreams within reach. I knew how much this opportunity meant to him. So, I encouraged him to come back home for the game. Prodigal supported my decision.

Later, I got a call from Cho saying that he was bringing with him his dad, another family member on his dad's side, along with his dad's girlfriend and their baby, Cho's sister. Of all the years he's played sports, his dad and his family had never been to a game. It was Cho's senior year and his last game. I knew that whatever we had going on, we couldn't let it get in the way of this experience. I saw the look on Prodigal's face as I told him about the news Cho shared with me over the phone. And I knew he was uneasy. Like me, he understood what was important here. But he also understood the potential danger of the situation. It was bad enough that he and Cho had to try to work through their hurts alone, but to add Cho's people to the mix would only make matters more difficult. The old him would've embraced the opportunity for chaos, confusion, and violence. The new him got out of the way. With only a look, he didn't have to say a word. I understood.

In our way, we were both sinking. As I washed clothes in the laundry room, he stopped by and told me he was going to get cigarettes or some milk or whatever men say when you know they are not coming back. I didn't argue. I just let him go because I understood it would be better that way, for now. I felt a heaviness in my chest as he walked away. That left us with only the younger kids, Nari, and me to do the packing.

The Thursday night before we were scheduled to close, I don't remember much. I just remember that I felt anxious, sad, hurt, abandoned, tired, and weak. Brooklyn and I got up that morning, and we drove to the closing. We arrived about twenty minutes late. I cracked some joke about Black folks always being late. No one laughed. It was awkward. But we jumped right in, signing a mountain of papers in a room that consisted of the sellers, their real estate agent, my real estate agent, Kelli, the title company representatives, and me and Brooklyn. The entire time, my adrenaline was rushing, and I was vigilant, trying to make sure I understood everything being said to me and everything I was signing. Whatever I didn't understand, I asked questions and didn't sign the respective document until my questions were answered. And then we were done.

There were congratulations all around. Kelli gave me a card and a small bottle of wine as gifts. Ruby gave me a card, a bag full of gifts for my children, a large bottle of wine, and a large wooden key that read, "This is Serious." As I held that key, I couldn't help but think of the lotus, finally blooming above the water but still bearing the marks of the journey through the mud. I was officially a homeowner.

CHAPTER 19

BREATHE

OCTOBER 2021

I'm on the phone with my aunt, apologizing for not calling as often as I used to. I explained that I had been navigating a difficult period—finishing my PhD, building my business—where anger and loneliness had often been my only companions. I told her that when people envision success, they often picture the shiny things: cars, houses, clothes, money, status, and power. But they rarely consider the trauma that shadows every step of the climb. Maybe they imagine the mountain lions lurking as we ascend, but they often overlook the nights stranded in the cold, the gnawing hunger, or the times we scale 10,000 feet only to slip back 15,000.

At some point, with persistence, faith, and a little bit of luck, many of us finally reach the summit. But then what? We pause, take in the view, and attend to our bruises, scrapes, and gashes. This final chapter isn't just about that moment of arrival; it's about what comes after. It's about the breath you take when the climb is over, the breath that signals it's finally time to rest.

When I finally held the keys in my hand, the moment wasn't the triumphant pinnacle I had imagined. The true emotional high had come earlier when we signed the paperwork, binding us to this property—a culmination of a lifetime's effort. The keys were lighter than I expected, far less in number than one would imagine for the size of the house. But what the physical keys lacked, the series of codes made up for, outnumbering the amount of metal handed over to me. They symbolized the start of a new chapter, yet held an intimidating weight with the responsibilities they unlocked.

The moment was fleeting. The celebration was cut short when the internet installer called, informing me he'd arrive earlier than expected. With little time to savor the milestone, I grabbed Brooklyn, our mountain of paperwork, and my new keys, and headed to what was now our home.

As I unlocked the door, the first thing that struck me was how beautiful the house was: the wooden floors, the tall windows, the sturdy wooden pillars. Everything seemed more magnificent than when I first saw it—perhaps because now they were mine.

When Brooklyn and I first used the keys to enter the house on our own, the moment hit me in a way I hadn't anticipated. This house, with its empty rooms echoing our footsteps, was now mine, yet it felt as though I was walking through someone else's life. I disassociated, a strange numbness settling over me as the reality of this new chapter seemed too vast to grasp all at once. As I let different people in, including Nari, I found myself shifting into problem-solving mode—a defense mechanism, no doubt. It was easier to focus on logistics, to compartmentalize my emotions, than to face the overwhelming realization that my life had changed in ways I was still struggling to understand.

Before I purchased the house, I had called all my aunts, uncles, and my mom, telling them I was about to be a new homeowner. Except for my mom, Aunt Business, Mistee, her mother Renee, Damian, and my cousin Ron, I kept the process to myself. But as we got closer, I called all the elders and told them I wanted them to come and bless our new home. I could hear it in everyone's voice, each separately, that the timing was terrible for them. But Aunt Word suggested I call her via video chat, and we walk through the house and pray together.

While I initially loved the idea, when I found myself alone, I realized that this moment needed to be intimate, just between me and God. There were things I needed to say, confessions that required the quiet of solitude, so I chose to bless my home alone.

"Father God, thank you for blessing me with a space large enough to accommodate all of my responsibilities. Bless this home and unify our family. You didn't bring us this far to allow us to tear ourselves apart. Let this space be for healing."

As I moved from top to bottom, room to room, I prayed for each person that I had intended to sleep in each room. I prayed for the completion of the basement and for women to come to our home and have a transformational experience through coaching and retreats. I prayed that the work we do personally in this

A POT TO P*SS IN

house would answer prayers, and I prayed for joy.

Burning sage has always been a sacred ritual for me. The dry leaves, tightly bundled, felt ceremonial—like a bridge connecting me, my ancestors, and God. As I lit it, the smoke curled upward, thick and lingering, filling the air with a sense of purpose. The scent was powerful, almost overwhelming, reminding me of the wild, thick smoke I'd seen when people smoked big, fat joints, blowing freely thick locks of smoke into the air.

I moved through the house slowly, holding the sage aloft as if it were an offering. My steps were deliberate, my pace reverent, like I was presenting myself to the gods in their throne room, except not. The atmosphere in the house began to change as the smoke spread, a tangible shift from the lingering anxiety to a growing sense of peace. I paused longer in the basement, the undeveloped space that had been the trigger for our family's divide. My hands trembled slightly as I raised the sage, praying for the strength to complete this space, to make it everything we had imagined and discussed. I held the sage high, as if it were the one being offered up as a blessing.

By the time I finished my prayer, a sense of peace had settled over the house. Mistee's call broke the silence. She and her husband had arrived in Madison, hungry from their journey, while I was starving from the day's emotional exertion. It was time for another kind of nourishment.

Mistee, her husband, and I decided to unwind with dinner at a local steakhouse. I couldn't resist ordering the salmon—a choice that had become a comforting ritual for me, no matter how unconventional it might seem at a steakhouse. The tender, juicy salmon, paired with broccoli, rice pilaf, and sweet potato, felt like the warmth I needed after a long, cold journey.

As we laughed and shared stories over the meal, the food and company provided a brief respite—a moment to savor before facing the evening's emotional challenges. Cho would be returning to Madison tonight, along with Big Cho and a few other family members who would be coming to watch him play his last football game of not only the season but his high school career, and they would be seeing him off for homecoming. I hadn't seen my son since the big family fallout, and I hadn't spoken to his relative since Yemi gave her a piece of her mind. Too ashamed to respond to Yemi, she immediately turned her wrath against me. Thinking about this reunion, I knew I should've been drinking something a lot stronger than water, with lemon and no ice.

The next morning, I found Mistee sipping tea at the dining room table with a knowing smile. While we had brought that table from the old home, along with a few other pieces of furniture, because the previous owners were downsizing, they left us an almost fully furnished home. It only made sense that Mistee and her husband stayed with us in our new place. In fact, everyone stayed—Big Cho, his daughter, his pregnant girlfriend, and the elder woman he brought with him. And my cousin was ready to fill me in on the drama that had unfolded while I slept, her voice laced with the humor that always brought light to any situation.

"The elder got up, and all I could hear was 'Come on, get up now. I'm ready to go,'" Mistee recounted with a shake of her head. "Big Cho, half-asleep, mumbled something like, 'But we're leaving later, right? Cho's got his dance tonight.' And she just snapped back, 'No, we're leaving now. Right now.'"

Mistee laughed as she recounted the scene, her voice full of mischief. "It was clear Big Cho wanted to stay, but she wasn't having it. Your success must have triggered something in her—a reminder of where she thought you'd never be." She laughed some more. "Is this the same woman who, when she saw where you lived all those years ago, looked at you and said, "Uh-huh. This is why Cho likes you. You're ghetto trash."

"And is," I said, laughing with my sister-cousin.

We found more things to laugh about together, and for a moment, the weight of the past lightened. But the day ahead still loomed large, and I knew this brief reprieve wouldn't last long.

With Big Cho gone, I felt the urgency of the day ahead of me, wishing Prodigal was here to help me sort through it all. Mistee, her husband, and I headed to the Pancake House for breakfast, a place that held memories for me. The last time I had been there was when I was announcing to my children that I was getting back with Prodigal. Now, Prodigal was not here, and neither were my other children. I fought back the pain and emptiness of that.

During breakfast, we continued to laugh about the elder who "had to go," and we planned out our day. Mistee's husband, who adored his pickup truck, agreed to let me put my desk in the back of his truck, which was a major concession for him, as he'd been very adamant that the back of that truck would not be used to haul anyone's stuff outside of his immediate family. I felt honored.

As we chatted, our server, who I've known for years, came over with a friendly smile I've grown accustomed to looking for whenever I arrive. Somehow, the server and Mistee started talking about all her animals—an unexpected mix of dogs, rats, maybe snakes, and birds. I can't remember. But I do remember thinking, *Wow, you learn something new about people every day*, as she told us about all the furry, scaly, and feather babies that lived with her.

After breakfast, we made our way to Office Depot to pick up the desk I had chosen. It symbolized the next step in my journey. I knew that once it was set up,

A POT TO P*SS IN   211

there would be no turning back. It would be time to build, time to work, time to turn this house into a home and a business.

The purchase was quick. I was in and out, and the desk was on the back of the truck, and we left.

Days later, as I began assembling the desk, the task seemed daunting. It was more than just putting together a piece of furniture—it was about constructing the foundation for the future I was building in this new chapter of my life. As each piece clicked into place, I felt a small but significant shift within me that, piece by piece, I was assembling not just the desk, but my future. I'm getting ahead of myself, though. We ran several more errands, laughed and joked, and then Mistee's husband and Ryland went over to the old apartment and started cleaning while Mistee, Cho, and I went to Walmart.

By the time we stepped into Walmart, I was cracking from the pressure of the weekend. They say that pressure either makes diamonds or busts pipes. I was a diamond about to explode.

Cho was in high spirits, eager to pick up the last few items he needed for his homecoming night. But with every step, I could feel my patience wearing thinner. My mind was a whirl of to-do lists: the moving truck that needed to be returned, the old apartment that still had to be cleaned, and the overwhelming reality of starting a new chapter in this house—all without the help I was counting on.

The fluorescent lights inside Walmart were harsh, casting a sterile glow that made everything feel too bright, too loud. The weight of the weekend bore down on me, heavy and unrelenting. Cho was chattering away in all his excitement and nervousness, but his voice seemed distant, lost in the cacophony of noise that filled the store. My head pounded, a dull ache that pulsed with every beat of my heart, and my limbs felt like they were moving through quicksand, each step more exhausting than the last.

I gripped the shopping cart tighter as I struggled to keep it together. My breathing became shallow, and each inhale reminded me of how close I was to the edge. Years of being a mother had trained me for how to have a meltdown while still taking care of my children. It's an art, really. I forced myself to speak calmly to Cho, even as the world around me seemed to blur, the lights and sounds closing in, spinning out of control.

As we neared the self-checkout, the world around me began to blur. Everything bled together until I could barely make sense of my surroundings. My vision tunneled, and the store was closing in on me. My body, always strong enough to push through, was finally giving out.

I didn't want to alarm Cho, but I knew he could see something was wrong. His towering frame seemed to shrink as he watched me struggle, his eyes wide with a mix of fear and helplessness. I couldn't bear for him to see me like this. With a forced calmness, I mumbled something about heading to the car and hurried out of the store, each step feeling like my internal organs would give out at any moment.

Before I knew it, a stream of urine ran down my leg as I fought back the urge to vomit. The moment I reached the parking lot, I couldn't hold it together any longer. The cool evening air hit my face, and my body seemed to unravel right there between the rows of empty cars. My hands shook uncontrollably, my vision blurred, and a strange, heavy numbness settled over me. I couldn't tell if I was having a panic attack or if my body was betraying me in some deeper, more dangerous way—a mild stroke, maybe? To this day, I still don't know for sure.

We had parked in a quiet, almost deserted corner of the lot, far from the main entrance and the flow of people. If anyone had been around, they either didn't notice me or chose to look away. The world kept moving, blissfully unaware of my breakdown. I was both invisible and entirely exposed, lost somewhere between panic and paralysis.

Mistee knew where to find me. She had parked with me, and when she couldn't find me inside, she naturally came to the car. Her face was a mask of concern as she took in the scene, but she didn't say a word—she didn't need to. With the quiet efficiency of someone who had seen people at their worst before, she helped me into the car, wrapping me in something warm and driving us home.

Cho sat in the back, uncharacteristically silent, his face still etched with the worry of what he had just witnessed. His silence felt like a block of cement falling to the bottom of the ocean, a reminder that while the world had kept moving, our little family had been thrown completely off its axis.

Back at home, I let Mistee take over. She handled everything. She made sure Cho was ready for his big night, took pictures of him and his date, and even drove them to the event. Meanwhile, I collapsed into bed, my body finally giving in to the exhaustion that had been building for days. I could hear the faint sounds of laughter and conversation on the other side of my bedroom wall as Mistee went about the business of keeping the night going while I drifted into a deep, dreamless sleep.

I woke up Sunday morning feeling thankful that Mistee had been there the night before. She and her husband were already at our old apartment, cleaning and working, trying to accomplish as much as possible before the couple got on the road back to Chicago.

I was thankful that it wasn't me handling that part. Mistee's husband, an old

A POT TO P*SS IN

213

friend of the Quiet One's from prison, was on the phone with him, filling in the details of the weekend. On the one hand, I was happy that the Quiet One was included, at least in some way. On the other hand, I was frustrated, angry, and annoyed that this man was giving my now ex-fiancé a play-by-play of everything, including Prodigal's absence. But I was too grateful for the help to rock that boat, so I didn't say anything.

I didn't clean, but I came over and watched the guys as they worked and noted the progress. Still, I worried that there would be so much more to do, and we were running out of time. Mistee and her husband would be gone in less than twenty-four hours, and it would take us at least thirty-six hours to close the apartment.

Meanwhile, Dianna, who still wasn't talking to me, was there with her siblings, helping them acclimate to their new environment. The day went on like that until the evening came when it was time for me to take back the U-Haul.

It was evening, and the cool October air wrapped around me as I stepped out of the U-Haul. Madison had that fall crispness in the air that signaled the beginning of sweater weather. The neighborhood, usually alive with the hustle of people on warm summer days, now felt lazy and still. Cars moved at a leisurely pace, and the sidewalks, once crowded, were almost empty. The only sound was the distant roll of a train moving over the tracks near the brown brick building that I had always admired—a small reminder of why I had been drawn to Madison in the first place.

As I handed over the keys to the U-Haul, a sudden jolt of panic hit me. My hand reached into my pocket, then my bag, searching desperately, but all the keys were gone—my new home, the old apartment, and my van—lost on the same ring. Although my van was safe at our new residence, I had errands to run and places to go. I needed those keys. My heart pounded in my chest, my back tensed up, and I could feel the wave of dread washing over me. How could I have lost everything so important all at once?

The U-Haul drop-off location, clean and organized, seemed to mock me with its sense of order and structure. A line of trucks, neatly parked and waiting for their next renters, stood ready, replenished after the weekend rush. The scent of gasoline faintly lingered in the air, a reminder of the busy days that had passed, but there was no comfort in it now—only the pressure of the chaos that my life had become.

Mistee and her husband were resting, preparing for their early morning drive, and I didn't want to disturb them. So I didn't want to call them to pick me up from the U-Haul location. My options were limited, but I knew I could count on Qiana. She had always been reliable. I dialed her number, hoping she wasn't too far away.

When she answered, I could almost feel the relief washing over me.

Minutes later, Qiana pulled up, her presence a calming force amidst the turmoil. Somewhere during the wait, I had made up my mind that with a good night's sleep, somehow, the keys would turn out. But I wasn't going to worry about them. Instead, I would focus on this big milestone, and I couldn't wait to show Qiana what I had accomplished. This house was more than just a place to live; it was the culmination of years of hard work, faith, and perseverance. It was meant to be an inspiration, a beacon for other women.

I used my code to walk through the door—grateful for the keyless technology on our main doors—but that didn't solve the problem for all the other doors in the house that still required actual keys to unlock them.

As we walked through the house, the smell of freshly cleaned floors greeted us. The house was silent; even our footsteps were quiet. I led her to the living room, pausing to let her take it in. The room was spacious, filled with potential, a place where I envisioned women gathering, sharing their dreams, and finding solace and strength in one another. Then, I pointed out the commercial space with rooms that would host community gatherings, meetings, and events. It was here that I saw a future filled with laughter, plans, and the kind of connections that change lives.

We descended into the basement, the coolness of the concrete floor seeping through my shoes. This space was special to me; it would be my contribution to the home. I had plans to leave my mark on the property, transforming it into a place of purpose.

As we walked, Qiana's voice broke the silence. "Do you really need all this space, especially with the kids getting older?"

I paused, her question hanging in the air. I couldn't quite read her tone. Was it curiosity, concern, or something else? But I took it as a legitimate question. *Layden's not even ten yet*, I thought to myself. *And this house has a purpose beyond just being a family home.*

I turned to her, considering her words before I spoke. "This space isn't just for us to live in," I explained, my voice steady. "It's for my business, for community gatherings, for when the kids come back home with their own families. It's a place for growth, for dreams, for the future."

Qiana didn't respond much, but her presence and attentive listening were enough. She was part of the IMverse, someone who had been with me through this journey, and now she was here to witness the fruits of that labor. Even without the keys, the house stood as a testament to everything I had worked for, and sharing it with her was a crucial step in grounding that achievement.

As we finished the tour, the sound of our footsteps was absorbed by the thick, plush carpet that cushioned the stairs. The house was quiet, but it wasn't empty. It was filled with the promise of what was to come. In that moment, despite the stress and chaos of the day, a sense of peace settled over me, as if the house itself was offering reassurance.

Monday morning came, bringing with it a soothing stillness tinged with melancholy. The transition from night to day was gentle, the light filtering softly through the windows. Mistee's presence had been a comforting anchor throughout the weekend, and now she was gone, leaving behind the keys that had caused so much turmoil. Finding them in her truck, she had quietly placed them on the edge of my bed as I slept, a silent gesture that brought both relief and the weight of responsibility. It held something old, something new, and even something borrowed in the form of Aunt Business's credit card. The move felt almost like a marriage—an intertwining of the past and future, of borrowed and earned. Even though my engagement to the Quiet One was over and my relationship with Prodigal hung in uncertainty, the house symbolized a commitment to myself and my future.

Standing in the stillness of the house, I realized this was my new reality—a home that was fully mine, a space echoing with the past and resonating with the promise of the future. It was time to take the next step. But first, I needed to embrace this moment of peace.

With Mistee gone, it was time to get back to work, to ground myself in the business I had fought so hard to build. The desk I had purchased felt like a necessary step—a physical manifestation of my commitment to both my business and this home. As I began assembling the desk, I initially felt overwhelmed. In the past, this would have been a task I tackled with Dianna or Yemi, but now, with our relationships strained, I had to rely on myself and the younger kids. Still, knowing that Ryland and Brooklyn were nearby provided comfort.

Piece by piece, as the desk came together, a sense of accomplishment began to take root. This wasn't just a piece of furniture but a symbol of the new beginnings I was forging—a step forward in establishing my new life and workspace. When the desk was finally complete, I felt ready to grow my business, ready to face whatever challenges lay ahead, and embrace my new role as a homeowner. The desk wasn't just functional; it was a declaration of intent, a commitment to myself and the future I was building.

After assembling it, I went to my room and prepared to take a shower. Entering my California closet to gather a towel and a change of clothes, I couldn't help but admire how far I'd come. *Damn, girl, this is a long way away from living out of bags and hampers. Everything is so neat and easy to see with all these shelves, drawers, and racks,* I thought to myself. And letting out a big squeal and then laugh, I screamed, "Yaaaaas, bitch. You did it! You motherfucking did that shit." Looking at the Gold N Hot hair dryer, bonnets, and Carol's Daughter hair products, it was obvious that the guard had changed.

A Black woman was now living in this mini mansion. And for the first time in my adult life, everything in my physical space was neat, organized, and in its place. The closet wasn't just a room; it was a sanctuary, a tangible manifestation of the order and stability I had fought hard to achieve. Each neatly folded garment, each carefully placed shoe, was a testament to the battles I had won.

Standing there, a deep sense of pride began to swell within me. This home, this ample, beautiful space big enough to see and accommodate all of me, was now owned by a single mother of six. Above all, it was a testament to my faith. Thinking back to the closet and looking at my life on display in it, I saw that a new chapter was being written on those shelves.

There was still so much ahead: bringing my family back together, unpacking the house, cleaning the old place, and starting on the basement renovations. All of that would come, God willing. But first, I needed to take a moment for myself.

After the intense weekend and the day's activities, I was eager to relax. Screw a shower. I needed to soak. And since I was the new owner of a beautiful spa bathtub, it was time to indulge in that luxury I had dreamed about since I first saw it. I filled the tub with warm water, added lavender bath salts, and lit a few vanilla-scented candles. The smell of lavender filled the room, mingling with the gentle flicker of candlelight, creating a soothing and surreal atmosphere.

As I sank into the warm water, it enveloped me like a cocoon, the lavender-scented steam curling around my skin, easing the tension from my muscles. I closed my eyes and let out a long sigh, sinking deeper into the tub, letting the water transport me away from everything I was going through. The day's chaos faded away, replaced by the soft, rhythmic lapping of the water against the tub's sides. It was an escape, a moment of peace in the midst of the storm.

For the third time this weekend, I allowed myself to simply be, letting go of the worries, plans, and endless to-do lists to embrace the peace that had been so elusive.

When I finally stepped out of the bath, I felt refreshed, ready for bed, and looking forward to a good night's sleep. Tomorrow would take care of itself. For now, I was at peace, the bath having solidified my sense of belonging in this new home, this new chapter of my life.

As I lay in bed that night, I thought back to the conversation with my aunt, the mountain lions, and the unseen dangers of the climb. I had faced those lions, battled through the cold nights and hunger, and now, finally, I was here at the top, taking that breath. This final chapter of this story was about that breath, that pause before the next climb. It was a moment of peace after the struggles, a moment that was entirely mine.

EPILOGUE

2027

I sit in Room One of my dream house, pen pressed to paper, my journal open to a fresh page. Early light pours through the window, soft and golden, brushing against the worn edges of the room. The house is quiet—sacred—like the pause between heartbeats.

"Dear God," I write. "Thank you for loving me. Thank you for guiding me. Thank you for protecting me. Thank you for your wisdom. Thank you for making the impossible possible in my life."

My pen glides over the page, each word a lifeline.

"I have such a deep respect and adoration for you because you have moved mountains for me. You have done things on my behalf that I, at one point, never thought about doing—like buying this house. I marvel at the skies, seas, lands, and oceans. I can't get over the stars, the universe, the galaxies. You are a marvel, the ultimate creator of everything, the artist of all artists, the visionary of visionaries."

I pause, a mischievous smile curling my lips.

"And since I am made in your image," I write, "I, too, have the power to create and do impossible things in all the best ways—with your blessing, of course."

I take a breath, steadying myself as I lean into the ask.

"And yet," I continue, "I still haven't accomplished that multi-million-dollar status, yet. And the other thing I haven't accomplished is transforming the lives of two million women by 2027. I think we're going to need a worldwide tour."

I set the pen down, resting my hands on the worn, wooden table. The house holds its breath around me. It knows, like I do, that this moment is more than ink on paper. It's a declaration. A battle cry.

But beneath the boldness is the truth—the weight of the battles we're still fighting. The ones that claw at the mind, rattle the spirit, test the body. The kind that make you sit in the dark, staring at nothing, wondering if you've already given everything you have.

"I need your blessing and your strategy, Daddy," I whisper to my Father, God, in the heavens, "if I'm going to pull this thing off."

I think of the new characters in this chapter of my life—Jo, with her steady coaching and unyielding belief that I'm not done yet. Joi, my niece, has always been there, but now, she has become an investor of my dreams when the numbers don't add up. And Mister, the quiet anchor in the chaos. God sent me a village when I needed it most.

"Thank you for sending them my way, Daddy. Because without those three being added to my support system, I wouldn't have survived this."

I close my journal, the weight of the words settling over me. But I don't linger on it. I've learned that survival isn't just about making it through. It's about building while you heal. It's about looking out over the ruins and daring to dream of skyscrapers.

I push back my chair, stretch, and take in the room around me—the castle that isn't quite the fairytale but is still my sanctuary. I can hear the house waking up, the soft murmur of life in the halls. I breathe it in, letting the gratitude fill my lungs.

I move to the window, pressing my hand against the cool glass. Outside, the sun has fully risen, drenching everything in light. The promise of a new day. The beginning of the next mission.

You ready, God? Because I am.

I laugh, a low rumble that shakes loose the last threads of doubt.

"We got the pot to piss in," I whisper to the room. "Now we're going to need a window to throw it out of."

And as I turn to leave, the journal remains on the bed, closed but not locked—because the story isn't over. Not even close.

To be continued ...

ABOUT THE AUTHOR

Sagashus T. Levingston is a cultural commentator, storyteller, and truth-teller who writes at the intersection of mothering, womanhood, power, and unapologetic living. With a PhD in English and a lived education shaped by the pursuit of wisdom and the quest to break—and design—generational cycles, she brings theory, practice and lived experience to the page—refusing to separate scholarship from soul.

She is the founder of *Infamous Mothers*, the visionary behind the *Without Apology Tour*, and the host of the "Books, Bullets, and Babies" podcast. Her work has been featured in classrooms, boardrooms, and living rooms—wherever people are ready to move beyond respectability and reckon with real stories.

*A Pot to P*ss In* is more than her next book—it's her next act of resistance. An intimate and incisive exploration of leadership, love, and leveling up, this book invites readers to sit with what society has tried to hide—and rise into their fullest, most unapologetic selves.

Dr. Sagashus Levingston lives in Madison, Wisconsin, with her six children, two fur babies, one partner, and a movement that refuses to rest.

Printed in the United States
by Baker & Taylor Publisher Services